1C

EFFECTIVE STUDY

EFFECTIVE STUDY

by

FRANCIS P. ROBINSON

Professor of Psychology
Ohio State University
Columbus, Ohio

HARPER & BROTHERS PUBLISHERS

New York and London

Effective Study is a revised edition of *Diagnostic and Remedial Techniques for Effective Study.*

CONTENTS

PREFACE

Efficient work skills are necessary in college, as in any occupation, in order that students may make the most effective use of their time and be able to understand the more complex ideas in their lessons. While it is not possible to make all individuals into equally good students, a training program can be set up to show each student how to work to his full capacity. The responsibility of the college must go beyond merely providing educational offerings; it must include showing the student how to take full advantage of his opportunities. This, in turn, will more than pay for itself by reducing the number of repeaters and by providing for more efficient progress in the classroom.

How-to-study programs have been set up in many colleges, one of the oldest and most successful being the one at Ohio State University. Evaluations of its effectiveness are summarized on page 2 of Project I. As the result of an extensive research program and of experience in applying the findings, a great deal of useful training material has been developed. This book represents a coordination of these diagnostic and training devices, and should be of use in other similar courses.

When this material was first presented in *Diagnostic and Remedial Techniques for Effective Study* (Harper, 1941) emphasis was placed on two general areas: (1) the diagnosis and remediation of skill disabilities which often cause students to limp along ineffectually in their work, and (2) the handling of problem areas which distract students from their studies. These areas are treated in Parts Two and Three in the present book, but Part One introduces a new and important idea in how-to-study work—higher-level work skills. Heretofore, goals in how-to-study work have been obtained by determining in what ways good students differed from poor ones, poor students then being urged to adopt the ways of the good students. Recent research, however, indicates that even good students have bad habits of study and are, on the whole, relatively inefficient in their study methods. An analogy to the outcomes of an old-time method of teaching swimming—the "sink or swim" method—illustrates this. A long time ago people were taught to swim by throwing them in the water. Each person gradually developed a dog-paddle swimming stroke from his desperate thrashing of the water in an effort to stay up. In those days such swimming methods were "good enough" to have fun and even permitted some to swim better than others. But since then experts have analyzed the problems of resistance and propulsion and devised new swimming methods which each year result in new swimming records. Students have similarly been thrown into assignments and each has had to figure out as good a method of studying as he could. Bright students, however, have easily been able to keep ahead, even with inefficient methods. Now the educational psychologist is stepping in and, on the basis of extensive creative experiments, is suggesting new methods of studying on a higher level of efficiency.

Such skills permit students to learn more rapidly, with deeper understanding, and with no more effort than with their present trial-and-error methods.

Such an emphasis on higher-level learning skills has caused two changes in the nature of the how-to-study training program at Ohio State University and might well be given consideration in other programs. Whereas how-to-study work once traditionally emphasized helping or "saving" the poor student, it now is of value to all students since even good students do not have efficient techniques. In fact, the students who take this work represent almost a normal distribution of ability, and those who make the most gains and feel the most satisfied with the program have tended to be the brighter students. A second effect has been the removal of the stigma which such training sometimes has with its emphasis on remediation and probation students. Remedial work is still carried on, but it is introduced as needed after the student has had some successful experiences with the use of higher-level study skills.

A program to develop effective study habits in students should also have other characteristics. The characteristics listed below have served as guideposts in the preparation of this book.

1. A how-to-study program must be individualized to each student's needs. Students have different programs of courses, they have different ability patterns and methods of learning, and they have different problems which need remediation or which are distracting them. Even in the field of higher-level study skills, the program must be individualized as a student progresses in learning a skill, much as coaching in golf takes individual instruction.

2. Although students are keenly aware of difficulty in studying their lessons, they usually do not know their actual level of skill nor the specific nature of their difficulties. For these reasons it is important that a student have some means provided for determining his level of skill and, if there is a difficulty, some knowledge of its nature. As he makes progress in learning a skill, he needs evidence of the nature of his improvement and of what is next needed. Self-evaluation tests are included in each project for these purposes.

3. How-to-study work has to go further than helping a student discover what is wrong or giving him information—through reading or lecture—on how to study efficiently. For, as is true of most skills, the mere possession of a desire to improve and information on how to do it will not guarantee that correct procedures will be used. How-to-study training demands much actual practice under supervision until the best skill is obtained and fixed.

4. To develop maximum motivation and to increase transfer of skills to actual studying, this work should be as closely allied as possible to a student's lessons in his other courses. That is, artificial exercises may produce gains on similar tests, but these gains do not transfer as well to actual studying as when the how-to-study suggestions are made in terms of the student's methods on other courses and his gains measured there. For this reason much of the student's practice and application is done outside this book. This book acts as an introduction, a basis for diagnosis, a presentation of study techniques, and a place to record progress; much practice will have to be carried on with other materials, preferably the student's actual textbooks.

5. Finally, this training in study methods can be of little value unless the student realizes its importance and believes it worth while to expend some effort toward improvement. The instructor's cajoling, making assignments, and giving grade penalties

have little place in such work. The student must, of his own volition, do the work. The projects are so arranged that he can select those of interest; the specific directions make it possible for him to go ahead on his own. These factors free the instructor so that he may become a counselor rather than a task-master. The purpose of this book is to provide a working aid for the student and counselor which will increase the efficiency of classroom and counseling sessions.

The arrangement of the projects and the emphasis on self-direction permit the use of this book either in a course or in clinical conferences. At Ohio State University several sections of a class (for college credit) meet daily for a full quarter in an informal labora- tory.[1] Various projects and tests are also used in the counseling of individuals who want help without being registered in the class on Effective Study.

This book is the product of the writer's ex- perience in how-to-study work over a period

[1] A description of this program and also one for counselor training will be found in the article, Two quarries with a single stone, *J. Higher Educ.*, 1945, 16:201–206.

of fifteen years. This program has grown until about 450 students a year receive training in a class on Effective Study and about 100 more are helped in the How-to- Study Clinic. In this work, the writer has been fortunate in having colleagues who have willingly and capably experimented with possible teaching methods and materials. The diagnostic and training materials in- cluded here are thus an outgrowth of many research adventures in personnel work; many persons have had their part in shaping the program. Tests that are not original with this program are used by permission of their authors and acknowledgment is made in the proper place. Special acknowledgment is due Miss Louise Edmundson, librarian at Ohio State University, for assistance in the prepara- tion of the library tests, and to Dr. Ray G. Wood of the State Department of Educa- tion for permission to reprint several of the Senior Survey tests. The writer is indebted to Dr. Loren S. Hadley, Mrs. Carolyn B. Robinson, and Mrs. Alice Seeman for valu- able suggestions in the preparation of the manuscript.

PROJECT I

INTRODUCTION

Almost all students have in their college life some problem or problems which so impair their efficiency that they are unable to make the most of their college experience. When asked to list their problems, as in the Problem Check List at the end of this project, students mention difficulties with their studies more often than any other type of problem.[1] And an objective analysis of students' behavior shows that they do have many such study problems. Furthermore, recent research in educational psychology indicates that new, higher-level methods of learning can be devised which are more efficient than those now used by even the best students. This book attempts to help the student who is worried and inefficient to make the most of his educational efforts.

Contrary to the opinion of many students, the way to achieve effective study is not by more study or more determined concentration, but by changing the quality of study method. For instance, good students study no more (usually slightly less) than poor students; they just use their time more effectively.[2] Ineffectiveness may be due to such defects as slow reading rate, poor grammar, or poor study habits; these cause

a student to limp along in his work when he might be able to go further, with an equal effort, if these deficiencies were remedied. Or a student, even one with good grades, may be trying to do his work the hard way, little realizing that there are better techniques. For instance, even good students seldom make use of headings in textbooks.[3] Finally, a student may be inefficient because some worry or outside interest so distracts him that he cannot concentrate on his work.

The Value of a How-to-Study Program

Colleges are sincerely interested in helping students "make the grade"; in fact, over a hundred colleges have remedial reading and how-to-study programs whose function is not only to rescue potentially successful students from failure but to help the many others work to their full capacity. Although many of these programs started out for the purpose of helping students on probation, a training in how-to-study can help anyone since every person is somewhat inefficient. There is evidence, in fact, that the brighter the student the more he gains from such training. An analysis of the records of several hundred students who have recently taken the how-to-study course at Ohio State University shows an almost normal distribution of intelligence (median percentile is 47 with slightly less than a fourth of the number in either the bottom or the top quartile) and

[1] Ross Mooney, *Problem Check List*, Norms, 1940; E. G. Andrews, Guidance survey of student problems, *Educ. and Psych. Meas.*, 1944, 4:209–215; Ruth Strang, *Behavior and Background of Students in College and Secondary School*, Harper, 1937, p. 21; C. G. Wrenn and R. Bell, *Student Personnel Problems*, Farrar & Rinehart, 1942.

[2] E. G. Williamson, The relationship of number of hours of study to scholarship, *J. Educ. Psych.*, 1935, 26:682–688.

[3] F. P. Robinson and P. Hall, Studies of higher level reading abilities, *J. Educ. Psych.*, 1941, 32:241–252.

grade point averages have ranged from .oo to 3.93 before taking the course. And the students with above average grades have been among the ones who gained the most.

How-to-study programs have met with notable success.[4] Some of the more outstanding ones have been those at the Universities of Buffalo, Chicago, Dartmouth, Illinois, Iowa, Minnesota, Ohio State, Stanford, and Yale. Measures of student progress have shown increased reading ability, greater skill in organizing work, better use of educational facilities, and more satisfactory personal and social adjustment. Further concrete evidence of improvement has been shown through higher grade point averages.

Some actual results over a period of years in such a course at Ohio State University may be of interest to the student. Ferguson found that remedial training for probation students produced positive results for the several quarters measured.[5] Making up a control group of probation students with background comparable to that of the trained group, she found that the grade point average of both groups before training was .77. The next quarter's grade point averages were 1.79 (trained group) and 1.04 (untrained or control group). The spring quarter grade point averages were 1.77 (trained group) and 1.43 (control group). Pressey gave how-to-study training to 50 probation students, but not to another

[4] The following sources provide excellent reviews of the many reports that have been published on how-to-study programs in high schools and colleges: W. W. Charters, Remedial reading in college, *J. Higher Educ.*, 1941, 12:117–121; J. W. Sherburne, *Problems and Outcomes of a College Remedial Program*, Ph.D. dissertation, Ohio State Univ., 1938, pp. 8–36; R. Strang, *Improvement of Reading in High School and College*, Science Press, rev. ed., 1940, pp. 136–177; F. Triggs, Remedial reading programs: evidence of their development, *J. Educ. Psych.*, 1942, 33:678–685.

[5] J. M. Ferguson, Probation students under guidance, *Educ. Rev.*, 1928, 75:224–228.

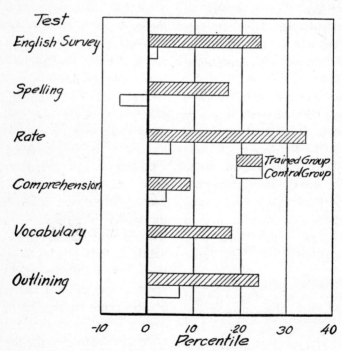

CHART 1. Changes in test percentiles after a how-to-study course, compared to those of a matched control group measured after the same period of time. (J. W. Sherburne, unpublished Ph.D. dissertation, Ohio State University, 1938.)

matched group.[6] She found three and a half years later that 58 per cent of the trained group had maintained a passing grade average or had left college with satisfactory grade records, but only 18 per cent of the control group did as well. Twenty per cent of the trained group graduated, but none of the control group did.

A more recent experimental evaluation of the result of this same how-to-study course, but with all types of students enrolled, showed that the students taking this course improved a great deal in various determiners of scholastic success.[7] Chart 1 summarizes some of these results. For instance, the median student, as a result of this training, improved 24 percentiles on a test of English skills, 34 percentiles in reading rate, 9 percentiles in comprehension accuracy, and 24 percentiles on an outlining test. A control group taking and retaking these tests over a comparable period of time showed very slight gains. The students in the how-to-study course received 17 per cent more A's and B's on a term paper in another course than a control group with comparable background. Fewer of the trained students withdrew or were dropped from the university than in the control group, and the grade point average of the trained students was .15 grade points higher for the year than that of the control group. Several aspects of the students' personal and social adjustment also showed improvement.

The Approach to Improvement of Study Skills

It takes more than knowledge to improve study skills. Not only must the student know what effective study skills are like but he must patiently practice until he has acquired them. He can quickly learn enough to tell some one else how to study but he will have to use continued effort in order to develop effective study skills in himself.

The program obviously has to be individualized to fit each student's needs. Students progress differently and vary in the errors they make while learning new skills. Methods which are of value in dealing with one student's problems may be of little use to another student. More than other courses, this program demands a highly individualized laboratory approach. And unlike other courses, it may be said that the subject studied is the student himself.

The situation in this class has a definite analogy to coaching in athletics. In teaching a swimmer the crawl stroke, a coach presents it as a new method and not as a patchwork modification of the dog paddle. And it takes more than one explanation or trial since continuing practice is necessary to develop polished skill. But practice alone is not enough because the swimmer does not recognize his errors; a coach, on the other hand, can spot difficulties and make definite suggestions. Similarly in study-skill training, higher-level work skills will be demonstrated and then, through the aid of tests and observation of work, further training suggestions will be made. The student can gain little without such diagnostic aid.

Another aspect of study skills, also analogous to coaching in athletics, concerns the importance of motivation in improvement. The writer's attitude toward his own game of golf will illustrate this point. Although the course of his ball may be likened to the meanderings of a child's tiddlywink, the writer does not see any great need to improve his game, or at least he does not want to take the trouble to work at it. In this case, no coach in the world can do much

[6] L. C. Pressey, The permanent effects of training in methods of study on college success, *School and Soc.*, 1928, 28:403–404.

[7] J. W. Sherburne, *Problems and Outcomes of a College Remedial Program*, Ph.D. dissertation, Ohio State Univ., 1938, 411 pp.

good. To state this principle in a positive form, it has been found that the student must sincerely desire to improve his study skills before these projects can be of much assistance. Mere exposure to such a program will not help him.

Finally, it is obvious that emphasis will be placed on developing effective skills, not just in finding out about them. Much of this book is devoted to helping the student discover his difficulties and learn what to do about them; some practice exercises are included but much of the actual practice should be done in his other courses. The student will get his practice by actually doing his work more effectively during study hours, in other classes, while reading at the library, and so on. Evaluation of achievement should be based on how much progress a student makes toward remedying his problems rather than on how much he knows in comparison to others.

Self Insight

Does the typical student know how good he is in various traits? How poor he may be in others? He doubtless feels that by the time he is in college he ought to know himself quite well. In such traits as height and weight, where he has had frequent measurements and has seen tables of norms, he probably does have a fairly accurate notion, but everyday life provides few opportunities for objective measures of abilities and other personality traits which affect school success. A person must be able to determine whether or not he needs help in developing study skills so the question of how accurately students estimate their own abilities becomes important in a how-to-study program.

The discussion of this topic will have greater interest and meaning for the reader when he fills out the following Check List. Checks can be lightly made and erased later; no one will ask to see the results. Ratings should be frank and honest. Later in the book, tests are provided for some of these traits; the reader may be interested in seeing how accurately he can estimate his relative standing.

How do you compare in each of the following traits with the other students in your college? If you feel that you are in the top fifth (20 per cent) on a given trait, check in the first or left-hand box; if you feel that you are in the bottom fifth on that trait, check in the third or right-hand box; but if you feel that you are in the middle 60 per cent on that trait, check in the middle box.

Interesting results have been obtained from using this type of rating sheet with high-school and college students. In several schools, the entire junior or senior class was asked to fill out such a sheet; since each student compared himself to the rest of the

	In My College, I'm in the		
	Top 20 Per Cent	Middle 60 Per Cent	Bottom 20 Per Cent
Speed of reading			
Ability to understand textbooks			
Vocabulary			
At ease with persons of own sex			
Honesty			
Note-taking ability			
Spelling			
Grammar			
Ability to recite in class			

class and everyone in the class answered, the distribution of rating in the three levels should have been 20, 60, and 20 per cent, respectively. Every effort was made to get as accurate estimates as possible; the students were told that they would not be asked to sign their names and that the data were to be used only as part of a research project. The actual results showed a marked tendency to overrate! For instance, only 11 per cent on the average rated themselves in the bottom fifth on a trait. Thus only 1 per cent felt they were in the bottom fifth in honesty, while 59 per cent felt they were more honest than the top 20 per cent of their classmates. Only 3 per cent felt they were in the bottom 20 per cent in being at ease with their own sex, but 45 per cent felt they were more at ease than the top fifth of their classmates. Only 8 per cent felt they were in the bottom fifth in ability to understand textbooks and 37 per cent felt that they were in the top fifth.[8] Such overratings are in part products of (1) an unwillingness on the part of a person to admit to himself (the results were otherwise anonymous) that he might be deficient and (2) the normal tendency to view oneself through rose-colored glasses. It is little wonder that a lecture or an assignment on how to improve usually does so little good when the advice seems to apply so much more to someone else than to oneself!

Even though there is a tendency to rate oneself high, is a person's self-rating related to his score on a standardized test which measures the same trait? Various studies indicate not. In one study in which students were asked to estimate how intelligent they were in comparison to other college students, only 40 per cent placed themselves within the correct fifth of where they actually belonged; 41 per cent overestimated and 19 per cent underestimated grossly.[9] In another study students' estimate of how many words they knew correlated only .50 with their actual test scores, i.e., these students could estimate their own scores only 14 per cent better than a blindfolded man could by pulling numbers from a hat.[10] Other studies of ability, English usage, and vocational interests show similar results.[11] This small relationship between estimate and score indicates that students may actually be strangers to their own relative abilities.

The function of this discussion is to point out the need for the use of diagnostic tests in how-to-study training. Such testing, however, is not to be used in grading—it is solely for the information of the student. To assure the reader of this fact, the keys for all tests in the book are printed in Appendix II.

One of the first steps in how-to-study work is to help a student discover his profile of abilities and skills. Such self-discovery is of value in itself and shows where training is needed. Feelings of security in schoolwork are promoted by knowledge of areas of competence, and energies can be focused where they will do the most good when specific difficulties are pointed out. A student with such knowledge will not need to feel, as some do, that he may be altogether "dumb." Because diagnostic tests show what needs to be worked on, a "rifle" rather than a "shotgun" approach can be used to pick off specific problems. Finally, a testing

[8] J. C. Wright, A Study of High School Students' Insight into Their Problems and Resources, Master's thesis, Ohio State Univ., 1944.

[9] T. H. Schutte, Students' estimates of their ability and achievement, J. Educ. Res., 1929, 20:394–396.

[10] R. M. Bear and H. S. Odbert, Insight of older students into their knowledge of word meanings, School Rev., 1941, 49:754–760.

[11] S. Arsenian, Own estimate and objective measurement, J. Educ. Psych., 1942, 33:291–302; N. D. M. Hirsch, Relationship between interest, ability, and self-estimated ability among maladjusted boys, J. Abn. & Soc. Psych., 1939, 34:395–399; R. C. Crosby and A. L. Winsor, The validity of students' estimates of their interests, J. Appl. Psych., 1941, 25:408–414.

program before and after training provides concrete proof of gains.

How to Use This Book

1. *Organization of the Book.* This book is designed to assist a student in learning how to secure the most from his college life: in the classroom, in his study, and on the campus. The projects will assist him in analyzing the effectiveness of various determinants of his success at college and in selecting suitable steps for improvement. The projects are presented in three general groupings: (I) higher-level work skills, (II) educational deficiencies, and (III) problems indirectly affecting scholastic success. Projects in Part One concern specialized work skills developed from research on techniques of learning, i.e., Survey Q3R Method of Studying, Effective Skills in Examinations, Skills in Attack and Concentration, Preparing Reports, and Classroom Skills. Projects in Part Two deal with deficiencies in reading, writing, and arithmetic which are surprisingly frequent among college students. Projects in Part Three relate to problems of health, vocational choice, recreational and social adjustment, and personal adjustment—problems which distract some students so much as to affect their success in college. These projects may be taken up in whatever order most interests a student. Some may wish to work in different sections of the book at the same time. For instance, while working on the Survey Q3R Method in the next project, a student may wish to work on reading rate in Project VII and also on making a vocational decision through Project XI. As a result, the individual members of a how-to-study class may not wish to emphasize the same projects nor take them up in the same order. In the final project, the student is given an opportunity to evaluate his progress in all these potential problem areas.

So much for a general description, but you, the reader, are more interested in your own diagnosis and treatment than in a general discussion of student problems, especially since each student's problems are so distinctly individual. In other words, what are your problems and what should you do about them?

The first step in using each project is evaluation; that is, how you stand in that skill or trait. With this information you may decide whether or not you are satisfied with that particular level of performance. The project will also indicate whether new higher levels of performance are possible beyond even the present level of good students. This information again provides a basis for deciding on which projects you wish to work, as well as giving useful diagnostic information for a starting point.

The second step is devoted to reading about how you may improve these abilities and skills. Space is provided in each project so that you may summarize the difficulties found and suggest the nature of the training program. The third and last step deals with practice and is, of course, the most important part of the whole project. Little written material can be prepared for this step because practice must be carried on in your actual courses in order to obtain the best results. This fact emphasizes that this is not a program of reading but of practice. You can rather quickly read a project and carry out the evaluative and diagnostic steps; but if you find a problem area, it will take constant application to obtain improvement. Furthermore, as you work on improving these skills, it will take continuing diagnosis to point out what still needs to be done to develop such skills fully.

In brief, your job is to find problem areas as soon as possible, to determine the specific nature of the difficulty and what higher-level skills are possible, and then to undertake a training program. This last task is the most difficult and time-consuming, but it makes the preliminary ones worth while. Aside from completing the diagnostic step, every student is not expected to put the same effort on all projects. You should select areas of need and there devote most of your time to programs of training.

2. *The Counselor and the Laboratory.* You may find it difficult to determine without help whether or not a given project will be worth while for you to work on. You may also find it difficult to decide just what training activity you should try. Further, you may have difficulty in deciding how much to do. As mentioned earlier, how-to-study training is in many respects similar to learning golf where an observer or coach can see what needs to be worked on and make suitable suggestions. Furthermore, more effective suggestions can be made if a student's actual studying can be frequently observed. For these reasons, how-to-study training is done most effectively in a laboratory situation with the aid of a counselor. A student can benefit from working with this book without outside assistance, but greater help will be obtained if he has some other person analyze his study methods, notes, examinations, and papers, and then make suggestions. Most colleges provide such help through how-to-study counselors or through courses on how-to-study. The exercises in each project are oriented to help the reader make effective use of this counselor or course.

The term "counselor" is used throughout this book instead of "instructor" in order to emphasize the characteristics this observer or coach must have. He is there to help you with your particular problems. He will not lecture merely to give you information and he will not urge you to do this or that; he is there, available for *consultation.* If you want help, he can check your methods and plans and so save wasted effort.

3. *Diagnostic Tests.* Many tests have been provided so as to give a picture of your study abilities. If as many of these as possible are completed early, a basis is provided for planning a training program. The counselor can also be more helpful if he has such test information and any further data which you feel will help explain your study difficulties. Whatever information is given will be considered confidential.

The materials necessary for using a test are included in the book: the directions for taking the test, the key for correcting the responses, the norms for interpreting results, and specific exercises for correcting errors. This arrangement enables you to take tests at the time they are most needed (except in a few instances where some assistance will have to be given in timing a test); it also permits you to score a test immediately so that you may go on with a minimum of interruption.

The following procedure is used in correcting tests. After filling out a test, tear out the key which appears in the back of this book. Fold it close to the column of correct answers, place the strip by your answers, and mark those that are incorrect. It is also useful at this time to write in the correct answer and, if designated on the key, the symbol for the rule that is violated. Place your score (usually the number of items right) in the place designated on the test.

The next step is to find out what the test result means, for a given score has little meaning by itself. Two bases for interpretation are provided:

1. All the items in the tests have been selected because they represent important aspects or factors in college courses. For instance, the items in the English Survey Test represent the most frequent major errors which students make in writing and are not merely a sampling of grammar rules. It might be said then that as a well-educated person

you should know or be able to do anything you may miss.

2. Another meaningful and possibly more interesting approach is to show how well you do in comparison with other college students.[12] To do this, tables of norms are provided for many of the tests. Your next step, then, is to find a comparative value (percentile rank, median, or quartile) in the table of norms and place this beside your test score. These norm terms have the following meanings: A "percentile" indicates the per cent among college freshmen who do poorer than you on that test. A "median" indicates the score of the middlemost person among college freshmen, and the "first quartile" and the "third quartile" refer to the scores made by the persons who had one-quarter and three-quarters of the freshmen below them respectively. This emphasis on comparison to a college group is important because students in higher education tend to be a select group. The percentile ranks show how you compare with your competition in college but not with the population at large. For instance, one may be at the tenth percentile in intelligence for college students and still be above average for this trait in comparison to the general population of the United States.

A table for summarizing your test results is placed on the back page of this book. Such a list permits a quick evaluation of tests taken and, when torn out, will provide a summary of your test results. Each time you take a test, write your result not only on the test but also on this Summary Sheet. (As other activities in this book are completed, they, too, should be recorded on this Summary Sheet.)

The final step in making use of a test result is to determine for yourself the level of skill you wish to attain. You may be satisfied with your present level and wish to do nothing further on that skill. In certain areas, however, you will feel challenged to improve your skills and so plan a training program. If, at the end of the school term, you wish to measure your gains and find what problems remain, you may retest yourself on the tests in this book, or second forms are available for some areas. (See Project XIV.)

Certain shortcomings of tests should be noted when you make interpretations. First, most tests are somewhat unreliable. That is, if the test or a similar test were repeated, one would not get exactly the same score because of differences in how hard one worked, accidental variations in the difficulty of the tests, etc. Not that your score has no value, for this unreliability will produce fluctuations of only a few points. Second, you may punctuate very carefully on the punctuation test, but in your letters home leave out most of these marks. The test will tend to give your best performance.

4. *Work to Be Completed in This Project.* Please fill out the following questionnaires with complete information. While this will be only a rough measure of information concerning yourself, the checking on the Problem Check List will help clarify your thinking and the information on both questionnaires will be of great help to the counselor.

---

[12] The function of some tests in this book is to help organize your thinking about certain topics. Others function as quick ways of giving your counselor information. These tests are not interpreted through percentiles; other directions accompany these tests.

STUDENT DATA SHEET: Date.......................

Personal: Name.. Age.......... Sex: M F

Major... Year: Fr. So. Jr. Sr.

School Address... Phone.......................

Home Address..

How many years have you lived in a city (over 10,000 population)...........................

town (1,000–10,000)..................,village or country (under 1,000)...................

Occupation of father..................................... Mother.....................

Education of father..................................... Mother.....................

Of whom beside yourself does your immediate family consist (i.e., father, mother, two younger

sisters, one older brother, grandfather, grandmother)?.....................................

Religious preference...

Educational: Which high school subjects did you like best?...................................

.... Like least?............................

What high schools or colleges have you attended?.......................................

....

What scholastic honors (valedictorian, honor society, scholarship) have you won in school?

....

What grades did you make last term?..

....

What courses in psychology have you had?...

Why did you enroll in this remedial course?...

....

Did someone suggest your enrollment?...

What courses are you taking this term?...

....

Vocational: What are your vocational plans?...

....

Why did you make this vocational choice?...

....

What other occupations have you considered?..

Have you talked over your vocational plans with anyone?................................

Whom?...

What work have you ever done (summer or regular; part or full time)?....................

....

Are you now working to help earn your way?........ If so, what are you doing?............

....

Social: To what organizations (community as well as school or college) have you belonged? List specific organizations such as 4-H Club, Boy Scouts, Epworth League, sorority, editorial board of school paper, debating team, football team, orchestra, dramatics club, Latin club, student,

government board, etc. Draw a line under organizations to *which you now belong*..............

....

....

What offices have you held in any organization (include chairmanships of committees)?........

....

To what social gatherings or affairs have you been in the past four weeks?...................

....

About how many days have you been away from home in the last year?.....................

Recreational: What magazines do you read fairly regularly?...................................

....

What are your favorite sports, recreations, and hobbies?...................................

....

Where have you traveled?..

Give below any other information about yourself you think of significance.

PROBLEM CHECK LIST

COLLEGE FORM

By Ross L. Mooney

Date..............................

DIRECTIONS FOR FILLING OUT THE CHECK LIST

This is not a test. It is a list of troublesome problems which often face students in college—problems of health, money, social life, relations with people, religion, studying, selecting courses, and the like. You are to go through the list, pick out the particular problems which are of concern to you, indicate those which are of most concern, and make a summary interpretation in your own words. More specifically, you are to take these three steps:

(1) Read the list slowly, pause at each item, and if it suggests something which is troubling you, *underline* it, thus, "34. Sickness in the family."

Go through the whole list, underlining the items which suggest troubles (difficulties, worries) of concern to you.

(2) After completing the first step, look back over the items you have underlined and *circle the numbers* in front of the items which are of *most concern* to you, thus, "㉞ Sickness in the family."

(3) After completing the first and second steps, answer the summarizing questions on pages 5 and 6.

Copyright, 1941, by
Bureau of Educational Research
Ohio State University
Columbus, Ohio

For Counselors' Reference—Space for Area Totals

Cir.	Tot.
HPD	
FLE	
SRA	
SPR	
PPR	
CSM	
HF	
MR	
ACW	
FVE	
CTP	

Total

First Step: Read the list slowly, and as you come to a problem which troubles you, underline it.

1 Tiring very easily	56 Not as robust as I should be
2 Being underweight	57 Not enough outdoor air and sunshine
3 Being overweight	58 Frequent illnesses
4 Not enough exercise	59 Threatened with a serious ailment
5 Not enough sleep	60 Afraid I may need an operation
6 Not enough suitable clothes to wear	61 Going in debt for college expenses
7 Too little money for clothes	62 Graduation threatened by lack of funds
8 Having less money than friends have	63 Needing money for education beyond college
9 Managing my finances poorly	64 Going through school on too little money
10 Needing a part-time job now	65 Doubting college is worth my financial struggle
11 Not enough time for recreation	66 Boring week ends
12 In too few student activities	67 Too little social life
13 Lacking a place to entertain friends	68 Awkward in meeting people
14 Wanting to learn how to entertain	69 Slow in getting acquainted with people
15 Being ill at ease at social affairs	70 Unskilled in conversation
16 Shyness	71 Unpopular
17 Being slow in making friends	72 Being made fun of
18 No real friends in college	73 Being talked about
19 Being called "high-hat"	74 Being watched by other people
20 Feelings too easily hurt	75 Feeling inferior
21 Too self-centered	76 Moodiness, having the "blues"
22 Taking things too seriously	77 Failing to get ahead
23 Nervousness	78 Not doing anything well
24 Getting too excited	79 Too easily discouraged
25 Not having any fun	80 Sometimes wishing I'd never been born
26 Too few dates	81 Too inhibited in sex relations
27 Not mixing well with the opposite sex	82 Uninterested in opposite sex
28 Lack of sex attractiveness	83 Doubting sexual virility
29 "Going steady"	84 Disturbed by ideas of sexual acts
30 Being in love with someone I can't marry	85 Wondering if I'll ever get married
31 Being criticized by my parents	86 Parents separated or divorced
32 Mother	87 Death in the family
33 Father	88 Father not living
34 Sickness in the family	89 Mother not living
35 Parents sacrificing too much for me	90 Feeling I don't really have a home
36 Belonging to a minority religious group	91 Wanting communion with God
37 Belonging to a minority racial group	92 Too little chance to develop my own religion
38 Affected by religious or racial prejudice	93 Wanting more chances for religious worship
39 Missing spiritual elements in college life	94 Confused in my religious beliefs
40 Bothered by vulgarity in college talk	95 Confused on some moral questions
41 Feeling lost in college	96 Getting low grades
42 Purpose in going to college not clear	97 Fearing failure in college
43 Disliking college	98 Enrolled in wrong courses
44 Don't know how to study effectively	99 Wanting to change to another college
45 Attending college on insistence of family	100 Wanting to leave college
46 Restless at delay in starting life work	101 Unable to enter desired vocation
47 Doubting wisdom of my vocational choice	102 Not physically fit for desired vocation
48 Family opposing my choice of vocation	103 Not interested in any vocation
49 Being told I will fail in chosen vocation	104 Dreading to think of a life of hard work
50 Doubting economic value of college degree	105 Doubting college prepares me for working
51 College too indifferent to students' needs	106 Hard to study in living quarters
52 Dull classes	107 No suitable place to study on campus
53 Too many poor teachers	108 Too few books in the library
54 Teachers lacking grasp of subject matter	109 Textbooks hard to understand
55 Teachers lacking personality	110 Inadequate high school training

				Cir.	Tot.

111 Poor posture
112 Poor complexion
113 Too short
114 Too tall
115 Not very attractive physically

166 Frequent sore throat
167 Frequent colds
168 Nose or sinus trouble
169 Speech handicap (stammering, etc.)
170 Weak eyes

221 Frequent headaches
222 Menstrual disorders
223 Lack of appetite
224 Digestive troubles
225 Not getting proper diet

276 Poor teeth
277 Poor hearing
278 Tired feet
279 Physical handicap
280 Being clumsy and awkward

HPD

---

116 Needing money for better health care
117 Having to watch every penny I spend
118 Poor living quarters
119 Family worried about finances
120 Disliking financial dependence on family

171 Living in an inconvenient location
172 Lacking privacy in living quarters
173 Too little money for room rent
174 Having financial dependents
175 Too many financial problems

226 Tiring of same meals all the time
227 Too little money for board
228 No regular source of income
229 Needing a job in vacations
230 Too little money for recreation

281 Doing more outside work than is good for me
282 Working late at night on a job
283 Working for all my expenses
284 Getting low wages
285 Dissatisfied with my present job

FLE

---

121 Living outside the stream of college life
122 Nothing interesting to do in spare time
123 Having no hobby
124 Not enjoying many things others enjoy
125 Wanting to learn how to dance

176 Unsure of my social etiquette
177 Awkward in making a date
178 Not knowing what to do on a date
179 Not knowing how to select clothes
180 Not fitting in the group with which I live

231 Not enough time to myself
232 Too little time for sports
233 Too little chance to enjoy art or music
234 Too little chance to listen to the radio
235 Too little chance to go to shows

286 Unable to lead a well-rounded life
287 Too little chance to do what I want to do
288 Too much social life
289 In too many student activities
290 Too little chance to read what I like

SRA

---

126 Being left out of things
127 Being regarded as queer
128 Being criticized by others
129 Hurting people's feelings
130 Losing friends

181 Not getting along well with other people
182 Disliking certain persons
183 Being disliked by certain persons
184 Getting into arguments
185 Being jealous

236 Wanting a more pleasing personality
237 Lacking leadership ability
238 Too easily led by other people
239 Being a poor judge of people
240 Picking the wrong kind of friends

291 Failing to get the confidence of people
292 Being snubbed
293 Feeling that nobody understands me
294 Have no one to tell my troubles to
295 Dislike talking about personal affairs

SPR

---

131 Unhappy too much of the time
132 Worrying about unimportant things
133 Daydreaming
134 Forgetting things
135 Afraid when left alone

186 Losing my temper
187 Stubbornness
188 Carelessness
189 Laziness
190 Not taking things seriously enough

241 Afraid of making mistakes
242 Can't make up my mind about things
243 Lacking self-confidence
244 Lost—no sense of direction in my life
245 Can't see the value of daily things I do

296 Too many personal problems
297 Unwilling to face a serious problem now
298 Bad dreams
299 Insanity
300 Thoughts of suicide

PPR

---

136 Embarrassed in discussions of sex
137 Insufficient knowledge about sex matters
138 Venereal disease
139 Afraid of close contact with opposite sex
140 Wondering if I'll find a suitable mate

191 Going with a person my family won't accept
192 Being in love
193 Deciding whether I'm in love
194 Thinking too much about sex matters
195 Finding it hard to control sex urges

246 Girl friend
247 Boy friend
248 Engagement
249 Marriage
250 Putting off marriage

301 Disappointment in a love affair
302 Breaking up a love affair
303 Petting and necking
304 Going too far in sex relations
305 Wanting love and affection

CSM

---

141 Friends not welcomed at home
142 Home life unhappy
143 Family quarrels
144 Not getting along with brother or sister
145 Not getting along with a step-parent

196 Heavy home responsibilities
197 Parents expecting too much of me
198 Clash of opinions between me and parents
199 Talking back to my parents
200 Parents' drinking

251 Not telling parents everything
252 Parents not trusting me
253 Being treated like a child at home
254 Being an only child
255 Wanting more freedom at home

306 Getting home too seldom
307 Living at home, or too close to home
308 Wishing I had a better family background
309 Relatives interfering with family affairs
310 Afraid of someone in the family

HF

---

146 Failing to go to church
147 Disliking church services
148 Being forced to go to church
149 Rejecting earlier religious beliefs
150 Doubting value of worship and prayer

201 Failing to see relation of religion to life
202 Doubting existence of God
203 Losing faith in religion
204 Science conflicting with my religion
205 Never having had a religion

256 Bothered by ideas of heaven and hell
257 Having a guilty conscience
258 Yielding to temptations
259 Can't forget some mistakes I've made
260 Getting a bad reputation

311 Moral code weakening
312 Trying to break off a bad habit
313 Sometimes being dishonest
314 Drinking
315 Cheating in classes

MR

---

151 Carrying too heavy a class load
152 Absent from classes too often
153 Not enough time for study
154 Poor memory
155 Not fundamentally interested in books

206 Slow in mathematics
207 Slow with theories and abstractions
208 Weak in logical reasoning
209 Not smart enough in scholastic ways
210 Unable to express myself in words

261 Worrying about examinations
262 Not getting studies done on time
263 Unable to concentrate well
264 Trouble in outlining or note-taking
265 Trouble in using the library

316 Afraid to speak up in class discussions
317 Vocabulary too limited
318 Weak in writing
319 Weak in spelling or grammar
320 Slow in reading

ACW

---

156 Wondering if I'll be successful in life
157 Needing to plan ahead for the future
158 Not knowing what I really want
159 Trying to combine marriage and career
160 Concerned about military service

211 Not knowing the kind of person I want to be
212 Not knowing where I belong in the world
213 Needing to decide on an occupation
214 Needing information about occupations
215 Needing to know my vocational abilities

266 Needing vocational training beyond college
267 Doubting I can get a job in chosen vocation
268 Wanting advice on next steps after college
269 Choosing courses to take next term
270 Choosing best courses to prepare for a job

321 Afraid of unemployment after graduation
322 Don't know how to look for a job
323 College of little help in getting a job
324 Lacking work experience to get a job
325 Doubting ability to handle a good job

FVE

---

161 Being without a good college adviser
162 Having no friends on the faculty
163 Teachers lacking interest in students
164 Teachers lacking understanding of youth
165 Too little freedom in classes

216 Not enough chances to talk to teachers
217 Classes too large
218 Teachers doing too much of the talking
219 Teachers too theoretical
220 Teachers not practicing what they preach

271 Wanting courses not offered by the school
272 Wanting courses I'm not allowed to take
273 Courses too unrelated to each other
274 Having an unfair teacher
275 Not getting along with a teacher

326 College system too arbitrary
327 Forced to take courses I don't like
328 Too much work required in some courses
329 Grades unfair as measures of ability
330 Having unfair tests

CTP

Second Step: Look back over the items you have underlined and circle the numbers in front of the problems which are troubling you most.

Total |

Third Step : Pages 5 and 6

Third Step: Answer the following five questions:

SUMMARIZING QUESTIONS

1. Do you feel that the items you have marked on the list give a well-rounded picture of your problems? ......Yes. ......No. If any additional items or explanations are desired, please indicate them here.

2. How would you summarize your chief problems in your own words? Write a brief summary.

3. If the opportunity were offered, would you like to talk over any of these problems with someone on the college staff? ......Yes. ......No. If so, do you know the particular person(s) with whom you would like to have these talks? ......Yes. ......No.

Note to Counselors: Normally the statistical summary is to be made by the counselor. In some situations, however, the counselor may want students to make their own summaries. In these cases, students should be given definite instructions and a demonstration of the method, preferably after they have filled out the check list.

Instructions for Making a Statistical Summary

For convenience in summarizing results on an individual case or on groups of students, the 330 problems are classified in eleven areas:

(1) Health and Physical Development (HPD)
(2) Finances, Living Conditions, and Employment (FLE)
(3) Social and Recreational Activities (SRA)
(4) Social-Psychological Relations (SPR)
(5) Personal-Psychological Relations (PPR)
(6) Courtship, Sex, and Marriage (CSM)
(7) Home and Family (HF)
(8) Morals and Religion (MR)
(9) Adjustment to College Work (ACW)
(10) The Future: Vocational and Educational (FVE)
(11) Curriculum and Teaching Procedures (CTP)

There are thirty problems in each area, these being arranged in groups of five items across the six columns of problems. The first area is the top group, the second area is the second group, and so on down the pages. On page 4, at the end of each group, is a box in which to record the count of problems marked in each area. In the left half of the box put the number of items circled as important; in the right half, put the total number marked in the area (including the circled items as well as those underlined only). At the bottom of the page enter the totals for the list. If desired, the area totals can be recopied to the first page for greater convenience in later reference.

PART ONE

HIGHER–LEVEL WORK SKILLS

Years ago many persons were taught to swim by throwing them in the water. After their initial terror they tried to propel themselves toward the shore while still thrashing the water to stay up. The result of such self-instruction was commonly known as the "dog paddle" and eventually permitted the swimmer to feel reasonably safe in the water and to enjoy it. Some undoubtedly became known as the best swimmers in the county, but in modern competition such dog paddlers would be left far behind. Modern methods of swimming were not found by comparing good and poor dog paddlers; they are based on scientific research on how to reduce the resistance of the body in the water and how to obtain the most forward push with the least effort. As a result, highly efficient swimming methods such as the crawl have been designed and taught. Because of further research and expert coaching, new swimmings records are constantly being set.

Present and possible future study techniques furnish an analogous picture. Typically, students have to learn to study as best they can, but such trial-and-error methods result only in a hodgepodge of inefficient techniques. Since everyone is about equally inefficient, however, a student can maintain his place in class on the basis of intelligence and effort. But what if this student could learn an "Australian crawl" method of studying! His work would seem much easier and his performance would be much better.

The reader may be surprised to find that even good students have bad habits, but several illustrations can be given. One study of soldiers assigned to ASTP training showed they were a highly select group in terms of intelligence, previous scholastic record, and present knowledge, but their study skills were no better on the average than those of other college students.[1] Inquiry brought out that, being brighter than their classmates, they had been able to get by in high school with their wits and personality. Other studies show that even good students pay little attention to boldface headings in books, i.e., they read as well when such headings are omitted, and they know few of the short cuts in term-paper writing. Of course, some people like to do things the hard way, but others—because they are lazy or want to get done sooner or want to do better—like to learn easier and more efficient ways of doing things.

The projects in Part One describe a series of higher-level work skills which have been devised from a scientific analysis of how persons learn and of the nature of school materials. They are called "higher level" because they represent an entirely different approach to studying than you have been using.[2] They will

[1] F. P. Robinson, Study skills of soldiers in ASTP, *School and Soc.*, 1943, 58:398–399; also C. W. Brown, The study habits of failing and successful students in the first two years of college, *J. Exper. Educ.*, 1941, 9:205–209; F. D. Brooks and J. C. Heston, The validity of items in a study habits inventory, *J. Educ. Psych.*, 1945, 36:257–270.

[2] The idea of higher-level work skills is not new nor is it limited to swimming and study skills. Time and motion studies of expert bricklayers showed many inefficiencies and, when new work arrangements and new techniques were taught, output increased 192 per cent. Similarly candy dippers were helped to increase their output 88 per cent and seemed to others to work less hard than regular candy dippers. Experiments have been carried out in which persons were taught methods of pitch discrimination, puzzle solving, and card sorting with resulting performance distinctly above what they had been able to do before. Finally, some experiments have been carried out in teaching persons techniques of analyzing problems with resulting improvement in the quality of their answers and the speed with which they were obtained.

be taught as new methods and not as an attempt to patch up your present techniques, i.e., the best way to teach the crawl is to teach it as a whole skill rather than as a modification of the dog paddle. Evidence as to the efficiency of these higher-level work skills will be brought out in each project. The first two projects take up the problem of school learning in its chronological aspects: selecting and comprehending the essential ideas, and remembering and demonstrating knowledge on examinations. The next three projects in Part One discuss skills in attack and concentration, skills in preparing reports, and skills in the classroom.

PROJECT II

SURVEY Q3R METHOD OF STUDYING

Have you ever noticed how students study? Everyone has his own techniques which typically are not very efficient. The following description (possibly somewhat exaggerated) may remind you of some of the ways your friends study if not of yourself.

A Typical Student

Let us for the moment skip over the difficulties of getting to the library, finding a suitable place to study, looking around at people, finding out what the assignment is, and getting settled down; these are discussed in a later project. Once started, how does our typical student go about studying? Having found the first page of the assignment, what does he do next? He probably looks for the last page, holds the assignment up to see how thick it is and then leaves a finger at the end of the lesson as a goal indicator. Have you ever noticed how students, after reading a while, will hold up the part read and the part to be read in order to compare their relative thickness? Also indicative is the student who, when asked what the lesson was about, looked at the length of the lesson and said "about thirty pages."

Note how many students follow the lines with their fingers as they read. One almost gets an impression of dutiful line following so that the next day they can truthfully say "I don't remember, but honest I read every word." Some so carefully mark the cadence of their plodding eyes that their fingernails seem to be plowing each line under. Not all are "line plowers" but certainly few reach the stage of using headings and context clues.

Most readers feel that they understand the material as they read; the trouble comes later in trying to remember it. Thus as they read along they can continually murmur "mmhm," "uhhmm" as they see each idea, much as a mirror passing over the book might clearly reflect what was printed. On finishing, the book is pushed aside with a sigh. To an impolite inquiry as to what ideas were discussed, the typical reader has a nebulous feeling that there was much he *had* understood but it now is jumbled. And rather than dwell on this discomforting fact, he prefers to say, "Well that's done, now for the next lesson."

Of course, there are a few really conscientious students who reread their lessons; some students read their lessons as many as four and five times in one sitting. But their testimony indicates that this approach is inefficient and not very fruitful. Other students laboriously copy out notes—as much as five pages on a lesson—only to find later that they would rather reread the book than their handwriting.

How Effective Are Typical Study Methods?

So much for a caricature of the composite, typical student. What are the facts as to the outcomes from such study methods? When several thousand high-school students were tested immediately after reading a selection they averaged only 53 per cent right on the quiz. Other experiments also show that the average student gets only about half of

13

the ideas asked on an immediate quiz.[1] Since probably every student felt that he understood each of the ideas as he read the selection, what can be causing the difficulty? A similar problem is found when a series of numbers, such as 8 9 4 1 6 5 8 7 3 5, is read once; each number is readily recognized as it is read but somehow by the end of the series the whole thing is mixed up.

And what little is learned seems to be forgotten so rapidly! The solid line in Chart 2

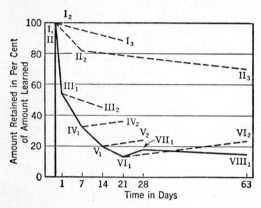

CHART 2. Curves of retention without intervening recall (solid lines) and with intervening recall (dotted lines) at various time intervals. (From Spitzer.)

shows how rapidly the several thousand high-school students mentioned above tended to forget what they had learned from a single reading. (The conditions which permit memory to persist as shown by the broken lines in Chart 2 will be discussed later.) Thus at the end of two weeks the average student could recall only 20 per cent of what he knew immediately after reading; and this, it will be recalled, was only 53 per cent right.

Some conscientious students try rereading their lessons in order to raise the level of their comprehension accuracy and to retard

forgetting. But simply rereading several times in one sitting does not help comprehension accuracy very much; thus in one experiment the average reader got 69 per cent right on an easy test after one reading of the text and only 74, 75, and 74 per cent right with two, three, and four successive readings, respectively.[2] (Later on it will be shown, however, that reading and then rereading at a different time is more effective.)

What then can be done? Is there some other more efficient method of studying than reading and rereading a lesson? It is evident that the average student, through trial-and-error learning, has not found an efficient way. One further experiment illustrates this point and indicates one source for building a better reading technique. In this experiment it was found that a superior group of students read no faster or any more accurately when a selection was printed with headings than they did when reading an equivalent selection without any headings.[3] But a boldface heading indicates the subject of the text which follows; it can be used to call to mind what is already known and to precomprehend or guess as to what will be said. Such a preorientation also helps a student discern what is and is not important as he reads.

Rather than analyze the skills of good students and suggest that poor students emulate them, the educational psychologist has more recently been conducting experiments to discover possible bases for devising more efficient study methods. New methods have been invented and their worthiness as study methods tried out. A higher-level method of studying will be presented later in this project but first it seems best to review the

[1] C. V. Good, The effect of a single reading versus two readings of a given body of material, *J. Educ. Meth.*, 1926, 5:325–329; H. F. Spitzer, Studies in retention, *J. Educ. Psych.*, 1939, 30:641–656; and see also the norms for the reading tests in this book.

[2] H. B. English, E. L. Welborn, and C. D. Killian, Studies in substance memorization, *J. Gen. Psych.*, 1934, 11:233–259.
[3] F. P. Robinson and Prudence Hall, Studies of high-level reading abilities, *J. Educ. Psych.*, 1941, 32:241–252.

two types of evidence used in devising this method: (a) cues provided by the way textbooks, lectures, and quizzes are prepared; and (b) new learning techniques obtained through extensive experimenting. These constitute the next two divisions of this project.

Cues in Course Materials

Rather than being an apparent piling up of line on line, textbooks are organized with definite cues, either in typography or in writing style, to point out what is important. One tends to read fiction straight along, but nonfiction is usually so written that the expert reader can know what the main idea is even as he starts to read a section and is able to skim, skip, or study in the right places. Training in the use of these cues will enable a student to speed up his reading, improve his comprehension of essential points, and—to be discussed more fully in the next project—predict quiz questions.

The three sources of these cues—in textbook, in class, and in previous quizzes—will each be discussed in turn.

1. Textbook Cues

Textbooks usually include many cues indicating what is important. If sensitive to them, a reader can readily increase his reading efficiency. An author in writing a textbook makes an outline of the six to ten major points to be developed and in the final printed copy has this outline inserted as the boldface headings starting each section. Major and minor points are differentiated by using centered and indented headings, and as further help these are often numbered. Some headings give the gist of the discussion which follows, others merely announce the topic but do not give the answer. For instance, the heading "Learning and Intelligence" indicates that these two topics will be discussed but does not say what the nature of their relationship is.

While headings which state the main thesis are more helpful with precomprehension, the mere indication of the topic can help the reader in looking for the answer.

Other cues are also used to indicate important points. Paragraphs typically have topic or summary sentences at the beginning or at the end which state the gist of the idea under discussion. Important statements or definitions are often put in italics or boldface type. Cue phrases and typographical cues are often used. For instance, watch for numbers as in "three kinds" or "four causes" followed by sentences or phrases set off by (1), (2), (3), or (a), (b), (c), (d). Or, sentences may begin with "First, . . . Second, . . . And lastly, ..." These represent dead giveaways as to equal and important subpoints in an outline. Authors frequently use a listing device to indicate briefly what is to be discussed in the next sections or as a summary at the end to show what has been discussed. Finally, the reader should pay especial attention to charts, diagrams, and maps; almost invariably the author uses them to present the *most important* ideas visually.[4]

It will be worth while to analyze several books to determine how these cues are used; some authors will prove to be more expert than others in their use. Sensitivity to these cues will do much to speed up reading and improve comprehension. In fact, it is through the use of such cues that phenomenally fast readers, the so-called "page-at-a-glance" readers, are able to perform; that is, by merely spotting these important cues

---

[4] Experience in writing manuals for the armed services has shown the value of these cue indicators. In fact, many of the manual writers adopted a plan of presenting points in short paragraphs which in turn were organized in an outline form. Cues such as numbering, boldface type, diagrams, etc., have also been much used. Research indicates that many textbook writers could improve the reading ability of students if they would modify their prose style through use of more cue indicators.

they can guess what will be said in between. But such skimming skill or, even more important, efficient study skill is not to be obtained through mere knowledge of these cues; there must be practice in their rapid recognition and use. Such practice will be provided at the end of this section and again later on.

2. Classroom Cues

A teacher's time in class is usually so limited that whatever he says should be important. Students may feel that this is not true of some lecturers, but even these professors meant to cover certain important points and may have wandered, or it may be that the students couldn't see the forest (main point) because they were too engrossed in the details of the trees (illustrations of the point).

A teacher will usually try to cover about half a dozen points more or less during a period. This may be represented by any combination from a couple of major points with several important subpoints to a series of equal ideas. The important skill to be discussed here is analysis of each teacher's lectures to determine if his lecture points are also emphasized in the textbook. If so, the student is doubly forewarned; both lecture notes and textbook should be studied thoroughly on these topics. If the lectures do not take up items in the book, it means that important supplemental points are being added which need to be known as well as those in the textbook. Suggestions on how to take lecture notes will be discussed in Project VI.

Finally, some cues as to the types of future quiz questions can be obtained by analyzing the questions which the teacher uses in class discussion. One can determine in general if the emphasis runs to definitions, lists, application, problems, or interpretation, and then study accordingly.

3. Cues from Previous Examinations

When a corrected exam is handed back, most students fail to recognize it as an important tool in studying. Many get little further than their test scores. Those who do look over the exam usually concentrate on what they did well, or feel like arguing with the instructor over items missed. On the other hand, an instructor's second quiz usually follows the same pattern as his first. Looking over the first test, one can see what types of questions are asked. Whether they are primarily true-false, completion, or essay is *not* important. But are definitions emphasized, or problems, or judgment questions, or lists? Do the questions come primarily from the textbook, laboratory book, or class lectures? Can you find where the topics for some of the questions appear in the text? Do they coincide with the headings? From such an analysis, one can often point up one's study technique for the next examination; one can then be more effective with no more effort.

Practice. In brief, then, three sources of cues—in textbook, lecture, and previous quizzes—provide the skilled student with means for promoting greater reading and listening efficiency and for pointing up his attempts to review for examinations. To sensitize you to these cues, you are asked to do four things at this time; further polishing exercises will be carried out later.

First, go back over this project to see what cues were used. Jot down the headings used in the form of an outline. Does this outline cover all of the important points as you remember them? Skim over the text and underline the other ones used, i.e., numbers, typographical cues, summary sentences, etc. Check these with your counselor for evaluation.

about reading that textbook in order to use the cues?

Second, rapidly glance over the selection used in the Art Reading Test and jot down a *brief* outline from the major cues there. Now compare this list of cues with the quiz used in the reading test; how many of the questions did you predict? The questions in the quiz are of two types: restating and illustrating points in the text. Do you feel that if you were to read more material by this author you could more easily prepare for a quiz? Check your outline with the counselor for suggestions.

Third, select a textbook from another one of your courses, mark the cues that the author uses to indicate important points, and check these with your counselor. Does this author give you good cues? What would be a good way to go

Fourth, in this same outside course and text-book, jot down the headings as a *brief* outline. Are there many important points? Compare this outline with your class notes on this same topic. Were many important points covered in class? Were they the same or different than the main points in the text? If you have a copy of the quiz questions over this section or can remember any of the questions, what is their relationship to the text or lecture outline?

EXPERIMENTS TO DISCOVER NEW METHODS

Analysis of the experimental attempts of educational psychologists to devise new learning methods provides a second basis for constructing higher-level study skills.

These experiments fall into two general categories: (1) techniques for selecting and comprehending what is important, and (2) ways to retard forgetting. The discussion will be organized accordingly.

SELECTING AND COMPREHENDING WHAT IS IMPORTANT

1. Value of Quick Preview

Several studies indicate that a quick preview of the headings or a look at the end summary is of help in reading a chapter. Thus in one experiment, 118 college sophomores were put in two equated groups, one group being shown how to skim over headings and summaries, the other not. When the two groups were then given a selection to read, the trained group read 24 per cent faster and as accurately as the students who read in the usual way.[5] Such a quick overview orients the reader and permits a partial precomprehension of what is to come; this head start speeds up the rate at which the selection can then be comprehended.

2. Value of Previous Questions

Of probably greater importance, however, is the discovery of techniques which im-

prove comprehension as well as rate. One idea tried by several experimenters has been to give questions to the readers before or as they read in order to give them a basis for selecting and organizing the ideas presented. Thus one experimenter divided 170 college students into two equated groups and had them read materials concerning science and the history of English literature. One group was given a list of 20 questions before reading; the other group was not. Comprehension was tested immediately after reading, and again two weeks later on a 40-item test (these 20 questions plus 20 other questions). As might be expected, the group given the questions did better on these questions, but they also did as well as the other group on the new questions. They were superior on the total tests, especially on the one given two weeks later; this is shown graphically in Chart 3. (Each bar represents a different selection for which results were obtained; all differences favor the method of using questions and a critical ratio of four is statistically significant.)[6]

Is there a *best time to introduce these questions*, i.e., before, during, or after reading? One interesting experiment sheds light

[5] H. Y. McClusky, An experiment on the influence of preliminary skimming on reading, *J. Educ. Psych.*, 1934, 25:521–529.

[6] E. Holmes, Reading guided by questions versus careful reading and rereading without questions, *School Rev.*, 1931, 39:361–371.

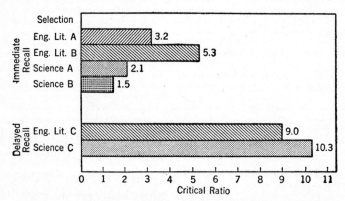

CHART 3. Reading, guided by questions, shows greater efficiency for both immediate and delayed recall than careful reading and rereading without use of questions. (Adapted from Holmes.)

on this problem.[7] In this study 1456 high-school students, divided into groups of equal ability, were given a selection about Florence, Italy, to study for 25 minutes. The selection read by each group, however, varied to this extent: For one group questions concerning facts and generalizations in the article were presented at the beginning; for another group these questions came at the end of the article; for a third group each question appeared at the beginning of the section in which it was answered; for a fourth group each question was placed at the end of the section in which it was answered; and for a fifth group no questions were given during the reading of the article. The test, which all the pupils took after reading the article, contained the questions already asked and other comparable questions. Of these patterns, the two most effective were: all the questions given at the beginning of the article; and each question placed at the beginning of the section in which it was answered. Furthermore, this and other experiments show that each of these two patterns has its unique advantages. A list of questions at the beginning of an article orients the reader to the whole subject in such a way that he can fit facts, not asked about, into a meaningful picture; this helps in their retention. On the other hand, it is difficult when reading a long assignment to keep a list of questions clearly enough in mind to help most efficiently in organizing the material. The use of questions at the beginning of each section gives an immediate questioning attitude and a core idea around which to organize the material which follows.

Two things seem evident, then. An initial overview of a lesson to determine "what it is about" speeds up reading and provides a general orientation that helps fit facts together so they will be better retained. Asking a question just before starting to read a section gives the *most* effective mental set for selecting and retaining the important facts and generalizations therein. As will be seen later, these two techniques can be combined into one effective study method.

What source can the student use to *find such helpful questions?* Teachers occasionally provide students with lists of questions to direct their study, or questions may be stated at the end of a chapter or in a laboratory manual. Such lists, if stated in a way to make the reader want to find the correct answers, are useful in providing an overview; true-false tests, on the other hand, are not helpful because the reader's attitude is one of acceptance or rejection of the statements.[8] But where can the reader obtain the all-important question he needs as he starts to read each section of the textbook? One excellent source has already been discussed. That is, authors place many "cues" in their writings to indicate the main theses under discussion; the most obvious of these are boldface headings and italicized phrases. It is a simple trick to turn each of these into a question as the reader comes to it; he then reads on seeking the major points which answer his query.

Another problem in learning is to determine the *most efficient size unit* which a given reader can handle in a meaningful way. Throughout our discussion there has been an emphasis on obtaining the larger ideas presented by the author. Students tend to get lost in detail and so miss the forest for the trees. Students vary, however, in the size of the bite of textbook stuff which they can assimilate at one time. Where material is familiar one can more easily take in bigger ideas than where it is unfamiliar. Some stu-

[7] J. N. Washburne, The use of questions in social science material, *J. Educ. Psych.*, 1929, 20:321–359.

[8] A. T. Jersild, Examination as an aid to learning, *J. Educ. Psych.*, 1929, 20:602–609.

dents, in addition, are not as well trained as others in grasping these larger ideas. Each reader has the problem then of finding how far he can read before he has, so to speak, to come up for air and reorient himself.[9] It is obvious that these spots should coincide if possible with the breaks in thought of the author, i.e., at the end of headed sections. If such headed sections extend over several pages, then the reader has to use paragraphing and other cues to find the best places for brief stops to summarize ideas and to reorient himself for the coming material.

Learning poetry illustrates how the most efficient sized unit may vary with age and training. In memorizing poetry it is generally best to read and reread the whole poem so that the total meaning can help with the learning. On the other hand, if the poem is long and the language difficult to understand, the total meaning will be hard to get, and reading and rereading the whole poem will not be particularly effective. In one experiment children at different age levels learned, by the whole method, four poems varying in length and difficulty. Other equated groups of children learned these same poems by the part method. The length and difficulty of the poem on which the pupils used the whole method most efficiently varied with the developmental level of the children; children in the lower grades found the whole method most effective on the simple poems whereas the pupils in the higher grades found it most efficient on the more difficult poems.[10] A student can train himself to handle larger and larger units as a whole with resulting increased effectiveness in his work.

3. Value of Outlining

The emphasis above has been on understanding the major ideas which the author presents and on seeing the relationship among these ideas. Various experimenters have tried to devise techniques which would help the reader clarify and verbalize his insights and which would give a visual picture of the ideas and their relationships. Of these techniques, outlining, underlining, and writing précis summaries have been the most frequently suggested.

Many students have definite opinions about the value of these techniques. While it is true that good students tend to keep notes on their readings more than poor students, many good students do not. Practically all students agree that taking notes is a lot of work; they often say that they scarcely have time to read the lesson and certainly wouldn't have time to read and take notes. Many students, having given note-taking a trial, report that it slowed them down and did not seem to help; in fact, some feel that the lengthened time and extra activity made it harder to get the lesson.

These observations have been verified by experiments in which students' effectiveness with various of these techniques tried more or less for the first time, was compared with simply reading and rereading. In one experiment 242 college students tried the techniques of underlining, outlining, writing précis summaries, and simply reading and

---

[9] Some students try reading straight along, possibly because of habits developed in fiction reading, only to end up with quite hazy notions as to the content of the lesson. Very often in desperation they resort to memorizing of key phrases and formulae. Probably every student can remember a time when he couldn't figure out an algebra equation or a chemistry formula and tried to "get by" with memorizing it; the only trouble was that the instructor changed the letters or numbers in the equation and the student was stuck. For example, in one group only 6 per cent didn't know the answer to $(x + y)^2$ but 28 per cent couldn't tell the answer when the question was $(b_1 + b_2)^2$. Furthermore, material which is memorized is forgotten much more rapidly than material learned by understanding it.

[10] M. L. Northway, *Difficulty of the Task and the Ability of the Subject as Factors in Whole-Part Learning*, M.A. thesis, Univ. of Toronto, 1934.

rereading on different selections equated for difficulty. Not much difference was found in the effectiveness of these techniques; the clearest difference was between reading and underlining compared to reading and writing a summary.[11] Analysis of students' behavior in this and other experiments showed that the students did not know how to use these other techniques very well and became so involved in indiscriminate note-taking and compositional efforts that their reading comprehension was actually hindered. Having tried these techniques once or twice, many students decide to rely on the one technique with which they are familiar, e.g., reading and rereading. These students are like the bashful boy who complained of great difficulty in talking to girls; on hearing arguments that it is easier to talk to a girl while dancing, he decided to try it on his next date although he was not a good dancer. Afterwards, when asked how it was, he replied, "Gosh! I was so busy placing my feet that I couldn't talk at all."

It is obvious then that any technique used must be so automatic and simple as to be subordinate to the task of reading. Rather than interfere with reading it should help. In the experiment reported above it was found that underlining was more effective than writing summaries, probably because the former merely requires the drawing of lines while writing a summary is a compositional effort. On the other hand, underlining has its disadvantages. Students tend to underline too much, to have difficulty seeing relationships among the scattered underlinings, and to memorize the author's words when studying.

To overcome these objections, a type of brief, topical outlining has been devised; it is called "working notes" to differentiate it from the type of outlining which most students know. To save time in writing and in later reading, headline phrases are used rather than complete sentences. To promote easy visualization of the main ideas in the lesson and again to save time, only the main ideas and main subpoints are jotted down; the notes on a chapter will cover a half page or at most a page, and the indentation of subpoints makes the major points stand out. To cut out clerical, slavish copying into a notebook, notes are jotted from memory after reading a meaningful unit such as a headed section. This type of note-taking is not what most students think of when note-taking is mentioned; it sounds much easier. A sample of such notes and a discussion of lecture notes will be presented later.

Such note-taking may not be particularly effective the first time it is tried; the newness of any technique tends to upset previous reading habits, just as trying a new but better grip in golf may temporarily spoil one's score. With practice, however, a student can develop a learning skill which is far more efficient than the usual student method; such engineered skills are here called higher-level learning skills. This need for practice and the possibilities of gain with it are shown in Chart 4. It shows that the first time three groups of students used outlining as a technique on study units in history it was not very effective, but after a month's practice the technique was highly beneficial (comparison is to the efficiency of equated groups who had not been shown how to outline).[12]

Evidence of increased efficiency possible with extended practice and of the transfer of efficiency to other courses is shown by still another experiment. Several hundred high-school students received intensive train-

[11] H. F. Arnold, The comparative efficiency of certain study techniques in the field of history, J. Educ. Psych., 1942, 33:449–457; also C. E. Germane, The value of the written paragraph summary, J. Educ. Res., 1921, 3:116–123.

[12] W. A. Barton, Outlining as a study procedure, Teach. Coll. Contri. Educ., No. 411, 1930.

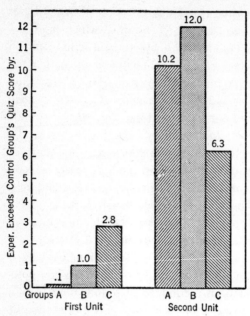

CHART 4. Gain in quiz grades when outlining is used as a study technique for the first time and after a month's practice; comparison is made to equated groups not taught the outlining technique. (Adapted from Barton.)

ing (daily lessons for six weeks) in outlining typical study materials. Emphasis was placed on the thinking side of outlining. At the end it was found that the trained group was better than a matched control group (received no training in outlining) in ability to comprehend what they read and in performance on study materials in other courses.[13]

Thus, in selecting and comprehending what is important, the student will find it helpful to make a preview of the headings and final summary before starting to read, to ask a question based on the heading as he starts to read each headed section, and to write brief summary phrases after reading each section so as to check his comprehension and to picture the relationship among the ideas. Further it was shown that any

[13] R. Salisbury, Some effects of training in outlining, Engl. J. (Coll. Ed.), 1935, 24:111–116; see also R. G. Simpson, The effect of specific training on ability to read historical materials, J. Educ. Res., 1929, 20:343–351.

method of outlining must be brief and easy to do and must be practiced before its benefits can be obtained.

WAYS TO RETARD FORGETTING

As every student is well aware, forgetting one's lessons takes place altogether too rapidly. Students occasionally reply when queried in class, "I knew it yesterday, but it's gone now." This rapid deterioration of learning was graphically shown in Chart 2; two weeks after reading a lesson a student usually remembers only about 20 per cent of what he knew immediately after studying the lesson.

The student's problem in studying is twofold: learning what should be known, and then fixing it in memory so it will be there when wanted. A student may develop facility at picking out important points so he can do well on an immediate quiz (this is one reason why many students cram before exams), but this does not necessarily insure that he will remember it. There is need to investigate the causes of forgetting and to develop techniques which will slow it down.

Nature of Forgetting

Contrary to popular opinion, forgetting is not simply a weathering away of once known impressions. The process of forgetting, like the process of learning, follows certain dynamic patterns whose study permits the scientist to develop techniques which retard forgetting. Several facts indicate possible directions for investigating: first, not all material is forgotten at the same rate, nor in the same way.[14] One study shows that

[14] E. B. Newman, Forgetting of meaningful material during sleep and waking, Amer. J. Psych., 1939, 52:65–71; J. M. Levine and G. Murphy, The learning and forgetting of controversial material, J. Abn. & Soc. Psych., 1943, 38:507–517; R. D. Williams and G. W. Knox, A survey of dynamic principles governing memory, J. Gen. Psych., 1944, 30:167–179.

eight hours after reading a story 86 per cent of the ideas essential to the plot can be reproduced but only 23 per cent of the non-essential ideas. Another study shows that persons tend to forget the content of an article on a controversial subject more rapidly when they disagree with its point of view than when they agree. Darwin said he found it necessary to jot down immediately any data which disagreed with his theory of evolution, but that evidence which supported the theory was much more easily remembered. Still other studies show that memories gradually change to fit previous knowledge and thought patterns. For example, the reddish hair of a long-absent friend tends to become redder and redder in memory because it is always thought of as "red." The bad acts of a "good" king are harder to remember (unless they are so atrocious as to stand out) than the bad acts of a "bad" king. The implication of all this for the student is that he should try to get a thorough understanding of the lesson since this will help him retain the essential ideas. Further, he should study carefully those items which tend to disagree with the general theme of a unit.

Secondly, not all students forget at the same rate. The student who remembers the most, immediately after reading, may not remember the most after two weeks; nor will several people who make the same score, immediately after reading, score the same two weeks later. A study of these people who tend to remember the most indicates that the prime factor in this superiority is not endowed superiority of memory but learned skills and attitudes. The three primary methods of attack to be discussed in the sections which follow are: interest, recitation, and distributed learning.

1. *Interest and Intent to Remember.* Every student intends to remember what he studies, at least until the next quiz is over, but students vary in the degree to which they mentally clarify the specific things they intend to remember and in the strength of this intent. Some students have little more than a vague urging from their conscience that they ought to remember what they are reading, but habits of reading for the moment's comprehension, as in fiction reading, really determine their behavior. Other students carefully select the points they feel they will need to know and definitely attempt to fix them in mind. The difference in efficiency is illustrated by a simple little classroom experiment. The teacher in one class asked the students to copy down twenty words in their notes, but no indication was given that they would later be expected to reproduce these words; the teacher in another class asked the students to copy down these same twenty words but they were told that a test on them could be expected later. On an immediate test, the warned group was 30 per cent better and on a delayed test one week later the warned group was 50 per cent better.

In addition to choosing which facts are to be remembered and carrying out activities which will strengthen memory, the interest a student has in a subject seems also to foster memory. Thus one more clearly remembers incidents from high-school dramatic and athletic events than he does from most of his classes. Material which is of interest is more apt to be meaningful and the student is more apt to remember it. Because this fact is well known, teachers attempt to make their material interesting to students; the student in turn should make every attempt to make the material meaningful, and therefore interesting, to himself. If he cannot see its value, he should ask the instructor to explain its possible relationships to the student's needs.

2. *Recitation.* One of the most effective devices to retard forgetting is very simple

yet few students make use of it, and scarcely ever do so at the best time. An axiom in preparing oneself for a task is to practice the way it will later have to be done. Since students have to show their learning through recitation in class or on tests, the student may well practice reciting beforehand. Students often mistakenly believe that, having understood something as a lesson is read through, it must be known and therefore will be retained. (Remember the example cited earlier of the list of ten numbers which were easily comprehended but learned with difficulty.) Such self-recitation insures that the material is understood and acts to fix it in memory.

The techniques of the expert at remembering names (how we envy him) are a good illustration here. Have you ever watched such a person? The first thing he does on being introduced is to repeat the introduced person's name *aloud* immediately; he wants to be sure he has it straight. Other persons are usually engrossed in their own thoughts when introduced because the stranger obviously means nothing to them at the time, or if they are paying attention they may feel sure they won't remember it anyway. There is no particular intention to remember as mentioned above. And to make matters worse the introducer is often so unsure of the name that he mumbles it so that a person doesn't get it in the first place. Little wonder that people have trouble in (learning and) remembering names. But to return to the expert again. He not only says the name immediately, he may try spelling it to be sure he has it straight and then during the course of the conversation he will use the new name several times. In other words, he learns and uses the name until it is fixed in mind.

Strong evidence of the value of self-recitation, and further clarification as to the best time for its use, is given by a study of several thousand high-school students in Iowa. Reference to part of this study was made earlier in order to show how rapidly students tend to forget after a single reading of an article (see Chart 2). In this experiment, the groups took an initial test at different intervals after the reading and then took it again at later times. The first test, therefore, acted as a recitation-review for the later tests. The results of such testing-review are indicated by broken lines in Chart 2, on page 14. For instance, group I took the test immediately after reading, after 1 day and after 21 days; group III took its first test on the first day after reading and again on the fourteenth day. Two things stand out: (1) The recitation-test acted to retard forgetting and (2) the earlier it came the better. It was found, in fact, that with a single reading the student is apt to remember only 20 per cent at the end of two weeks, but with a single reading followed immediately with a recitation test, he will remember 80 per cent! Or as the author says, "More is forgotten in one day when retention is unaided than is forgotten in 63 days when retention is aided by recall." Such a gain is far beyond what rereading will produce and yet it takes less time.[15]

The best time to use recitation to retard forgetting, therefore, is immediately after reading a lesson. But just *where in the lesson should this self-recitation take place?* That is, after the lesson is read clear through, or after each headed section? If the student waits until the end of the lesson before jotting down an outline from memory, he will find that he has too hazy a notion of the details. On the other hand, the student should not stop to recite each time he finds an important point. It seems best to read

[15] H. F. Spitzer, Studies in retention, *J. Educ. Psych.*, 1939, 30:641–656. See also G. Forlano, School learning with varying methods of practice and rewards, *Teach. Coll. Contri. Educ.*, 1936, No. 688, 114 pp.

through a meaningful unit, such as a headed section, and then try self-recitation. This forces the reader to organize his thinking in terms of main ideas and does not interrupt study so often as to break the train of thought.

What form should this self-recitation take? Many of the characteristics found necessary for an effective technique in organizing comprehension are also pertinent here. Any such technique should be simple and automatic; it should be an aid and not a distraction to thinking. The easier a recitation technique is and the less time it takes, the better. Recitation techniques of complete outlining, underlining, writing summaries, jotting down summary phrases, and discussion have been tried, and the system of reading a headed section and then jotting from memory a key phrase or so in the reader's own words has been found the most effective.[16] If the reader feels unsure as he writes these summary phrases from memory, he can check back over the reading material. And as he progresses through the chapter these cue phrases are arranged in outline form in order to present the ideas of the total lesson in an easily visualized form. Underlining is not particularly effective as a recitation technique because the reader has merely to check back over the material and recognize important points and is not forced to check his understanding of the section.

It is comforting to note that the technique which was found to promote comprehension (turning headings into questions which are read for and recited on) can also be used to retard forgetting. One general

technique serves several ends: The heading turned to a question tends to cause reading for important meanings. After reading a section, this same heading-question can be used as the basis for self-recitation to check whether the answer is known. The self-recitation tends to fix the knowledge in one's memory. And (to be discussed more fully later) these heading-questions are useful in predicting quiz questions for later review. This varied value of a single technique is used to advantage in a later section which presents an over-all technique for going about textbook studying (Survey Q3R).

Two other ways are also useful types of self-recitation, but demand the assistance of another individual. Whenever the teacher or author provides a list of questions covering the main points of an assignment, these can be used for self-recitation. If quizzes were used as learning aids rather than as end measures for purposes of grading, they could be useful in checking comprehension and in review. Discussion is another effective device because it is so easily done and emphasizes understanding rather than memorizing. It is usually difficult to find at convenient times for study another student taking the same course, and the urge to visit may be so powerful as to prevent an efficient use of study discussion.

3. *Distributed learning.* A relatively simple way to increase learning and to improve retention is to distribute the learning over a number of short periods instead of trying to master the entire task at one time. Common sense would accord with the results of research in suggesting that this distribution would be favorable for routine memorizing since in such boresome tasks attention is likely to wander after the first few minutes; several short attempts with attention presumably fairly high would be superior to long periods during which the student becomes

---

[16] H. F. Arnold, The comparative efficiency of certain study techniques in fields of history, *J. Educ. Psych.*, 1942, 33:449–457; M. Bridge, The effect on retention of different methods of revision, Melbourne Univ., *Educ. Res. Ser.*, 1934, No. 28, 55 pp.; C. O. Mathews, Comparison of methods of study for immediate and delayed recall, *J. Educ. Psych.*, 1938, 29:101–106.

bored and inattentive. However, the same situation seems to hold for "logical" learning —not verbatim memorizing—as well. In one experiment two groups of adults were called upon to read passages of a technical nature five times—one group five times consecutively in one sitting and the other once each day for five days. A test given immediately after the fifth reading showed a superiority in retention of only 4 per cent for the group using distributed readings; however, at the end of two weeks this group showed 20 per cent greater retention, and 25 per cent after four weeks, as compared with the group who did all their reading in one day.[17] This experiment is suggestive of the defects of cramming—there is reasonably good immediate recall, but rapid subsequent forgetting.

The distribution of study sessions will vary as they are used to serve either of two functions: the most efficient arrangement to obtain clear comprehension or quick learning, and the most efficient arrangement to renew learning through review. Suffice it to say here, since a thorough discussion of reviewing for examinations will be presented later, that the rate of forgetting and the value of review near examination time are prime factors in determining the distribu-

tion of review sessions. When it comes to trying for the first time to understand some difficult problem or learn some task demanding exact reproduction as in a poem or foreign vocabulary, a quite different distribution of learning sessions is needed. Time enough should be taken on the first reading to get a meaningful view of the whole task and, rather than reread the lesson, evidence already discussed indicates that an immediate effort at self-recitation is very worth while. But how long should the student then wait for the next session? If he waits too long there will be so much forgetting that studying again will seem like a new task. If too soon, the factors of fatigue and boredom may be operative. One experiment shed some light on this problem. Different equated groups tried reading a lesson as follows: four times in one session, once a session each three hours apart, once a session each one day apart, and once a session each three days apart. As will be seen in Chart 5, the four study sessions three hours apart was the best of the four plans.[18] In general, then, it would seem wise for a student with a difficult problem to give it a thorough try, then return to it later.

In planning distributed learning periods, some consideration should be given to what

[17] S. D. McAustin, A study in logical memory, Amer. J. Psych., 1921, 32:370–403.

[18] English, Welborn, and Killian, op. cit.

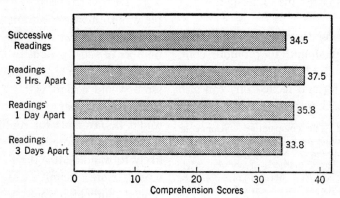

CHART 5. Comprehension scores made by equated groups who read a selection four times but with different spacings between the readings. (Based on data from English, Welborn, and Killian.)

is done immediately after each period of study. A similar task may interfere with the previous learning, especially if it is one demanding rather exact reproduction; thus in memorizing a poem there will be more rapid forgetting if it is followed immediately by study of another poem than if some other activity follows.[19] The usual ten minutes between classes not only provides time for travel but also lets what is learned become "set" before the student has to start on new material. When studying in the evening, the student may well reward himself with a brief respite after finishing a lesson and before starting a new one. A rest at this time will make a break in the middle of the new lesson less likely.

It has been shown that forgetting can be retarded if a student becomes interested in the material he is reading, intends to remember it, and distributes his study time. Of further help, and probably most important, is the use of a self-recitation technique after reading each headed section, the preferred form for such self-recitation being "working notes." The experimental findings of this and of the preceding section on selecting and comprehending what is important provide a basis for devising a new, total method of studying which is highly efficient. This is the subject of the next section.

HIGHER-LEVEL STUDY SKILLS

Various books have been written on special skills useful in reading books.[20] Some have emphasized increased speed of reading; others, techniques for getting the most stimulation from an author's ideas. Students, however, want a skill which will be particularly effective with school *textbooks*.

[19] J. McGeoch and F. McKinney, Retroactive inhibition in the learning of poetry, Amer. J. Psych., 1934, 46:19–30.

[20] M. J. Adler, How to Read a Book, Simon & Schuster, 1940; M. A. Bessey, Active Reading, Appleton-Century, 1941; N. Lewis, How to Read Better and Faster, Crowell, 1944; I. A. Richards, How to Read a Page, Norton, 1942.

A new technique must be devised, since the methods of good students are too often inefficient and no one of the experiments above used the perfect method. The findings of these experiments, however, contribute a scientific foundation from which a higher-level study skill can be devised. They showed that a quick survey of headings and summaries before starting to read gave an orientation which speeded up reading and aided retention. They showed that asking a question before starting each section also helped reading. Other experiments showed that the very rapid forgetting which is so typical after reading can be markedly slowed down by the simple expedient of forcing oneself to recite from memory after reading. Other experiments showed something as to the best timing of this self-recitation during the study period. Various studies emphasized the importance of understanding the larger meanings in the selection, and of seeing their pattern of relationship. Outlining, relating the material to one's interests, and a brief review when through reading were shown to help with this. Still other experiments showed the value of distribution of effort in studying.

The creation of a study skill which uses these findings, which satisfies the demands of school study, and which pleases the student with its efficiency is a challenge to the reading specialist. The student wants any suggested method to help him (1) select what he is expected to know, (2) comprehend these ideas rapidly, (3) fix them in memory, and later (4) review efficiently for examinations. The method must be more efficient and less time consuming than rereading lessons. And it should not be difficult to learn.

For years the writer has had students try out various methods which such experiments have suggested; such trials have led to further refinements and suggestions. One method has finally been devised which fits the criteria above, is more effective than typical study methods, and has found student approval. Further research may show other possible refinements but it is felt that this now represents a higher-level skill of great effectiveness for schoolwork. The ma- terial which follows is devoted to a descrip- tion of this study technique and to exercises directed toward developing such skill. Fol- lowing this there will be some discussion of special techniques in studying foreign- language and non-prose materials.

THE SURVEY Q3R METHOD

The title for this new higher-level study skill is abbreviated in the current fashion to make it easier to remember and to make reference to it more simple. The symbols stand for the steps which the student follows in using the method; a description of each of these steps is given below:

SURVEY   1. *Glance over the headings in the chapter to see the few big points which will be developed.* This survey should not take more than a minute and will show the three to six core ideas around which the rest of the discussion will cluster. If the chapter has a final summary paragraph this will also list the ideas developed in the chapter. This orientation will help you organize the ideas as you read them later.

QUESTION 2. Now begin to work. *Turn the first heading into a question.* This will arouse your curiosity and so increase comprehension. It will bring to mind information already known, thus helping you to understand that section more quickly. And the question will make important points stand out while explanatory detail is recognized as such. This turning a heading into a question can be done on the instant of reading the heading, but it demands a conscious effort on the part of the reader to make this query for which he must read to find the answer.

READ   3. *Read to answer that question,* i.e., to the end of the first headed section. This is not a passive plowing along each line, but an active search for the answer.

RECITE   4. Having read the first section, look away from the book and try briefly to *recite the answer to your question.* Use your own words and name an example. If you can do this you know what is in the book; if you can't, glance over the section again. An excellent way to do this reciting from memory is to jot down cue phrases in outline form on a sheet of paper. Make these notes very brief!

NOW REPEAT STEPS 2, 3 AND 4 ON EACH SUCCEEDING HEADED SECTION. THAT IS, TURN THE NEXT HEADING INTO A QUESTION, READ TO ANSWER THAT QUES- TION, AND RECITE THE ANSWER BY JOTTING DOWN CUE PHRASES IN YOUR OUT- LINE. READ IN THIS WAY UNTIL THE ENTIRE LESSON IS COMPLETED.

REVIEW   5. When the lesson has thus been read through, *look over your notes to get a bird's-eye view* of the points and of their relationship *and check your memory* as to the content by reciting on the major subpoints under each heading. This checking of memory can be done by covering up the notes and trying to recall the main points. Then expose each major point and try to recall the subpoints listed under it.

These five steps of the Survey Q3R Method—Survey, Question, Read, Recite, and Review—when polished into a smooth and efficient method should result in the student reading faster, picking out the important points, and fixing them in memory. The student will find one other worthwhile outcome: quiz questions will seem happily familiar because the headings turned into questions are usually the points emphasized in quizzes. In predicting actual quiz questions and looking up the answers beforehand, the student feels that he is effectively studying what is considered important in a course.

Its Effectiveness

Evidence of the success of this method has been obtained from several studies. In one experiment several sections of a how-to-study class measured their reading ability (reading rate and comprehension accuracy) on a test which dealt with the history of Canada; they were then given practice in the use of the Survey Q3R Method for several days after which they took another comparable reading test. Before training, the average rate of reading for the classes was at the 34th percentile and after training it was at the 56th percentile; before training the average accuracy of comprehension was at the 43rd percentile and after training at the 53rd percentile. In another experiment an attempt was made to measure the effectiveness of this method for examination preparation. Two quizzes of equal difficulty were prepared; for the first quiz the students were permitted to study in their own inimitable ways but for the second quiz they were shown how to predict questions. The average number of errors on the first quiz was 15 but on the second quiz only 6. One of the most convincing arguments to the writer has been the comments of students who have tried it and found that it worked. Students have

walked into class and said "I predicted 15 of the 20 questions he asked," or "Boy, oh boy, I've been getting D's in chemistry but I got a B yesterday," or "It looked like he had picked the quiz questions from my list."

Further Details of the Method

The description above has given an overall picture of the method. Experience in teaching its use, however, shows that certain typical errors may occur, usually because old study methods interfere. Indicating these critical points, so the student can be particularly careful concerning them, is helpful in learning a skill. These cautions are arranged according to the steps in the method:

a. *Survey.* A survey of headings in a lesson should take only a minute. Some students are so in the habit of reading on once they get started that, until they have learned how, they need to make a conscious effort to look just at the headings and then to estimate what the lesson is about. It is worth while to practice this skill by itself: Take some reading material on topics with which you are familiar, e.g., newspapers, digest magazines, previously read textbooks, etc., glance over the headings in an article or a chapter, then make guesses as to what the material will actually say. Check to see how well you have done.

b and c. *Reading to answer questions.* Changing a heading into a question should be a conscious effort to orient oneself actively toward the material to be read. The reader should definitely have in mind what he wants to learn as he reads each section and not just passively read it line by line. Habits from reading fiction often make it difficult to read textbooks, for it has been found that most people read fiction in order to forget their troubles and not to remember what is in the book. Such an attitude of comprehending for the moment, when carried over into textbook reading, gives rise to a delusion that since the ideas are comprehended as they are read they will, of course, be remembered and unconsciously organized as answers to questions. Such is far from the truth. Reading textbooks is work; the reader must know what he is looking for, look for it, and then organize his thinking on the topic he has been reading about.

d. *Reciting*. The tendency in reading is to keep going, but one should stop at the end of each headed section to see if he can answer the question asked at the start of the section. As indicated before, this tends to check whether the reader has comprehended the material, and the recitation fixes the ideas in memory. Furthermore, this insistence on answering the question makes it easier to force oneself to read with an active, inquiring attitude.

Self-recitation may consist of mentally reviewing the answer or writing it out. The latter is more effective since it forces the reader actually to verbalize the answer whereas a mental review may often fool a reader into believing that a vague feeling of comprehension represents mastery. Furthermore, the more sensory channels used in learning, the more effective it is; in writing notes one provides visual and kinaesthetic (muscle) cues as well as verbal imagery in thinking about it. But it is very important that this note-taking require little time and energy; the notes should be exceedingly brief. It is here, in fact, that many students have the most difficulty with the Survey Q3R Method. Some think they are to use old habits of lengthy note-taking where all details are copied from the book, usually as complete sentences. This technique so disrupts the progress of reading that the train of thought is lost. Other students, when they spy something important, are in the habit of stopping then to copy it into their notes—with one finger marking each phrase as they look back and forth between book and notes. It can truthfully be said that many such students copy a sentence into their notes without ever having read it (for meaning) because as soon as they see something in italics they start copying.

The student will have to practice the type of working notes, as they are called, recommended here. First, no notes are written until the whole headed section is completely read. Second, the notes are jotted down from memory and not from the book. And third, the notes should be in the student's own words and should be brief, i.e., little more than a word or phrase. Just as a public speaker's notes usually consist of a list of topics as reminders of what to talk about next, so the student's notes should include only cue words and phrases to demonstrate to his own satisfaction that he knows what points are included. Knowing a topic, the student can easily supply an explanation of it. Such brief wording also keeps the notes in compact form so that they can be easily visualized later in review.

The following sample of working notes based on the first five pages of the Art Reading test shows how points can be made to stand out (key words are italicized for emphasis) and how the indentations make visualization of the subpoints easier. The brief wording will not convey full meaning to a stranger, he should read the article; but the cue phrases are sufficient reminders of what is in the article to the student who made the notes.[21]

Notes on Art Test

A. *Art*—joining together; signify experience
B. *2 classes:*
  1. Useful arts
  2. Fine arts—attempt to express beauty, triumph
    a. Artist identifies self with object; observer also
    b. Shows effect not causes
    c. Shows inspiration nature gives
C. Character of art:
  1. *Unity*—one idea, no distractions in picture
  2. *Composition*—process of selecting and arranging
    a. *Harmony*—consistency of character
    b. *Balance*—consistency of attractions
    c. *Rhythm*—consistency of movement
  3. Message of art is mood

It is difficult to maintain an attitude of active attack on any type of work over long periods of time. In industry it has been found more efficient to alternate periods of working at different activities. The change of activity is less boring and one can start each new period with zest. In studying, an alternation of reading and note-taking makes it easier for the student to keep at his lessons and to maintain an attitude of active searching for ideas. It is easier to keep at reading until a headed section is finished than it is to complete the whole lesson, therefore breaks in at-

tention are apt to come at logical places in the reading material and so do not disrupt the student's thinking as much. This alternation of tasks, in fact, helps make concentration much easier in studying lessons.

e. *Review.* Review immediately after reading should be brief; probably not more than five minutes will be needed. This is certainly much faster than rereading the lesson. The total outline should be looked over to get an over-all, easily visualized picture, but the review should not be limited to this. As indicated in the directions, another attempt at self-recitation makes sure that the material is better fixed in memory.

Later reviews are also worth while because of the forgetting which takes place. The factors influencing the efficiency of these delayed reviews will be discussed in the next project.

Exercises

In spite of all these do's and don'ts, the Survey Q3R Method probably sounds simple, but so does golf or swimming. Just as in learning any skill, this one will take much practice to make it highly effective and as habitual as your present methods. And as with any new skills, this one may seem awkward and ineffective when it is first tried. So a series of practice exercises has been set up to give you training in the use of the method.

Laboratory materials will be used at first because they are constructed so as to show what is wanted and the counselor can more quickly check errors in method. As soon as possible, however, practice will be carried out on your actual courses.

1. The first step in learning to use the Survey Q3R Method was described on pages 16–17. Here you learned to recognize cues in textbook writing.

[21] Some students find even this amount of note-taking too laborious! Another technique is to jot down, or underline in the text, cue words or phrases which represent probable quiz questions. The answers are not written. These lists then provide a good basis for review. If in reviewing, the answer doesn't come immediately to mind, the student reads in the book.

2. The second step was also completed then when you jotted down the list of cues in outline form. This was in reality a first attempt at working notes. It also showed how such brief notes can predict quiz questions.

3. Now that you understand what textbook cues and working notes are, the next step is to get some practice doing the whole skill. As in coaching baseball, your whole delivery should be observed and suggestions made on pertinent difficulties. Practice will be of two types:

a. Special reading assignments will be used in class for a series of practice exercises on the use of the Survey Q3R Method. You will be observed while doing this, your notes will be evaluated, and, if time permits, quizzes will be given over these "assignments."

b. During the weeks to follow you will also practice this method on some one of your courses, preferably one with much reading in it. Keep checking with your counselor as to further ways to improve your skill with the Survey Q3R Method.

While a student may become particularly interested in improving one aspect of the total skill, educational psychologists have found that a skill is learned most readily if it is always practiced as a whole. Thus in studying a lesson, you should carry out the whole Survey Q3R Method as rapidly and efficiently as possible. When a lesson is completed you can note the time it took and so obtain a measure of rate, your notes can be evaluated by the counselor, and later quizzes can be analyzed to see how well the correct points have been predicted.

Evidence of Improvement

You will, of course, be interested in seeing evidence of improvement from use of this technique. This may show up in various ways: reading rate may be faster, comprehension accuracy may be higher, notes may be better, and quiz questions may seem more familiar because they have been predicted. Charts for designating progress are provided below or are referred to elsewhere in this book. Although minor fluctuations may occur in a graph due to chance differences in difficulty or variations in your own efficiency, you should find in time that the lines representing performance will gradually progress upwards. Charting progress provides assurance that your efforts are getting results and will help you and the counselor discover where there is still difficulty.

1. *Rate of Reading.* Note how many words a minute you are able to read on the average while completing a lesson. Plot this on the chart on page 112. Rate with and without note-taking will be quite different; it will be interesting to keep two lines on the graph: one for rate with notes, the other for straight reading rate.

2. *Notes.* The check list for rating working notes is on the following pages. In evaluating working notes as a part of the Survey Q3R Method, two characteristics are emphasized: Do they cover the essential points? And are they in a good format, i.e., writing reduced to a minimum, major points standing out with subordinate points indented, and written so that self-recitation can be carried out easily. Have the counselor rate your notes on this chart so you can see which aspects need further work.

3. *Comprehension Accuracy and Prediction of Quiz Questions.* On the second chart below, record such measures of comprehension accuracy as test scores and estimates of the per cent of questions asked which you were able to predict. Great care must be taken in what is compared to what; success may be greater on a quiz in one course than it is in another because the quizzes in

the first course are easier. So in plotting below be sure to mark each item with enough descriptive detail so that later comparable predictions may be joined up with it by a line. The chart will eventually have several lines on it indicating progress in predicting quiz questions in one course, accuracy of comprehension on a series of reading tests, etc. To keep these lines from becoming confused it may be well to make them of different colors or of different types.

Scores are not always obtainable or best presented as per cent right. Thus grades may be given only in a letter form of "A," "B," and "C"; or the instructor may indicate the average score for the class with which your score can be compared; or the test score itself may be used. You may plot any of these on the chart so long as they provide you with a visual evidence of progress.

4. *Memory.* Students occasionally find that their notes agree with the questions asked, but they had trouble on the quiz when it was given. This is evidence that they once knew the material but it was forgotten. Some such forgetting is normal, but if this difference is extreme it represents an aspect needing remediation. Whenever you find missed quiz questions actually listed in your notes, turn to Project III for assistance.

CHECK LIST FOR ANALYSIS OF STUDENT NOTEBOOK

Each time the student's notebook is rated, use a separate column. In general, rate the same subject each time. The rating is done by checking each of the deficiencies found, and double-checking particularly bad aspects. Count the number of checks in each section and put this number in the box for each boldface heading. Then add all these numbers for the total score. Plot this score on the graph; successive evaluations and plottings will show any improvement made.

Name of course rated, and date

General Format:

Handwriting illegible

Too many notebooks

Notebook too small

Pages overfilled

Unorganized notes; courses mixed together

Loose, odd-sized pages

Too much time on notes

Too spread out

Too compact

. . . .

Organization or Form:

Poor labeling at top

Need more indentation

Just a listing of points

Not in outline form

No numbering system

Use emphasis marks

Hard to see organization

Subtopics unrelated to head

. . . .

Phrasing of Notes:

Unnecessary wordiness

Wording does not convey
meaning of section

Missed some of main ideas

Not finishing headed sec-
tion before writing notes

Start with cue word

In author's words; not own

Too meager for material
covered

Too much detail

. . . .

General Quality of Notes

Rating on 10-point scale,
with 0 as excellent, 5 as
average, and 10 as ter-
rible or no notes.

Total Score:

**Graph Showing
Improvement**

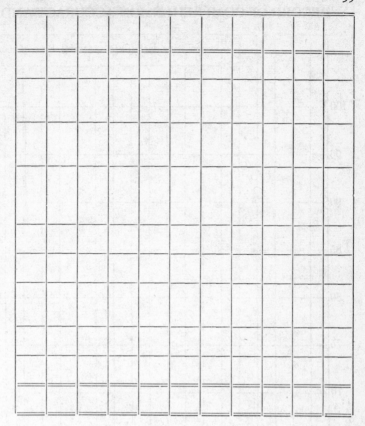

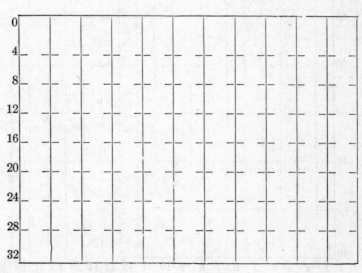

Date

RECORD OF COMPREHENSION ACCURACY AND QUIZ PREDICTION

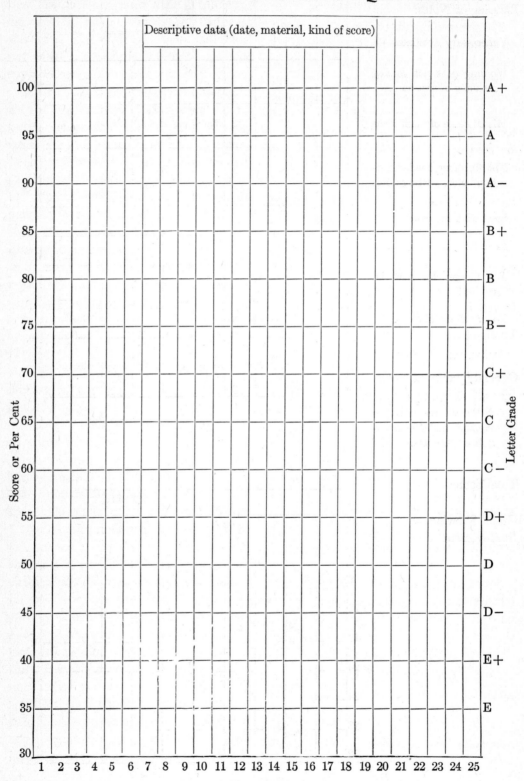

The previous discussion has dwelt at length on techniques of studying the usual college textbook. Some reading material, however, is heavily loaded with diagrams, charts, and formulae, and some is even written almost entirely in a foreign language. Such materials demand different study skills than are used with prose. That is, the principles of learning still apply, but the total study method is redesigned to fit these special materials. The need for this is well illustrated when students try to read a formula at the same rate as the prose which precedes it. The material which follows first discusses skills in foreign-language study and then study methods with diagrams, charts, and formulae.

Foreign-Language Study

While some students find the study of a foreign language easy and interesting, others find it one of their most difficult subjects. Some of this latter group spend hours each day studying the strange language and yet find that they have made little progress. Part of this is due to differences in facility at linguistic learning, but learned factors also determine success in language courses. While occasionally a student may feel that he is aphasic to foreign languages, the causes actually lie elsewhere and are usually remediable.

Some indication of the nature of these difficulties is shown in a series of experiments on factors related to success in German classes.[22] In the first experiment two groups

of students, equal in ability but differing markedly in their success in German, were measured in a large number of characteristics that might be related to success in language. The only areas in which the two groups showed significant differences were: English proficiency, desire to master a foreign language, daily preparation of lessons, habit of studying corrections made on their papers, and reading German for ideas rather than translating words. In a second experiment, an analysis was made of the methods which students use in studying German. The results showed that: (a) The poor students tended to postpone study but the good ones mastered each lesson and actually studied German when they sat down to do it. (b) The poor ones said they had lots of trouble with grammar while the good ones didn't, and said they saw grammar as a means rather than as the end purpose of their course in English. And (c) the poor ones said they made no special effort to study declensions while the good students did, and also had a plan to use in attacking new German sentences and studied any corrections which the instructor made on their papers.

In brief, these factors are of three general types: motivation, English training, and special skills in foreign-language study. Each of these will be discussed in turn.

Some students have difficulty because they really are not interested in foreign languages and only study them to fulfill requirements for a degree. And even for those who are interested, the necessary routine practice does not provide interesting new facts such as the budding scientist finds in his study of chemistry. It is little wonder that a student sometimes prefers to study other more interesting courses first and finds it difficult to keep his mind on his language study. As a first step in making language study easier, a student must clarify in his own mind the

[22] R. P. Larsen, J. R. Wittenborn, and E. G. Giesecke, Factors contributing to achievement in the study of first semester college German, *J. Exper. Educ.*, 1942, 10:265–271; J. R. Wittenborn and R. P. Larsen, An empirical evaluation of study habits in elementary German, *J. Appl. Psych.*, 1944, 28:420–430; J. R. Wittenborn and R. P. Larson, A factorial study of achievement in college German, *J. Educ. Psych.*, 1944, 35:39–49.

values he expects to obtain from the study of a foreign language. Since this whole problem of getting down to work and learning to concentrate is the topic of Project IV, turn to that project if you are having trouble with language study.

Training in English, more specifically in English grammar, is another important factor determining success in study of a foreign language. Because greater use is made of grammar terminology in teaching a foreign language than in the teaching of English, experiments show that knowledge of English grammar is actually more highly related to success in studying a foreign language than in studying English.

But the necessary grammatical terminology is not as extensive as the size of a grammar book might indicate. Following is a list of grammatical terms that an analysis shows are frequently used, and which teachers consider important, in foreign-language study.[23] This

[23] L. C. and S. L. Pressey, *Essential Preparation for College*, Farrar & Rinehart, 1932.

list is in addition to the grammatical terms which a college student would know from his work in English composition. Test yourself on these terms to see if you can think of an illustration for each. Any terms which cause difficulty can be looked up in an English grammar book, a dictionary, or in J. A. Meredith and W. S. Jack's pamphlet, *Outline English Grammar for Foreign Language Students* (published by its authors, 1936).

Other practice materials dealing with English usage will be found in Project VIII; turn to it if you feel that English usage is a factor in your language-study problem.

Special techniques for language study are also important. The suggestions which follow deal with the twin problems of learning to read for meaning and learning vocabulary and conjugations. A first suggestion is to read constantly for meaning rather than plod along looking up English equivalents. Some students feel that they have read their lessons when they have dutifully looked up each

Technical Vocabulary in Foreign Language Composition

1. masculine gender	22. indirect objects
2. feminine gender	23. negatives
3. neuter gender	24. interrogatives
4. possessive pronouns	25. prefixes
5. possessive adjectives	26. suffixes
6. relative pronouns	27. positive degree
7. interrogative pronouns	28. comparative degree
8. demonstrative pronouns	29. superlative degree
9. definite articles	30. imperfect tense
10. indefinite articles	31. perfect tense
11. transitive verbs	32. pluperfect tense
12. intransitive verbs	33. active voice
13. regular verbs	34. passive voice
14. irregular verbs	35. subjunctive mood
15. nominative case	36. imperative mood
16. objective case	37. indicative mood
17. impersonal verbs	38. inverted word order
18. reflexive verbs	39. syllable
19. auxiliary verbs	40. declensions
20. infinitives	41. conjugations
21. predicate nouns	42. inflection

word, but such translating gives little meaning and does not develop habits of expecting meaning; it is not learning to read. Since reading for meaning is difficult the first time through a lesson, an immediate rereading provides this experience and helps fix the material in mind. Thus rereading, which is *not* effective in studying other textbooks, *is* effective when learning a foreign language. Further practice at reading for meaning can be obtained by reviewing previous lessons and by reading easy stories and newspapers.

A second suggestion is the study of any specific aspect of the language which causes trouble. Thus, even in chemistry, it is important to study the technical vocabulary, but in a foreign language it is imperative to put special study on vocabulary, conjugations, and idioms. Much of this is learned in reading selections, but some additional practice is necessary to fix in mind the meaning of frequently recurring foreign terms. Self-recitation practice on such word lists is extremely valuable. While only brief use of self-recitation was shown to be very effective immediately after reading a headed section in history, in learning such things as foreign vocabulary or poetry it is most efficient to spend as much as four-fifths of the time in self-recitation! That is, in learning a foreign language much time will be spent in actual reading and rereading, but that part of the time spent in vocabulary study should emphasize reciting from memory rather than mere reading of definitions.[24] A good way to do this is to make a pack of vocabulary cards: on one side of the card is written a foreign term and on the other its English equivalent or the desired declension or conjugation. Such cards are made for all important or frequently recurring words. Drill is carried on by looking at the foreign term, thinking of its meaning and then checking on the reverse side. The cards for those words that were not known are kept separate for a second trial; cards for known words are put in a separate pile and given an occasional review.

A third technique in foreign-language study is the development of a three-level plan of attack on new material.

1. Try to foresee what is going to happen in the selection. Before starting to read, it is helpful to read the title and briefly skim over the selection; this general orientation greatly helps in recognizing the meaning of words or in guessing at the meaning of entirely strange words. And as a student reads further in a selection, the story or theme becomes clearer so that anticipation is easier; this attitude should be maintained throughout the reading.

2. Techniques of attack on sentences are also important. In some languages the sequence of subject, verb, and object differs from the pattern in English; the student should have this pattern clearly in mind and with difficult sentences make it a practice to look for the words in that sequence rather than in the simple chronology of left to right. The position of modifiers in some languages also differs from their position in relation to nouns and verbs in English; attention to this detail also helps with difficult passages. With sufficient practice or with easy material, however, the language will seem so familiar that the student can get the sense of the sentence as he reads straight along much as he already does with English.

3. The third level of attack concerns methods of dealing with unknown words. Very often the context of a selection can indicate the probable meaning of a strange word; use context to guess at words and

[24] H. A. Peterson, Recitation or recall as a factor in the learning of long prose selections, *J. Educ. Psych.*, 1944, 35:220–228; L. C. Seibert, A series of experiments on the learning of French vocabulary, *Johns Hopkins Univ. Stud. Educ.*, 1932, No. 18, 106 pp.

finish the sentence or paragraph before using the dictionary to verify your estimate. Very often a familiar word root will represent part of a strange word or a known word may be linked with other unknown words to form a compound word. In either instance, such analysis of the unknown word may be sufficient to suggest the correct meaning which can later be verified. Hunches as to what a word means are right so often that a student should trust his first hunches and read straight along for general meaning, then check for more exact meanings. This is more effective than translating each word, with much turning to the back of the book or to a dictionary.

Foreign languages are taught by different methods and with different emphases. For instance, some instructors make much use of grammar or of exact translation while others emphasize rapid reading for whatever meaning can be obtained. Some emphasize silent reading ability while others emphasize pronunciation. It is obvious that each emphasis demands a somewhat different approach in studying. If you are having trouble with a language course, ask your instructor for suggestions as to the best methods of learning the language as he is teaching it.

The following references provide further discussion of techniques for learning a foreign language:

C. Bird, *Effective Study Habits*, Appleton-Century, 1931. Pages 78–83.

W. E. Bull and L. E. Drake, *Aids to Language Learning: Spanish*, College Typing Co., 1941, 57 pages.

C. C. Crawford, *Studying the Major Subjects*, published by the author, 1930. Pages 72–102.

C. C. Gullette and L. C. Keating, *Learning a Modern Language*, Crofts, 1938, 24 pages.

P. Hagboldt, *Language Learning*, Univ. Chicago Press, 1935, 165 pages.

Studying Non-Prose Materials

Most textbooks include charts, diagrams, tables, maps, and formulas as part of the text which the student is to read, and a survey of current textbooks indicates that these forms of presentation are being increasingly used. Students, however, have certain difficulties in studying them. Some students skip them because they want to keep on reading the text; other students read them as if they were prose; still others randomly glance over the tables and charts. There are as definite techniques for studying charts, diagrams, tables, and formulae as there are for prose.

There are two aspects to studying these non-prose materials: ability to read them and effective study techniques. Knowledge of how to read these materials is discussed in Project VII along with other remedial reading problems. This section deals with the study techniques which most effectively use this reading skill to learn quickly what is important, i.e., an over-all plan of studying assignments which include charts, tables, formulae, etc.

Non-prose forms usually supplement a prose text in order to emphasize and summarize important points. They may illustrate what several paragraphs or pages of text have discussed. Obviously they should never be skipped as a half page which doesn't have to be read. One approach in studying a lesson is to read a headed section, then look over the tables and charts before using self-recitation. With a question in mind and having read the background discussion, the important points should seem to stand out in the charts and tables. It may become obvious, in fact, that these non-prose materials are being used to emphasize and summarize the important points. Thus, rather than a random glance, non-prose materials warrant an analytic attack based on questions suggested by the author's headings.

In some courses, diagrams may be the fundamental means of presenting essential material. In zoology, botany, and physiology, for example, a drawing of an organism may be the primary device used to present structure; or in industrial arts a wiring diagram may be used. The prose text in these instances may be supplementary to the drawings. If the course requires ability to reproduce this material in whole or in part, then certain techniques of study are important. Some students waste time staring at a drawing, possibly hoping, on the principle of time exposure in photography, that such a method will make the material sink in. The important thing is to practice what you will have to do later—practice reciting. Look the diagram over trying to figure out its organization, i.e., the electrical circuit or the blood circulation system, then push your book aside and try sketching the diagram from memory. Part will be easy, but part will probably be too vague to be reproduced. Now look back at the drawing with particular emphasis on the parts that were vague; then try sketching it again from memory. Very soon a complete sketch can be made from memory. This technique is the same general pattern used in prose reading: ask a question about how it works, look over the diagram to find the answer, then recite from memory to check what is known and not known. This self-recitation also helps to make the material stick in mind. If the course requires only that you correctly label parts of a diagram, then practice self-recitation by covering up the labels in the book and naming the parts.

Formulae cause particular trouble in reading because they seem so small and are put right in with the prose text. A reader tends unconsciously to read them at his prose rate and in his prose manner, i.e., at a glance. A formula, however, is a short cut for saying a great deal; the only way to read one is to take it slowly and analyze it. For instance, in a chemical formula the interaction of the constituent parts of the left-hand side need to be studied until the result or right-hand side is understood. When a formula is not easily understood, students often try memorizing it, hoping that this represents comprehension. Since teachers typically alter the components of a formula when using it in a quiz, such memorization leaves the student unprepared. To overcome this tendency and to insure comprehension, it is useful to make up a simple problem and then apply the formula. Since formulae tend to be so important, it is a good idea to be sure to cover them in review.

PROJECT III

EFFECTIVE SKILL IN EXAMINATIONS

A project on examinations follows rather naturally a project on how to study textbooks. Since students typically differentiate between studying a lesson for the first time to understand it and reviewing it later for an examination, the skills needed for each of these tasks are presented as separate projects. The skills dealing with examinations are of three general types: (1) preparing for examinations, (2) taking examinations, and (3) making use of returned examinations. Each of these areas will be discussed in turn.

A. Preparing for Examinations

Knowing that an examination will come sometime after he has read the lesson, a student wants to set up a review schedule which, with the least effort, will place him at a peak of efficiency for the examination. Research studies indicate not only the best timing for these reviews, but also something as to the most effective types of review.

Timing of Reviews

Since forgetting takes place so rapidly after learning it is evident that reviews should come early when review will be easy and most effective. The time-honored custom of cramming also has the value of returning memory to something of its original freshness just before the examination. Research studies show that both of these timings are more effective than review in between.[1] The student's problem is to distribute his review

[1] H. A. Peterson and others, Some measurements of the effects of reviews, *J. Educ. Psych.*, 1935, 26:65–72.

times so that no single review takes much time and so that studying before an examination does not become a hectic and fatiguing effort.

The best way of going about immediate reviewing after reading a lesson was discussed in the preceding project. It was evident in Chart 2 that the immediate self-recitation and review which are parts of the Survey Q3R Method are of great help in keeping memory at a high level. Another method frequently used is rereading the lesson. Reading and rereading during the same study period was shown not to be very helpful, but spacing this rereading with several hours in between was more effective than any other distribution.

Certain principles are also of value in determining the distribution of review time as the student approaches an examination. The very size of the task of reviewing for a midterm or final examination tends to lead to procrastination. The lengthy cramming session which finally occurs just before the examination greatly fatigues the student so he cannot be as alert the next day on the test. And during a given study period there is a tendency to get the next day's lesson before starting to review; then there is rarely time for review. The following principles have been found to help with these difficulties: Several review times should be scheduled rather than one lengthy session. A review time should be scheduled separately from study time. A definite segment of the lesson should be assigned to each review time so the task looks possible of completion and does not lead to procrastination. And finally a student probably should not review for more than an hour or two the night before an examination.

Between immediate review and review just before the examination there is need for some intermediate review to keep the material fresh in memory. Because, as indicated in the previous project, memories tend to become reorganized in a dynamic way with the passage of time, such intermediate review tends to keep ideas in line with the actual facts read. An occasional looking over of one's notes, with rereading on obscure points, will do much to reduce forgetting and will tie in previous material with what is then being studied.

Kinds of Review

Just as there are most efficient methods for studying a lesson for the first time, there are most efficient methods of review. Furthermore, it has been found that the closeness of the review to the original time of study determines which method of review will be most effective. In the Survey Q3R Method it was shown that an immediate self-reciting was much more efficient than rereading; on the other hand, if review does not occur for some time after reading, so much may be forgotten that self-recitation cannot be fully effective. This is demonstrated in an experiment in which large equated groups read a selection and were tested on it 42 days later; in the meantime the various groups used different methods of review spaced at different intervals. The results, summarized in Chart 6, show that recitation is more efficient than rereading as a method of review soon after studying a lesson, but some two or more weeks later rereading is more efficient.[2]

An active, organizational attack on material is more effective than a passive approach both in reading and in review. In review there should be a prediction of quiz questions with an active searching for, and an organization of, the answers. In review a student should use his notes or textbook headings to indicate probable questions. Whenever an answer is recalled immediately, he can pass on quickly to the next question. Whenever recalling an answer is difficult, the student can skim and reread until the answer is found. Such review through question answering provides a feeling of completeness when the job is done that does not usually follow attempts to reread a whole book. Students who undertake to reread six weeks' or a term's work usually find the task so enormous that they resort to skipping

[2] A. M. Sones and J. B. Stroud, Review, with special reference to temporal position, *J. Educ. Psych.*, 1940, 31:665–676.

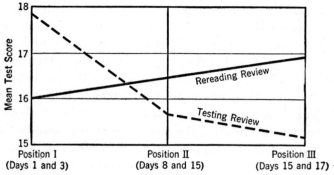

CHART 6. Relative effectiveness of two kinds of review at three different intervals after initial learning. (From Sones and Stroud.)

about and merely glancing at pages here and there. The increasing accuracy with which a student finds himself studying the right questions (shown in the chart of question prediction in the preceding project) also gives him a feeling of energy well spent in review. Rather than an attitude of "There's no telling what he'll ask" or "One has to know everything," the student predicting questions feels definitely oriented with a realization that "These twenty things are sure to be asked."

Too much cannot be said of the value of notes for review. Rather than being overwhelmed with a hundred or more pages to reread, the student with three to five pages of notes easily obtains an outline picture of this material. Indentations in the notes make major points stick out and relationships among the major points easily seen.

What effect should the type of examination have on review method? Most students believe that one should study differently for an essay than for an objective examination.[3] They feel that the objective examination is easier and therefore one has to study less hard; that is, one has only to recognize rather than recall the points. There is also a feeling that one should study details rather than organization of ideas when preparing for an objective examination. Actually, it is equally hard to make good grades on either type of examination, and a method of study which emphasizes understanding the main ideas and their relationships should be used for both. That is, scores tend to be higher on true-false examinations because it is easier to recognize answers than to recall them and because of opportunities for guessing, but since all students have these same

[3] E. C. Class, The effect of the kind of test announcement on students' preparation, *J. Educ. Res.*, 1935, 28:358–361; G. Meyer, The effect on recall and recognition of the examination set in classroom situations, *J. Educ. Psych.*, 1936, 27:81–99.

advantages, a given student will find himself in the same relative position to the other students as if he took an essay examination. And while objective questions may seem to deal with "small points," actual comparison of the topics of these questions with headings in the text will show a close similarity.

Preparation for Final Examinations

The principles which apply to preparing for quizzes also apply to final examinations, but because the latter so typically cover the whole course and count so much on grades, many students get excited and fall back on rather childish methods of cramming. Because of its importance, a special section on final examinations is included. You may feel at this time, however, that final examinations are a long way off; this section can be read now as a summary of the discussion thus far and should be considered more carefully near the end of the school term.

Use the charts below to plan your review time for the last two weeks of the school term. Write in your regular classes and the times for the final examinations. Write in any other necessary activities, such as work and meetings. Now, write in your study and review times. In doing this be sure to differentiate between study time for daily lessons in the last days of the term and review sessions; also label what course and materials are to be reviewed at each time. Wednesday evening might look like this: "7–8:30 Study Chaps. 17 & 18 History; 8:30–9:30 Review Chaps. 1–5 History; 9:30–9:45 relax; 9:45–10:15 study French verbs and idioms; 10:15–10:45 relaxation and so to bed." Reviewing for a given course should be divided up and assigned to three or four spaced sessions; the last session before the examination may well be spent in looking over notes for the whole course. No review session should be very long; the task of recalling and organizing many ideas is so fatiguing that efficiency goes down rapidly after an hour, or an hour and a half, of review.

This ten-day period should be one in which you live normally. The extra review time may cut down somewhat on your recreation, but you should be careful to maintain usual habits of eating, exercise, and sleeping. Examinations demand a "clear head" for thinking; staying up half the night will not produce this. Do not fret and worry about examinations. The night before examinations is too late to learn much in preparation; review the material thoroughly and then relax.

✓ Review selectively. Review the important points, especially those you have trouble recalling. A good way to do this is to take the main headings in your notes or in the

Schedule of Review for Finals
Before Exam Week

	Wednesday	Thursday	Friday	Saturday	Sunday
8:00					
9:00					
10:00					
11:00					
12:00					
1:00					
2:00					
3:00					
4:00					
5:00					
6:00					
7:00					
8:00					
9:00					
10:00					

text and see if you can recite the main ideas from memory. Look up those items with which you have trouble and try reciting again. Or as previously suggested, guess what questions will be asked on each chapter and recite the main points from memory. The headings in the textbook, your class notes, and previous quizzes are all useful in this prediction of questions.

Mere rereading is time consuming and not very efficient. Reread sections only if, after looking at a heading, you have trouble remembering what it is about. Thus you will tend to review in a different way than the lesson was first studied. Ask questions, make up illustrations for each topic, diagram relationships, and discuss the points with a friend.

During the school term you will have tried question prediction many times and should

Exam Week

	Monday	Tuesday	Wednesday	Thursday	Friday
8:00					
9:00					
10:00					
11:00					
12:00					
1:00					
2:00					
3:00					
4:00					
5:00					
6:00					
7:00					
8:00					
9:00					
10:00					

have found it effective (see the chart on page 36). It should also help with your final examinations. To provide further supervised practice, select some one of your final examinations and write out your predictions of *all* the major points which may be asked. This can be done by jotting down topics or by marking these points in your notes with colored pencil. Predictions made for previous quizzes can be used here. Have your counselor check these for further suggestions.

B. Taking Examinations

Did you ever thank a teacher for giving an examination? In theory one ought to be grateful for the hours an instructor spends in giving a test so that you and he may know what has been learned and where further work is needed. Almost all students, however, look forward to tests with trepidation and find the taking of the test somewhat of an ordeal. Rather than seeming like a cooperative effort, students often feel that teachers' tests seem more like a battle in which each tries to outwit the other. In any case the role of tests in determining grades places so much pressure on students that they often become upset during an examination. All too often they remember after the examination what they should have said. On other questions, they know the material but can't see what the questions are driving at, or later, can't see why points were taken off their grades. Skills in taking exams, which will help with these problems, are discussed below.

Emotional Excitement During the Examination

All tests are not equally upsetting. If the questions cover familiar material, the student hurries to write down all that he knows. Unexpected questions, on the other hand, scare him so that sometimes he is blocked completely. In the last project it was shown that reading to answer questions helps to organize learning so that it is remembered much better. If these study questions cover the same topics as in the examination, then it will seem familiar and easy. Therefore one of the most effective ways of combating a tendency to "blow up" on examinations is to predict quiz questions and study up on their answers. As indicated previously, this can be developed into a highly effective skill. And on questions not predicted, it has been shown that studying in this way is as effective, if not more so, than the usual student attitude of "study every little thing because there's no telling."

Students are sometimes bothered because, as they say, they know so much they don't know how to begin to express it. Or they get so engrossed in answering the early part of an examination that they have to hurry with the last part or omit it. Habits of calm and systematic attack on a test help here. A good instructor builds an examination which can be answered in the allotted time although it is usually planned so students shouldn't dawdle on any questions.

A first step in starting an exam is to glance over the test to get some idea as to how long it is and to see if certain parts count more or will take more time or may be easier to answer. On the basis of such a thirty-second survey, you should then roughly budget time to each essay question or to each page or section of an objective test. It pays to remember that although all the questions are not equally easy, they all usually count alike; it is better to work on many easy items and omit a few hard ones than vice versa. A final suggestion on attitude is just to do your best. Although every student would like to get every question right, it must be remembered that the test has been made difficult enough to give a range of scores for grading. Think and write on one question at a time.

Don't worry about questions further down the list until you get to them.

Students often get unnecessarily excited just before an examination. They hurriedly compare ideas as to what the answer is to some expected question and find themselves in disagreement. The ensuing frantic argument among partially informed and mistaken students produces a feeling of insecure preparation which only serves to upset the student's ability to think. So, if you get to the examination early, keep cool with small talk. Other students try to keep calm by delaying their arrival at the ordeal until the last minute with the result that they often arrive late. This is upsetting and they may also miss opening instructions.

Essay Examinations

Each type of examination requires certain unique skills and has its special difficulties. One common error in writing on essay questions is to waste time writing away from the subject. Because of the press of time during an exam, the instructor has to limit what he asks for; he therefore directs the student not to write everything he knows about the topic but specifically to "*list* the causes," "*compare* the outcomes," "*illustrate* these terms." These key words, as they are called, must be watched for in essay questions; they help the student to write exactly on what is wanted. Furthermore if the question says "list" or "outline," the teacher is expecting a list or an outline and is annoyed at having to search out the answer in a rambling essay.

Any question which asks for more than a brief definition needs to have an organized answer. Yet most students start writing on the first idea that comes to mind after reading a question and then continue with whatever ideas come to mind next; as a result some weird sequences of ideas are produced. The grader who has a list of points which

should be covered, finds it difficult to determine how many points are included in such essays; the labor of checking back and forth to find the items puts him in a frame of mind to give a low grade. It has been the writer's own experience that when he finds a test paper whose answers follow an organized sequence, he often feels like giving, and does give, a higher grade than the points listed would warrant. An easy and effective way to obtain this organization is first to jot down quickly a sketchy outline of key words which stand for the ideas to be covered. These ideas remind the student of further ideas which he inserts at the correct spots in his list. Writing the essay then becomes a matter of expounding on each of the ideas listed. Since the grader has to read many papers, he appreciates any cues which will speed up his reading. It pays, therefore, to number the main points in an essay or to use some visual system, such as outlining, to show the organization of the answer. Often a hastily drawn diagram will do much to demonstrate that you see the relationships among the ideas being presented.

There is some correlation between length of answer on an essay question and its grade. Of course, the student who knows the most will usually write the most, but one common failing of students is to feel that a few words carry as much meaning to the teacher as they do to the student himself. A student may feel that quoting a definition from the text is enough, but the grader wonders if these words have been really understood or merely memorized. Adding an illustration helps a great deal. In a question which asks for "discussion," do not list points only, but explain why they are important or how they are interrelated. Elaboration to show full understanding is different from "padding," which is readily recognized and resented. "Padding" means to bring in irrelevant points or to repeat points already made in order to fill up space. Explaining what you mean, giving illustrations, or showing the implications of your points are different and much appreciated by the grader.

Simple mechanics in writing examinations may markedly affect grades. For instance, in one experiment on the effect of legibility on grading papers, 43 teachers were asked to grade the same compositions at two different times—one time the compositions were written legibly, and the other time the same compositions were written somewhat illegibly. The compositions in legible handwriting received an average grade one letter higher than the compositions in illegible handwriting.[4] Examinations written in ink are more easily read than those in hard pencil. Also, take a few minutes at the end of the hour to proofread your paper. An accidentally omitted "not," or some other word, may grossly affect your grade. Be sure that the questions and their parts are numbered correctly.

Objective Examinations

There are also certain principles which assist in taking objective examinations. Since every question usually has equal weight you should work straight through the list of questions and not hesitate too long on those whose answers do not immediately come to mind. These hard questions should be checked in the margin and returned to later. Such a system insures that all the easy questions on the examination will be completed; later questions may remind you of the answers to the ones skipped. Be sure to go back over the examination to answer questions that were omitted the first time through.

Find out if there is a correction (a subtraction) for guessing. If the correction is not greater than rights minus wrongs on true-false questions, and rights minus 1/3 wrongs on four-choice multiple choice, do your best on each question. With corrections no greater than these, you should do as well by guessing as not guessing, and there is good psychological evidence that you will get more than a chance number right because of the operation of certain residual memories from material read. If there is an overcorrection for guessing, such as rights minus 2 × wrongs on true-false questions, you should leave unfamiliar questions blank.[5]

If a true-false question causes difficulty, the following principle is often helpful. Most such questions are built on the pattern of briefly describing two things and their degree of relationship to each other, i.e., "*Some* cats are black." The two "things" in each statement are usually true; statements are made false by changing the modifier so as to overstate or understate the degree of relationship. The following series of modifiers are typically used:

　All—most—some—no
　Always—usually—sometimes—never
　Great—much—little—no
　More—equal—less
　Positively related—not related—negatively related
　Good—bad
　Is—is not

When a student sees one of these in a sentence, he can usually test whether the statement is true by substituting the other words in that series. If none of them makes a better statement than the modifier already in the sentence, the statement is true. Thus when the above statement "*some* cats are black" is tested by substituting as follows: "*All* cats are black," "*Most* cats are black," and "*No* cats are black," the original state-

[4] H. W. James, The effect of handwriting upon grading, *Engl. J.*, 1927, 16:180–185.

[5] G. M. Ruch, *The Objective or New-Type Examination*, Scott, Foresman, 1929.

ment is shown to be true. Knowing this common pattern a student can go to the *key word* in true-false statements and not have to worry about possible exceptions to each word in the statement.

Many students have learned to look for the key words "no," "never," "every," "all," "entirely," because they usually cause the statement to be false. That is, it is difficult to make any statement which is true of all or no items to which it refers. Knowing this tendency of students to look for these specific words, however, many instructors work hard to formulate some statements in which the use of these terms makes true statements, i.e., "An island is entirely surrounded by water." "All men are mortal."

Care should also be used in answering a true-false statement containing two independent clauses. If one of these is true and the other false, the whole statement must be marked "false."

In answering multiple-choice questions, certain choices can often be crossed out as obviously wrong. This may reduce your immediate evaluation to one or two possibilities. Read the directions. If it says mark the one best answer, do not put more than one answer in the space provided. Such inconsistencies are marked wrong. In answering matching questions in which a given answer may be used only once, it will obviously be helpful to answer the known questions first, and then study the few remaining choices as answers to the hard questions. Mark out the answers as you use them. In answering completion questions, it is better to fill in the best answer you can think of than to leave it blank; such answers often get complete or partial credit. If the question calls for a word with a certain number of letters, use another word which carries a similar meaning if you cannot think of the correct word. If the answer is quite familiar to you, but for the moment you are unable to recall it, go on and return to this question later. Your changed point of view may assist in overcoming the previous mental block.

New Types of Examinations

Analysis of typical examinations shows that about 95 per cent of the items deal with knowledge of facts. Though the average instructor hopes that his students are also learning certain attitudes, points of view, ways of thinking, and ways to apply information, he assumes that students who know the most facts must be equally good in these other characteristics. This is far from the truth, however, because experiments show that these characteristics are not apt to be learned unless there is teaching and testing for them. For these reasons many teachers are changing their testing practices to include measures of these other aspects.

Students have trouble with these new types of examinations not only because they may not have the characteristics which the tests are attempting to measure, but also because they just don't know how to take these tests. Students who are familiar with true-false examinations are often stymied by questions which give all the data needed right on the test blank and ask the student to determine with fine discrimination whether an accompanying statement is "true," "probably true," "probably false," "false," or there is "insufficient evidence" to say. The writer has found that many students feel they don't understand what these test items are all about and so resort to guessing. On the other hand, a little explanation of how these tests are constructed has been found to increase students' scores markedly. Thus students at Ohio State University who analyzed their errors on a 45-item test of this type were able on the average to improve their score on a second test by 10 points; furthermore such practice on examples in physics transferred to similar items in zoology. The purpose of this section is to show that with a little training a student can demonstrate his ability on these tests as well as he now demonstrates his knowledge on true-false tests.

Techniques for measuring points of view, ways of thinking, and ability to apply information are not as well worked out or as standardized as they are for the usual objective or essay examination. So the form of these tests tends to vary from campus to campus and from course to course. Two currently emphasized examples are given below as illustrations of these new types of tests. Both attempt to measure accuracy and the kinds of constant errors which students make in thinking. They are known as "interpretation of data" and "application of principles" tests.

An interpretation of data test gives all the necessary information right in the test and asks the student to determine in terms of this whether each of a series of statements is true or false, probably true or false, or whether there is insufficient evidence to say. The test is scored not only as to the number correct but also as to the frequency with which a student is "too cautious" and "too gullible" in handling data. That is, the test measures whether a student has learned to use data without reading too much or too little into it. In making these test items, a standard pattern is used: If a statement is directly verified or denied by the data given it is "true" or "false." On the other hand, it is "probably true," or "probably false" under the following conditions: (a) a slight extrapolation of a curve, (b) an interpolation between points in a graph, (c) the behavior of a major part estimated from the behavior of the whole, and (d) an experiment repeated under comparable conditions. And a statement has "insufficient evidence" under these conditions: (a) comparison made between data given and data not given, (b) a cause is attributed for the data, (c) a value judgment is made in terms of the data, and (d) a too extended extrapolation is made. A student who knows these patterns will more easily recognize what a given item is driving at and so be able to react to it more intelligently.

In an "application of principles" test, the student not only answers a question but also checks the reasons for his answer from a list which is provided. These reasons are also constructed to fit a pattern; in this case, the incorrect ones are worded so as to resemble the types of erroneous arguments that people commonly use. These variously disguised arguments thus represent potential "booby traps" to catch the unwary thinker; some diagnosis is possible from an analysis of the types of errors for which a student tends to fall. Following is the pattern of errors commonly used: (a) reasoning by false analogy, (b) merely restating the conclusion, (c) reference to similar happenings, (d) appeal to authority, (e) use of ridicule, (f) teleological reasons, (g) irrelevant reasons, and (h) untrue statements. Again it has been found that students who understand how these items are made are better able to demonstrate their ability on these tests; they at least know for what they are being tested.

Many instructors vary the form of their items from that indicated above and other types of tests are being constantly experimented with. It is therefore difficult to know what a student will run into on a given campus. Rather than provide specific training exercises, it is suggested that the student analyze his exams to see if they include items which attempt to measure these non-informational aspects and with which he has trouble. Have your counselor assist you in analyzing how such items are constructed;

then make a definite attempt to improve your skill on such tests.

C. Making Use of Returned Examinations

Your score on a test does not in itself indicate how well you have done. Tests differ in length and difficulty so that a score of 70 may be excellent, average, or failing. You need some standard with which to compare your score, i.e., letter grade equivalents for your score, the average score of the class, or something as to the range of scores in the class. Having determined your level of performance, your next step is to determine what was wrong with your attack on the examination. Most students, however, don't take this step. Having seen their grade, they compare notes with other students, argue with the teacher that a certain question wasn't fair, or brood on the thought that they hate exams.

A quiz is a quick and easy way of reciting on what is important in the course. The items missed are those that need further study. Questions that give difficulty are often repeated later to see if students have mastered them. If you do not see how the correct answer is derived, ask the instructor for an explanation. But in any case use each quiz as a practice review which shows where further study will be needed before the final examination.

Much can also be learned from a test as to what the next one will be like. What kinds of questions were asked: definitions? interpretation? discussions? problems? Were they primarily from the text or from the lecture? Were they the ones you had expected? And of those you hadn't expected, where did they come from? What was wrong with your answers: not complete enough? poor distribution of time on the important parts of the test? questions omitted and

careless mistakes? Very often the instructor will write suggestions on the paper for improving your answers. If not, and you cannot determine what to do, ask the instructor sometime after class.

Practice. So much for a great deal of advice; the important thing is to try these skills out on actual tests to see if they work and to polish them to a level of efficiency. Much of what is stated here ties in directly with the methods of study discussed in the preceding project; skills which improve comprehension and retention are also useful with examinations. Some practice exercises have already been referred to in this project. To aid students, the whole program of practice on examination skills is summarized here. Set up a regular practice program along the following lines and check with your counselor for suggestions.

1. Look up the question topics from some old quizzes in the index of your textbook. Do these topics stand out in the text? Do they represent headings or other items set off by typographical cues?

2. Select some outside course in which you will make regular predictions of questions on quizzes. Check these predictions with your counselor for suggestions or additions and for ways to speed up making the predictions. Make such a set of predictions for a final examination, also.

3. After each such predicted quiz is returned, count or estimate the per cent that has actually been predicted. Record this on the chart on page 36.

4. If practice examinations are used, answer the following questions:

   a. Did you do better on the second than the first test? Did the class? Do you see how the Survey Q3R Method can easily be used?

   b. Analyze these practice tests for key words in the true-false items. Can you tell which words in a statement make it false or if changed would easily make it false?

c. Analyze these practice tests for key words in the essay questions. Did you write directly to the point in your answers? Did you give what was wanted and in the form requested? Have your counselor go over your essay answers and make suggestions as to possibilities for improvement in style.

5. Bring in available tests, essay and otherwise, from other courses for suggestions from your counselor as to possibilities for improvement in method.

6. At the time of final examinations, reread the section on final examinations and fill in the time chart.

7. Students wishing to read further on how to take examinations will find the following references interesting and worthwhile.

S. L. Crawley, *Studying Effectively*, Prentice-Hall, 1936. Pages 72–83.

R. W. Frederick, *How to Study Handbook*, Appleton-Century, 1938. Pages 291–348.

H. C. McKown, *How to Pass a Written Examination*, McGraw-Hill, 1943.

A. W. Ham and M. D. Salter, *Doctor in the Making*, Lippincott, 1943. Chaps. 5, 6, and 7.

PROJECT IV

SKILLS IN ATTACK AND CONCENTRATION

Many students complain that they have difficulty in settling down to work and in concentrating, that in hurrying from one thing to another they seem to get very little accomplished, or that with so much to do they cannot relax and enjoy themselves. On the other hand, almost every underclassman admires some senior who appears to complete all his work at a high standard, who has time for social activities and recreation, and who seems unflurried and unworried about his work. Since this senior was probably a typical freshman at one time and since skill in concentration is acquired and not inherited, what skills must he have learned to enable him to succeed so much more easily?

Basically much of his success is due (1) to the development of work-study skills, (2) to the development of habits of efficient time use, (3) to the setting up of better study conditions, and (4) to motivation. When this senior studies, one finds that he wants a quiet room, that he gets right to work, that a voice has to be raised to attract his attention, that he emphasizes the most important parts of his assignments rather than reading every word, and that he finishes a job without unnecessary interruptions. Every student would like to be that way too—it would make life so much easier!

The first of these areas, the development of work-study skills, has already been discussed in Projects II and III. The other three areas, i.e., habits of efficient time use, study conditions, and motivation, will be discussed as separate divisions of this project.

Since inability to get down to work or to concentrate may be due to many possible causes, an analysis of each individual's difficulties is necessary. Each division will start with some queries or other forms of self-analysis in order to focus attention on the issues which are of primary importance to the reader. Following this, means of improvement will be discussed.

HABITS OF EFFICIENT TIME USE

Students' difficulties in the use of time tend to be threefold: (1) they have feelings of guilt because they think they don't study enough, (2) they waste time in moving from one activity to another, and (3) they have difficulty in settling down to work even after they have made up their minds to start.

Most students feel that they ought to study more than they do. Many have feelings of guilt whenever they stop to talk or go to a movie. But as has already been indicated, good students actually don't study more than poor students, they are just more efficient when they do study. The primary remedy for study difficulties is more effective methods of study rather than more study time. Good students have good times in school and it is characteristic that they usually worry less about needing to study than students with lower grades. It is not a purpose of this project to try to get you to study more hours; in the case of "grinds," in fact, part of the remedy is to get them to spend less time in study.

The average person usually feels that the

hours in the day pass rapidly with too little accomplished. Part of the difficulty lies in the lack of a planned routine of activities. With a continuing attitude of "what next?" one has to be constantly making decisions about next steps. Such a person responds sensitively to distractions about him; he no sooner starts something than he is reminded of several other pressing matters. With little or no system to a person's activities, everything seems to demand immediate attention. Two examples will show how, without some habitual routine, time seems to be frittered away. The average student with classes at nine and eleven behaves somewhat as follows: converses after class (10 minutes), smokes a cigarette (5 minutes), mails a letter (15 minutes), starts for the library but meets a friend (15 minutes), then because of the time starts for the next class. Or, in the evening this typical student starts prodding himself to go to work immediately after supper, begrudgingly gives himself until seven to talk, then with self-recrimination extends this time until 7:30 and then at 8 finally drives himself to work. On settling down he finds that he doesn't know the assignment and has to fill his pen, once started he has to stop in order to help his roommate with some algebra. Study is further interrupted by the "necessity" of planning a week-end trip and telephoning for a date. Later he passes up going out to eat with some friends but then finds that he can't study after that so he goes out to eat alone. The next day he says he spent the whole evening trying to study.

Concrete evidence of the difficulty students have in settling down to study and then keeping at it is given in the following studies.[1] Students entering a library room to study were observed during their first ten minutes; it was found that little more than half of this time was spent productively. And efficiency after the first ten minutes was not much more effective.

[1] F. K. Berrien and J. L. Kennedy, How quickly do students start studying, School and Soc., 1942, 55:482–483; D. C. Troth, A ten-minute observation in the library, School and Soc., 1929, 29:336–338; Helen Randall, A Study of Reading Efficiency Over Various Time Intervals and Under Different Work Conditions, Master's thesis, Ohio State Univ., 1943.

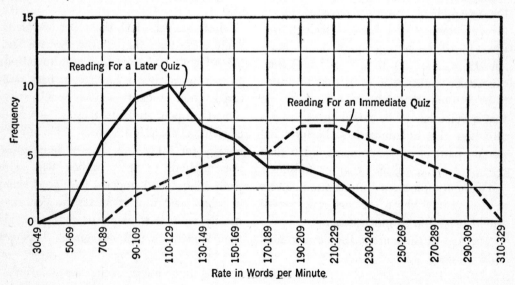

CHART 7. Rates at which students read comparable selections during thirty-minute periods under different conditions: (a) reading for an immediate quiz, and (b) reading for a later quiz in an apparently untimed situation and with more study the next day seeming possible, i.e., similar to normal study conditions. (Smoothed curves adapted from Randall.)

In one experiment, students reading for a test several days hence and not knowing that their rate of reading was being measured (i.e., similar to the usual study situation) read only 60 per cent as fast during 30 minutes as they did on similar material when they knew they were taking a reading test. (See Chart 7.) Indicative that individuals differ in the degree to which they apply their reading skills while studying is another finding in this same study. Knowing a person's rate on a test, one can predict his rate of reading during apparently untimed study only 5 per cent better than just guessing! It's a case of the tortoise and the hare; some plod steadily along to finish first and others, more hare-brained, interrupt their work to do this and that.

Self-Evaluation

Fill in the accompanying time chart to show how you now spend your time. Select several days this week during which you agree to make an effort several times a day to mark down by 15-minute intervals how you have spent your time. Be accurate—include loafing, talking, walking to class, recreation, etc.

A first reaction to a time diary like this is to see if there has been enough or too little study, sleep, or recreation. As a matter of fact, peoples' interests and requirements differ so much that no norm can be set; what is the best distribution of time for one individual will not be particularly efficient for another. Table 1, which summarizes the distribution of time of several hundred women in a state university, shows how variable the use of time can be for students. Critical judgment cannot be made of the total time which a student gives to different types of activity, but it can be made of extremely unbalanced patterns, i.e., all work and no play or vice versa.

Much more productive to the average student is an analysis of this time diary to find examples of inefficient mixing of activities during a unit of time. Thus a student may find that instead of spending an evening at study as he intended, he has actually interrupted this activity so often that he spent less than half of the period productively, or he may find that some extra hours between classes have been frittered away. Try rearranging the times you studied or enjoyed recreation into more consecutive periods. Does more time seem available than it did during the hectic rush on those days?

Later on, principles for the placement of different activities during the day will be presented; on the basis of this information other inefficiencies in this time diary can then be noted.

TABLE 1. Week-Day Distribution of Time in Hours and Minutes of Freshmen Women; Data Given for Median, First Quartile, and Third Quartile.[2]

	Median	Q1	Q3
Sleep	8 hr 0 min	7 hr 30 min	8 hr 30 min
Meals	1 hr 13 min	1 hr 0 min	1 hr 26 min
Class	3 hr 07 min	2 hr 39 min	3 hr 35 min
Study	3 hr 05 min	2 hr 18 min	3 hr 52 min
Recreation	3 hr 26 min	2 hr 34 min	4 hr 18 min
Work	1 hr 39 min	57 min	2 hr 21 min
Personal	1 hr 50 min	1 hr 26 min	2 hr 14 min
Travel	52 min	33 min	1 hr 11 min
Miscellaneous	2 hr 08 min	1 hr 15 min	3 hr 03 min

[2] From unpublished data of M. V. Bean and E. A. Gaw. Used with permission. The times do not total 24 hours because "work" and "travel" were calculated only from those time schedules listing them.

PRESENT USE OF TIME (CLASSES, STUDY, RECREATION, WORK)

	1st Day	2nd Day	3rd Day		1st Day	2nd Day	3rd Day
6:00				3:00			
6:30				3:30			
7:00				4:00			
7:30				4:30			
8:00				5:00			
8:30				5:30			
9:00				6:00			
9:30				6:30			
10:00				7:00			
10:30				7:30			
11:00				8:00			
11:30				8:30			
12:00				9:00			
12:30				9:30			
1:00				10:00			
1:30				10:30			
2:00				11:00			
2:30				11:30			

Name.. Days...

Study Habits Questionnaire [3]   No. right out of 23......

Answer each of these questions by writing in one of the following words (or its number): (1) never, (2) seldom, (3) sometimes, (4) often, or (5) always.

Time Distribution

..... 1. Do you have a plan of work for each day?

..... 2. If so, do you stick to it?

..... 3   Does your work prevent you from engaging in social activities?

..... 4. Do you allow time for exercise?

..... 5. Do you get enough sleep?

..... 6. Do you have certain hours that you regularly spend in talking and recreation?

..... 7. Do you eat at the same hours each day?

..... 8   Do you tend to spend too much time on social and recreational activities?

..... 9. When you study at night, how long is it usually from the time you close your book until you are in bed? (Indicate the time in minutes.)

Attitudes

.....10 Do you feel that you have to spend too much time studying?

.....11 Do you feel that you ought to spend as much time as possible studying?

.....12 Do you get tense and nervous when you study, or worry about your work?

.....13 Do you feel incapable of doing your work?

.....14. Do you try to complete a lesson before allowing interruptions to take place?

.....15 With a four-hour French assignment, would you try to complete it at one sitting rather than at several different times?

Work Habits

.....16. Do you study during the hour between two classes, say between a 9 and an 11 o'clock?

.....17 Do you have trouble "settling down to work" at the beginning of a study period?

.....18 When you study, do you frequently get up, walk about, glance at a paper or magazine, or do other things which interrupt your work?

.....19 Do you daydream in class or when you should be studying?

.....20. Do you study a given course each week day in the same place and at the same time?

.....21 Do you get to class or sit down to study, only to find that you do not have your notebook, pen, textbook, or other material?

.....22. Do you get your work in on time?

.....23 Do you immediately go on to the next lesson when you have completed the one you are working on?

[3] These and the questions used later concerning study conditions are adapted from S. L. Pressey and M. E. Troyer's Study Questionnaire which appears in the *Laboratory Workbook in Applied Educational Psychology*, Harper, 1945. Used with permission.

The questions whose numbers are followed by periods should be answered "often" or "always" while those question numbers not followed by periods should be answered "seldom" or "never." The answer to question 9 is "30 minutes or longer." There is seldom a paragon, even among good students, who can honestly answer all of these correctly. The items missed indicate which suggestions in the following discussion will be most pertinent.

Program for Improvement

Developing habits of efficient time use is a somewhat different proposition than many students believe it to be. A person is efficient not because of any superb display of will power used to force himself to keep on the job, but rather because he has developed habitual patterns or sequences of activities. A person who knows what he wants to do next and who gets down to work quickly usually goes about his work with no particular feeling of effort in "keeping his nose to the grindstone." Two homely examples of activities in which most people are efficient will illustrate: The average person doesn't have to be constantly reminding himself to remember to eat; even when engrossed in some activity his attention turns to eating at the right time. This occurs because he has built up habits of eating at a regular time. He also has little trouble concentrating on eating because every day at this time and place he has always devoted himself to eating. Another example is the greater ease one has in following a time schedule of classes which meet daily at the same times than in following a schedule which changes daily. After several weeks on a constant schedule, the student goes by habit from one class to the next one; he does not have to prod himself to go, he seems to follow the routine without much thought. One would say that this student finds it easy to concentrate on

getting to class and he is less easily distracted by friends and activities he sees on the way.

It should also be evident that ability to concentrate and use time efficiently does not mean drudgery or following a dreary routine. In fact, these habitual skills should make life seem more interesting. Thus some people let habit get them to their accustomed eating places on time while they visit and joke. Other people, because of a habitual routine, are even able to get to an 8 o'clock while still enjoying a half-sleep.

There are three steps in developing skills in effective time use: working out an efficient time schedule, following this schedule until work habits develop, and applying conscious effort to certain work rules. Each of these will be discussed in turn.

1. *Development of a Time Schedule.* School programs are so planned that every student should be able to have a suitable balance between study, recreation, eating, and sleeping. When a student feels too hurried, he will probably find that rearranging his use of time—his whole time—will help. The time diary filled out earlier shows where inefficient use of time tends to occur. With this information and a little experimenting, an efficient time schedule can be worked out. Use the first of the following Time Charts to write out this proposed schedule. Experience in using it will probably suggest the need for some revision, so after a week's use of this initial time chart make a final time chart.

In making out these charts, the following steps and principles will be of help. First, write in those activities for which the time is more or less set, such as eating, sleeping, class hours, and outside work. In doing this, be sure to allow adequate time for eating and sleeping.

Next indicate the hours during which you expect to study each subject. That is, don't just say "Study from 7 to 11" but say "Study

PLAN OF STUDY, CLASSES, AND RECREATION

	Monday	Tuesday	Wednesday	Thursday	Friday	Saturday	Sunday
7:30[a]							
8:00							
9:00							
10:00							
11:00							
12:00							
12:30							
1:00							
2:00							
3:00							
4:00							
4:30							
5:00							
5:30							
6:00							
6:30							
7:00							
7:30							
8:00							
8:30							
9:00							
9:30							
10:00							
10:30							
11:00							

[a] Enter classes in red pencil.

Name.. Week beginning....................................

PLAN OF STUDY, CLASSES, AND RECREATION

	Monday	Tuesday	Wednesday	Thursday	Friday	Saturday	Sunday
7:30[a]							
8:00							
9:00							
10:00							
11:00							
12:00							
12:30							
1:00							
2:00							
3:00							
4:00							
4:30							
5:00							
5:30							
6:00							
6:30							
7:00							
7:30							
8:00							
8:30							
9:00							
9:30							
10:00							
10:30							
11:00							

[a] Enter classes in red pencil.

Name.................................... Week beginning....................................

history from 7–8:30" and "Study chemistry from 8:45–10." Typical students average somewhat less than two hours of study for each hour of class—an often-quoted university standard. Furthermore, research shows that good students differ from poor students more in effective use of study time than in the amount.[4] Rather than planning to study extra hours if doing poorly, you should learn to make more effective use of your time. Any student who is averaging much more than two hours daily in preparing for a given subject should look to other projects for more effective study skills.

Having filled in these various activities, you will normally find that there are still some hours left over. These are your reward for time well spent; these hours are for recreation. Students with heavy outside work schedules may find little time left over. Such students report that outside work normally affects hours of recreation more than anything else. Studies of working students, however, show that they, with few exceptions, make as good grades and are as well-adjusted socially as the non-working student.[5] And it is interesting to note that students with work schedules usually complain less about problems of concentration than non-working students; their full schedules require them to follow a habitual routine and so form concentration habits.

In assigning definite hours to study and recreation, certain principles are of assistance.

a. Normally, it is better to study an assignment just after the class in which it is given if the class is usually a lecture section, or just before the class in which it will be used if emphasis is on recitation or discussion.

b. In studying over long periods of time, it is worth while to stop for a few minutes between chapters or between change of subjects.[6] Such a period of stretching and relaxation allows one to attack the next lesson with renewed energy and, more important, it prevents the immediate study of a different subject matter from interfering with the process of remembering—a psychological effect known as retroactive inhibition.

c. It is better to study a subject every day at the same time than to have occasional long sessions. This daily routine develops habits which facilitate deciding what next to do, in getting down to work, and in concentrating.

d. Allow a "slowing down" period between the end of studying and starting for bed. Such a period of relaxation is apt to make going to sleep much easier.

e. Make use of vacant hours between classes. That is, the hour between a 9-o'clock and an 11-o'clock class is a poor time for visiting; it can be spent in study so as to reduce the evening's work.

f. From 4 to 7 P.M. is the usual period for recreation during the week. Plan to use as much of this period as possible for such purposes.

2. *Habitual Use of Time Schedule.* Having developed an efficient time schedule

[4] A. C. Eurich, The amount of reading and study among college students, *School and Soc.*, 1933, 37:102–104; J. G. Jenkins, Student's use of time, *Personnel J.*, 1931–1932, 10:259–264; D. G. Ryans, Some observations concerning the relationship of time spent at study to scholarship and other factors, *J. Educ. Psych.*, 1938, 30:372–377; E. G. Williamson, The relationship of number of hours of study to scholarship, *J. Educ. Psych.*, 1935, 26:682–688.

[5] S. C. Newman and R. L. Mooney, Effects of self-help employment on the college student, *J. Higher Educ.*, 1940, 11:435–442; M. E. Wagner, H. P. Eiduson, and R. J. Morris, The effects of Federal Emergency Relief Administration employment on college grades, *School and Soc.*, 1937, 45:25–26.

[6] I. A. Gentry, Immediate effects of interpolated rest periods on learning performance. *Teach. Coll. Contri. Educ.*, 1940, No. 799.

for the school term, the next step is to follow it until you habitually turn from each activity to the next one. It is a good idea to place the proposed time schedule where you will see it frequently, e.g., in the front of your notebook or on the wall of your room. Try to follow its pattern each day. Gradually the habit of turning from one particular activity to another will develop; getting down to work and concentrating will begin to seem much easier.

It cannot be emphasized too strongly that this aspect of developing skill in concentration and effective use of time is not based on merely understanding how important it is to study, nor is it a matter of making a decision really to get down to work. It is a matter of habit development. This will take much practice and, to keep yourself at it, you should check your use of time occasionally or have your counselor do it.

A time schedule should not be an inflexible thing which gets in the way. When special events or opportunities occur, rearrange your schedule, but during the normal course of events use the basic habit pattern to guide the flow of the day's activities.

3. *Applying Work Rules.* The purpose of the above program is to develop a tendency to turn habitually to a next scheduled activity; a student can help this tendency along by knowing and consciously applying certain principles of time use. As William James once said, the way to develop a habit is to do the act at the first opportunity and to let no exception take place. A right mental set will go a long way toward helping the above habit formation. For instance, don't wait for a suitable mood before studying; begin studying at your regularly set time. Likewise, try to finish all your work within the time limits set; do not rob yourself of recreation time. Don't worry about all the work to be accomplished—there is a time

scheduled for everything. Don't carry extra books around—you should know which are scheduled for studying. And don't waste time trying to figure out what to study first —take the subject scheduled.

Once you are at the study table, try to go right to work; force yourself to postpone other activities until later. Check yourself whenever you start to daydream. Set a time or page limit on your work because it is easier to keep at a lesson for 20 more minutes or five more pages than it is to promise yourself to study all evening. Try to finish your work within the time limits set; if you should finish early take a short rest period.

STUDY CONDITIONS

Study conditions affect in three ways the ability to get down to work and to concentrate: (a) Distractions tend to draw the student's attention away from his work. (b) Poor lighting, inadequate ventilation and noise tend to be fatiguing. (c) Study materials not readily available cause the continuity of work to be broken in order to hunt for them.

Self-Evaluation

A self-evaluation can be only preliminary at this point. Some technical information as to the best conditions for study will be presented, then a summary section for self-evaluation will be provided in conjunction with the section on plans. The questions which follow, however, will help indicate which suggestions are most pertinent in the discussion of study conditions.

All the questions below should be answered "seldom" or "never" except for questions 11, 13, and 14. Question 13 should be answered "usually" or "always" and the answers to questions 11 and 14 will be found in the discussion below.

Study Conditions Questionnaire   No. right out of 15......

Answer each question by writing in one of the following words (or its number): (1) never, (2) seldom, (3) sometimes, (4) usually, or (5) always. A few questions are to be completed by writing in other answers as directed.

Distractions

..... 1. Do you prepare for bed before doing some of your studying?

..... 2. Do you study some of your lessons while in bed or while stretched out on the davenport?

..... 3. Is your room used for many informal meetings during the evening?

..... 4. Is your room near some disturbing source of noise?

..... 5. Do you have pictures or things that you like to look at on or near your study table?

..... 6. Do other people in your study room distract you?

..... 7. Does the temperature of your study room make you feel uncomfortable?

..... 8. Is your studying interrupted by thinking about various personal problems and worries?

..... 9. Is your studying interrupted by thinking about various interesting events in the near future?

Materials

.....10. Do you have trouble obtaining the materials that you need for study?

.....11. How much clear table space do you have for study? That is, about how long and how wide is the free space on your desk?

Fatigue

.....12. Do you have much glare on your book?

.....13. Does enough light fall on your book when it is in the position in which you normally have it when you study? (See directions below on use of the light meter.)

.....14. What type of lighting do you have? (a) gooseneck or study lamp; (b) overhead light; (c) indirect lighting; (d) _____

.....15. Is it generally noisy where you usually study?

Background Information

1. It is often difficult to concentrate on studying because it is more fun to concentrate on other doings in college. A textbook just isn't as interesting as a photograph on the study table or a talk session in the same room, and at the library there are other distractions. Something as to the range of these distractions in a library is summarized in Table 2.

TABLE 2. Types and Frequency of Distractions Interrupting the Library Study of College Men and Women. (Adapted from Troth.)

Distraction	Per Cent of Total		
	Men	Women	Both
Conversation	32	26	29
Aimless looking around	15	15	15
Aimless leafing through books	14	10	12
Students walking by	12	7	10
Vanity cases	0	16	8
Attracted by certain individuals	9	5	7
Daydreaming	7	5	6
Reading and writing letters	4	7	5
Arranging hair and clothes	2	7	4
Miscellaneous	5	2	4
	100	100	100

These results might seem to indicate that any place but the library would be better for study. But actual evidence indicates that students who study in the library get better grades than students who study elsewhere.[7] The experimenter found that these two groups did not differ in intelligence, yet the ones who studied in the library obtained grades .4 of a grade point higher, i.e., almost half the distance between a C and a B. This greater effectiveness of library study is probably due to various things, besides having fewer distractions than the student's room. The environment is one always used for study, so the surroundings act as stimuli which set off habits and attitudes of study. All necessary study materials tend to be more readily available there. And there is more desk space. The experiment has its moral, however; some consideration should be given to determining how distractions in the library can be cut down. Probably the best solution is to seek a small reading room

in the library, find a corner and face the wall. Later, if you wish social contacts, move to the center of the main library room.

Distractions in the student's own room can also be cut down. Fix it so while sitting at the study table you can't see any pictures, souvenirs, or blotters with football schedules on them. Face your study table to the wall and not looking out into the room or out of a window. A book can seem more interesting if it has only to compete with bare surroundings. It is nice, on the other hand, to decorate one's room, but divide it off into different areas. Place pictures and souvenirs where studying won't interfere when you want to meditate upon them with affection. Eliminate all interesting sounds, i.e., radio programs and conversations, during study hours.[8] Arrange with fellow students to set

[7] A. Eurich, The significance of library reading among college students, *School and Soc.*, 1932, 36:92–96.

[8] P. Fendrick, The influence of music distraction upon reading efficiency, *J. Educ. Res.*, 1937, 31: 264–271; H. B. Hovey, Effects of general distraction on the higher thought processes, *Amer. J. Psych.*, 1928, 40:585–591; Brother Richard, The relationship between freshman marks and study environment, *J. Educ. Res.*, 1935–1936, 29:589–592.

up a few house rules to maintain quiet during periods restricted for study.

In spite of all these precautions, some sounds are bound to occur and will naturally tend to be distracting, but a student can rise above such minor interruptions by challenging himself to keep at his work for the designated study period.

2. Various stimuli can also be used to promote concentration. Study habits are developed and set in motion not only by repeating a sequence of activities (discussed earlier) but also by repeating the same surroundings every time one studies. If the same situation is always and only associated with studying, it has been found that a student becomes conditioned to concentrating on his studies whenever he is in that situation. A frequently used example of this phenomenon is the manner in which a standard situation promotes sleep: Before going to bed one may not feel particularly sleepy but changing to bed clothes, lying down on a soft bed and pillow with covers over one, and turning the light out all produce a combination of stimuli to which people are conditioned to respond by going to sleep. Note how much harder it is to go to sleep in a strange bed and surroundings! Similarly in studying, if students study the same subject in the same place at the same time every weekday, the surroundings all tend to suggest study and so help concentration. It also seems evident that the place in which one studies should not also be used for letter writing, card games, day dreaming, etc.; if used only for studying, one is reminded only of studying.

Posture can also produce stimuli which remind you of work; other postures may suggest relaxation. Take a cue from the way people behave when listening to an interesting lecture—they sit erect or even strain forward to obtain each idea. Similarly it is advisable to sit erect in a straight chair while at the study table. It is even a good practice (and not bad etiquette) to put your elbows on the table while studying. That is, studying demands an attitude of active work; using the above posture helps to maintain this attitude. Relaxing in an easy chair, on the other hand, is not conducive to concentration. Worst of all is dressing in pajamas before starting to study in the evening and then lying on the davenport or bed while studying. Being conditioned to go to sleep when in this garb and position, the student has difficulty concentrating. If he learns to stay awake while doing this, he may also tend to stay awake when he retires.

3. Allow adequate space for all the materials you will have to use. Kraehenbuehl concludes, on the basis of a study of the needs of over 2300 students at the University of Illinois, that the "desk should be, for a single individual, approximately 30 by 48 inches in size." [9] Collect all necessary materials before starting to study, so that they will be at hand when needed.

4. Noise and poor lighting are two unnecessary causes of fatigue in studying. Noise not only tends to distract the student from his work, but the energy demanded in trying "not to pay attention to it" wears a person down quite rapidly. For instance, in one study it was found that stenographers working in a noisy room hit the keys harder and fatigued more quickly than did stenographers working in a relatively quiet room.

There are three criteria for good lighting: (a) adequate and well-distributed illumination, (b) absence of glare, and (c) light placed so as not to shine into the eyes. Kraehenbuehl's survey of the kinds of lights students use showed that only about 5 per cent would be considered satisfactory in these terms. Gooseneck lamps and those

[9] J. O. Kraehenbuehl, *Study Facilities in College Dormitories*, Publication No. 232, National Society for the Prevention of Blindness.

with "cute" silk shades were the most frequently used types of lights and were among the poorest in lighting efficiency. Studies at the University of Minnesota show that a student should "never read with less than 5 foot-candles of light. Where diffusion of light is quite unsatisfactory, use 5 to 10 foot-candles. When the illumination is well distributed, use 10 to 15 foot-candles. If no glare due to faulty distribution of light or to other factors is present, higher intensities may be employed with safety, but without gain in efficiency and comfort." [10] These studies also show that: (a) Indirect or well-diffused lighting is best; fatigue is fostered by lights that shine in the eyes or cause glare on the paper. (b) There should not be too much contrast between the lighting on one's work and that on the surroundings; there should be an over-all illumination in the room of about 3 or 4 foot-candles. (c) Colored (monochromatic) light does not have any advantage over daylight or common forms of artificial illumination in producing more efficient reading or less fatigue.

A light meter must be used to measure the amount of light given off by a lamp, since type of glass, distance from the book, and efficiency of reflecting surfaces affect the amount of light produced. A light meter may be obtained from the counselor to measure the illumination in your study room.[11] If this illumination is inadequate

and you wish to impress your landlord, the following clause, written into each housing contract at the University of Illinois, may be of use: "Each man, if he so desires, is entitled to 100 watts of electric light."

Since the gooseneck lamp is so frequently the study lamp available, the following suggestion is given for making it more effective. Face the lamp toward the wall at your side and place a shiny white sheet on the wall to act as a reflector. If necessary, increase the wattage of the bulb, and you will have a fairly satisfactory lighting system. Or the light can be diffused by placing tracing cloth over the face of the reflector. In this case, some way will have to be devised to allow the air to circulate about the heated bulb.

Program for Improvement

Some specific activities are listed to help demonstrate how study conditions do affect concentration and to suggest remedial possibilities to the reader. Carry out each of the following projects.

1. It is surprising and enlightening to see how often students are distracted as they study. Seeing this in others will make you more sensitive to distractions in your own case. For the following exercise go to a library and watch an individual for a period of 10 or 15 minutes as he studies. If it is a person in this how-to-study class, your checking will later be of use to him. It is better to have the person at some distance so that your observing will not be noticeable to him. Every time there is a change in his behavior, even though but a brief glance about the room, tabulate it below. This check list is similar to the list in Table 2; an interesting

---

[10] M. A. Tinker, Illumination standards for effective and comfortable vision, *J. Consulting Psych.*, 1939, 3:18.

[11] To measure illumination, stand the light meter vertically to the surface being read and the candle-power illumination will be indicated by the pointer. Readings can be made above 75 foot-candles by clipping the metal plate over the light-sensitive cell of the meter and multiplying the foot-candles on the scale by 10. When not being used, the plate can be clipped to the bottom of the meter. While a carefully worked-out illumination survey for a room is quite involved, sufficient accuracy can be obtained for student use by measuring the illumination on the surface being read and in the immediate surroundings.

The student should use care in handling the light meter. Although the cell is not easily damaged, it should not be exposed to bright sunlight for any appreciable length of time; the cell cover-glass should be kept clean, and the meter should not be subjected to sudden jolts or blows.

comparison can be made with it when this checking is completed. If this observation proves interesting, something as to individual differences in distractibility can be obtained by observing and tabulating the behavior of several individuals.

Check List of Work Behavior

	Individual "A"	Individual "B"
Work Activities:		
Reading		
Note-taking		
Self-recitation		
Working problems		
Distractions:		
Conversation		
Aimless looking around		
Aimless leafing through books		
Students going by		
Vanity cases		
Attracted by certain individuals		
Daydreaming		
Reading or writing letters		
Arranging hair and clothes		
Miscellaneous		

Time Use:
  About what proportion of the time was spent in studying?

While it is not convenient to tabulate each thing which tends to distract your own studying, you should take mental note of the things which take your attention away from studying. Possibly you can arrange with a friend to observe your studying and check the number of times you are distracted, giv-

ing some indication of the causes. Or one of the other students in this course may use you as a subject for observation and will turn his ratings over to you.

2. Survey your own study room for evidence of surroundings which are distracting. Are there pictures, souvenirs, etc., near where you study? Is a radio played or do students talk while you try to study? Also survey your room for adequacy of lighting, ventilation and clear table space for study.

3. On the basis of the earlier self-evaluation questions, the above checks, and your own observations, fill in the evaluation of your study conditions (page 70) and what you plan to do about them. Be specific as to difficulties and plans.

MOTIVATION

The discussion thus far has suggested improving use of time and concentration through developing an efficient time plan, following it until habits develop, and removing distractions which interfere with concentration. But something like leading a horse to water, he really has to want to drink before he will consume any. The will to study is an important, if not the most important, determiner of effective use of time.[12]

Many students say that college work is not interesting to them. By a characteristically human projection, they often state that this is due to their uninteresting courses and teachers. It is a mistake, however, to assume that a course must be entertaining to be interesting. Students in medicine and law are vitally interested in their courses, but the material is not sugar coated with jokes and stories. The college authorities, by presenting a subject, certify that the content is

[12] D. D. Feder and J. S. Kounin, Motivational problems in student counseling, *J. Appl. Psych.*, 1940, 24:273–286; M. E. Wagner, Studies in motivation, *Univ. of Buffalo Studies*, 1936, 13, No. 5.

EVALUATION OF STUDY CONDITIONS AND PLANS FOR CORRECTION

Area	What's Wrong	Specific Plans
Auditory distractions in room		
Visual distractions in room		
Personal worries and interests which distract		
Auditory distractions at library		
Visual distractions at library		
Constancy of study conditions to stimulate study		
Posture while studying		
Adequacy of lighting		
Adequacy of work space		
Availability of materials		

useful and therefore of interest. The cause of lack of interest in college work almost always lies with the student himself. If he is not interested in college, or if he is unable to apply himself to his work in spite of an expressed interest in it, he needs to undertake a serious evaluation of his problem.

The purpose of this section is not to try to convince any student that he *ought* to be interested in college work. Rather a student needs to think through what his interests are and what they mean for him. The material which follows will be of some assistance in such "thinking through."

Why Isn't College Work Interesting to Some Students?

There are many possible reasons. The following are the primary explanations of why some students can't get interested enough to study while other students in the same courses are interested.

1. In the first place, few people are completely unmotivated, or not interested in anything. Laziness is an expression of lack of interest in immediately available activities, not a cause of it. It is characteristic that one likes to do some things and dislikes to do certain others. Occasionally one of the latter is college work. A general apathy or lack of energy would strongly suggest the need for a medical examination.

2. Personal problems seem of such importance that worry about them dispels interest in college work. Such threats to personal security must be eliminated before continued interest in study can return. See Project XIII for a discussion of this.

3. Many people are not interested, and rightly so, in doing college work. For some, college attendance may not represent the best step toward attainment of success. They might like business or trade schools much better. These schools provide training for entering well-paid occupations for which some people have the ability and interest. Such training can usually be obtained in less time than in college and it often results in faster advancement for these individuals than if they had attended college. In other instances, direct entry into work may be the best path toward success. In our democracy, these various forms of education do not have any superiority over each other; each prepares for different aspects of life, and different types of persons are best suited to each.

Other students are not yet vitally interested in preparations for adult living and a vocation; they are, therefore, little interested in the work of college classes. Some students go to college apparently for no better reason than because their friends are going or they can think of nothing else to do. Each student needs to determine, for himself, what he expects of further education and, in terms of this, what he should do. Project XI on Vocations will be of value in helping the student to determine his best potential areas of preparation.

Sometimes a student realizes that it is a waste of time for him to continue in college but feels that it would be a disgrace to leave. In this case, it is only necessary to point out that the majority of students who enter college do not graduate; most of these leave quite voluntarily. One study of the academic history of freshmen entering a college at Ohio State University found that only 35 per cent graduated from the same college they had entered as freshmen, 17 per cent transferred to other colleges in the university but all did not graduate, 33 per cent withdrew voluntarily from the university to turn to other means of preparation, and 15 per cent were dismissed.[13]

4. If the analysis of your plans indicates the need for further college attendance but you still cannot become interested in your studies, you may find the following discussion helpful. It briefly describes some aspects of the genetic development of interests which affect college work. Some of the points discussed may give insight into the origin of your own difficulty.

It is obvious that people's interests differ with their age; a study of these changes shows that they tend to follow certain definite sequences. While the subject is much too complex for a thorough discussion here, five examples are given of ways in which interest in schoolwork may increase or de-

[13] R. D. Bennett, Mimeographed report, Ohio State Univ., 1939.

crease with such maturation. The student may see in these examples a basis for his own or, at least, others' lack of interest in college work.

   a. Childhood interests tend to center about immediate rather than delayed goals. A penny in the hand for candy is preferred to a nickel in the bank toward a pair of roller skates. As a person grows older, he becomes more aware of the importance of delayed goals. Yet some adolescents, although highly valuing ultimate school success, are unable to resist putting off their studying when other more immediately interesting activities present themselves, i.e., going along with friends to a movie instead of studying for a mid-term the next day. The mature adult, however, has the ability to weigh values in terms of his own future welfare and can plan his time and direct his energies accordingly. Thus a person may study because of the future social or vocational values of the subject. It must be admitted, however, that even adults find it difficult to make textbooks seem as interesting as attaining some immediate goal. And for the less mature it is even more difficult.

One common misconception about good students needs to be corrected here, however. Good students have good times and do not spend their time in dreary drudgery. For instance, fewer good than poor students answer "yes" to the question "Do your studies tend to prevent you from participating in social activities?" And analysis of the activities of Phi Beta Kappa students shows them to belong to and be leaders in more extracurricular activities than the average student.[14]

   b. Young children seem to be just naturally curious about the nature of things, but as older students, many become hesitant about asking questions. Sometimes this is due to having previously received too many inadequate answers, sometimes it is due to a dislike of admitting a deficiency, and at other times questions are withheld for fear they will be interpreted by other students as a form of "apple polishing." Each of these instances is unfortunate; if any one of them strikes home with you, it may be well to back up and give learning about the world a new try. Learning can be fun!

   c. Personal qualities which are thought important differ at various age levels. This provides a third illustration of a genetic change which tends to affect interest in college. Physical prowess is admired by young children. During adolescence, appearance and good fellowship are apt to be weighted heavily because these traits are considered important for acceptance by a fraternity or by the opposite sex. Adults also consider the reactions of others to themselves as important but are apt to put it in better perspective. Intellectual competence is given its greatest emphasis among adults. These trends are illustrated in Chart 8 which shows the relative degree to which various traits are admired at different grade levels.

Since a person will work hardest for what he most values, college courses may or may not appeal to a student. For the adult who desires intellectual competence, college work will seem vital and interesting; this has recently been dramatically illustrated by the in-

[14] M. Newcomer, The Phi Beta Kappa student, School and Soc., 1927, 25:24; W. R. Voorhis and

A. C. Miller, Influence of college training upon success after college as measured by judges' estimates, J. Educ. Psych., 1935, 26:377–383.

tense motivation of many returned war veterans in college work.[15] At the other end of the distribution are some college students who are still adolescently engrossed in belonging to a group and in being esteemed for prowess in high-school-like activities. Such individuals are not ready for college work and will not find it interesting. In between these two extremes are ranged the rest of the college students. That interest in doing schoolwork is not the strongest motive in the life of the average student is illustrated by a study comparing how hard students will work for a professor and for a fraternity.[16] Ten freshmen fraternity initiates, on the last evening of a very strenuous "hell week," were required to spend about two hours in

working arithmetic problems; they were told that the tests were a part of their evaluation for admission to the fraternity. Later 54 students working under normal classroom conditions were asked to do the same tasks. The fraternity neophytes, although fatigued and harassed, did a third more problems than the group working under normal classroom conditions.

Another interesting illustration of how differences in motives may influence studying is shown in the grades made by social fraternity initiates before and after initiation and those made by Phi Beta Kappa candidates under the same conditions.[17] Fraternity and non-fraternity freshmen were matched as to year of matriculation, grade point average, and hours of credit the first semester. The grades of these two groups were then compared through

[15] L. S. Hadley, Scholastic adjustment problems of the returning veterans, *Educ. Res. Bull.*, 1945, 24:87–92.
[16] F. B. Knight and H. H. Remmers, Fluctuations in mental production when motivation is the main variable, *J. Appl. Psych.*, 1923, 7:209–223.

[17] H. C. Lehman, Motivation: college marks and the fraternity pledge, *J. Appl. Psych.*, 1935, 19:9–28.

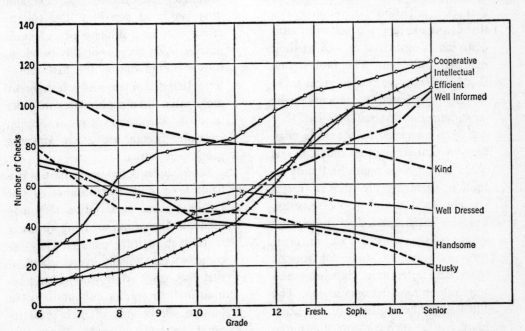

CHART 8. Changes in the degree to which traits are admired at different grade levels. (Adapted from unpublished data of S. L. Pressey.)

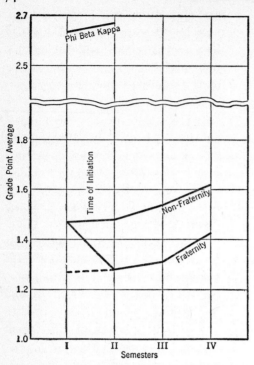

CHART 9. Effect of initiation into a social fraternity and into Phi Beta Kappa on grades in succeeding semesters. (Adapted from Lehman.).

successive semesters. Chart 9 shows that after initiation (based on grades the first semester) the fraternity students never again did as well as their matched colleagues. The broken line is inserted as a reasonable guess as to how well the fraternity students might have done the first semester had they not been interested in becoming eligible for initiation; the difference is about .2 of a grade point. Fraternity initiation standards are thus a useful stimulus to studying for one semester, but this experiment also shows that many college students are in great part motivated to study for reasons other than interest in knowledge and preparation for after graduation. The Phi Beta Kappa students, on the other hand, had no such letdown after initiation. One can more nearly assume for them an interest in learning for learning's sake.

d. Although the usual sequence of development during adolescence is from being primarily interested in social acceptance toward being interested in working on deferred goals, entrance to college may temporarily cause a regression in behavior for some students. The average high-school senior has friends and is respected in his community; he therefore feels secure enough to go about selecting an occupation and preparing for it and for other aspects of his projected adult life. He eagerly looks forward to his college studies. But when first away at school this feeling of social acceptance disappears much to his distress and, if his efforts to make friends and obtain status are constantly denied, he yearns for the security of home, i.e., is homesick. And little studying will be done until this personal problem is settled. Through "ice-breaker" parties and other informal activities, the college attempts to help students make friends quickly. Also because of this problem, it is expected during the first school term that freshmen will return home more often than sophomores in order to rebuild this feeling of social security. In time, friends are made and the problem is settled.

Some students, however, have a difficult time of it. For instance, if not bid by a social organization they may spend all their time worrying and may even want to leave college. They become so emotionally tense about it that they can't study, and getting behind in their studies only adds to the tension. Or because of their great interest in being accepted they may emphasize all the methods and behaviors that made for popularity in high school; absorption in such activities makes them appear more immature in orientation than they were in high school and certainly is not conducive to college achievement. Some realization of this psychological mechanism may help bring about a more realistic adjustment.

e. A fifth illustration of a genetic change in interest which affects college work is the shift from the desire for parental praise to a desire to stand on one's own feet. Opportunity to obtain praise from adults is one among many reasons why young children like school. Also while the child is in school in the early grades, the teacher becomes something of a parent substitute and so the child will work under authoritarian suggestion. But during adolescence, adult praise becomes less important than praise from companions, and there may even be a reaction against parental authority as the adolescent tries to become an independent adult. Many students unconsciously generalize the object of their rebellion to include any form of superiority—teacher, schoolwork, rules, and law. They feel that they know as much as adults; hence they resent suggestions. Since they believe that they are already fully mature, this stage is characterized by lack of interest in college work. But it is interesting to note that while sophomores often feel this way, professional and graduate students rarely do.

Adolescents are typically ambivalent, however; they want to be independent yet are so used to being told what to do at home and in school that many feel lost in college when someone doesn't keep after them. The writer recalls one student who announced that he had enrolled in the how-to-study course because he needed someone to get after him now that he was away from home; college authorities refuse to be the "Jimminy Crickets" for students.

The last two examples of genetic changes in motivation have emphasized difficulties which sometimes occur when adolescents change in their attitudes toward persons their own age and toward their parents. As indicated, such students may have difficulty with schoolwork until their immediate problem is solved, but other individuals may immerse themselves in their schoolwork in order to forget their troubles. Such persons, however, usually show other signs of immaturity and their intense interest in schoolwork is not healthy. They need as much help in making these transitions as do students who show other types of overcompensation.

Self-Evaluation

The above discussion gives some notion of how different motives affect student behavior and of the changes which take place in their emphasis as a person grows older. It is difficult to evaluate one's own pattern of motives because the average person has not given much thought to it and wants to think as well of himself as he can. Moreover, motives are so nebulous as to be difficult to evaluate. In fact, it is usually easier to recognize others' motivational patterns than one's own. It will be helpful, however, to attempt some evaluation. Some may discover that they have been kidding themselves with verbalizations about vocational preparation whereas they really have more important interests. Others may realize that they have been continuing activities based on earlier interests and are not giving their present values much consideration.

The following analyses are easy to complete but difficult to answer frankly. Unless you are candid with yourself, however, they will be of little value.

1. Evaluate your own interest maturity in terms of the five sample developmental sequences listed below; they are the ones which were just discussed. Look back over things you used to enjoy or thought were important; see how much you have grown. Do you have to go back many years before you can see a change? Compare yourself to other adults; are you able to see comparable steps for further growth?

SOURCES OF LACK OF INTEREST IN SCHOOL

1. Health condition
2. Distracted by personal problems
3. Not interested in college
   a. College is not the most suitable source of training
   b. Came only because friends came and nothing else to do
4. Maturity level of motives

a. Immediate goals much stronger than delayed vocational goals
b. Curiosity inhibited
c. Value other characteristics more than scholarship and intellectual development
d. Upset by lack of friends and chance to participate in worthwhile group activities
e. In process of emancipation from adult supervision

2. In order to make more concrete a study of the strengths and conflicts of motives, ten situational questions are listed below. Don't answer them the way you think your counselor wants you to, or your mother would want you to, or even the way you think you ought to. The "right" answer to all these questions might well be "yes," but the writer has found few undergraduates who could honestly answer all of them that way. The value of the "no" answers will be to suggest how motivational patterns may conflict with schoolwork.

MOTIVATIONAL CONFLICTS

Yes   No.   1. You discover at 5 P.M. that you have no assignments to prepare for the next day but have a mid-term exam for day after tomorrow. A friend wants you to go to a movie. Normally in such a situation, would you study?

Yes   No.   2. A regular two-hour laboratory class is cancelled one day because of difficulty with plumbing. Normally in such a situation, would you study?

Yes   No.   3. When you spend an evening in study, do you spend more than three-fourths of the time in actual reading and study?

Yes   No.   4. A basic but not required course in your major is given only at 8 A.M.; another course which is acceptable in the major but actually not quite as good for your needs as the other is available at 10 A.M. Would you take the 8 o'clock course?

Yes   No.   5. Do you spend more time a week (not counting Sunday) in studying than in all types of social recreation?

Yes   No.   6. You haven't been home for three weeks and there is as much school work for the coming week end as usual. Would you stay on the campus and study?

Yes   No.   7. When an instructor asks if there are any questions about what he has just presented, you do not hesitate to ask about something which you do not understand.

Yes   No.   8. You would rather have a grade point average .5 of a point higher than be elected to a well-known, semihonorary campus organization.

Yes   No.   9. Twins of your own sex and with pleasing personalities are in your class. You would rather have as a friend the one who is outstanding as a student than the one who is popular with the opposite sex and in activities.

Yes   No.   10. Assuming that it took an equal amount of effort and would produce equally successful results, you would rather write for publication a short paper in your major field than manage the campaign of a candidate for president of the student government.

3. "Why do you want to make good grades?" A list of typical reasons given by students is indicated below. Which ones of these most motivate your schoolwork? Which ones are the least important? Rank these reasons in their order of importance as they affect your schoolwork. This rank order need only be rough and approximate since it is difficult to interpret and weigh these values carefully. While such a rating device is too unreliable for accurate measurement, it will tend to stimulate your thinking.

I WANT TO MAKE GOOD GRADES

..... To secure a better future recommendation for a job

..... To indicate that I am actually learning something: new facts, how to think, etc.

..... To win out in competition with some other person or persons

..... To please my family

..... To be eligible for initiation and student activities

..... To uphold a reputation already gained among my associates and friends

..... To win special honors and recognition

..... Just to meet the requirements for a degree

..... To gain the respect of my instructors

..... It is a matter of little interest to me

If interested in comparing your rating to those of other college students, look at Table 3 which summarizes the reactions of over five hundred students to this question. Their method of rating was more elaborate than you were asked to use, therefore their ratings have some significance for this discussion. In the method of paired comparison which was used each statement was paired with every other statement and the student chose from each pair the stronger reason for his schoolwork. The importance of a reason was then obtained by adding up its number of first choices. Table 3 shows

TABLE 3. The Rank Order from Highest to Lowest of Reasons Given by Different Groups of Students to the Question "Why Do I Want to Make Good Grades?" [18]

Reason	Freshman	Junior and Senior	Women	Men
Job recommendation (JR)	JR	JR	JR	JR
Evidence of learning (EL)	EL	EL	EL	EL
Competition (C)	C	PF	PF	C
Please family (PF)	PF	C	R	PF
Be eligible (BE)	BE	R	BE	R
Reputation (R)	R	RI	JG	JG
Win honors (WH)	WH	JG	RI	BE
Just to graduate (JG)	JG	WH	C	WH
Respect of instructor (RI)	RI	BE	WH	RI
Little interest (LI)	LI	LI	LI	LI

[18] Adapted from S. C. Eriksen, An experimental study of individual differences in scholastic motives, J. Educ. Psych., 1940, 31:507–516.

the relative importance of these reasons for freshmen, juniors and seniors, women, and men. The letters in each column refer to the keyed list of reasons to the left. It will be noted that wanting good grades for "job recommendation" and for "evidence of learning" rank first and second for all groups. The changes in relative importance of "be eligible" and "respect of instructor" between the freshman and later years may be partially indicative of changes in scholastic motivation with increasing maturity. The differences between men and women are also interesting.

4. The three exercises above have been little devices for increasing your insight into your motivational pattern. Little of the total picture of your motivational pattern, however, has been covered. If lack of interest in schoolwork is a real problem with you, little progress can be made unless there is a thorough exploration of the whole problem. A discussion with your counselor will be of help. Another particularly effective device is to make an outline summary of your interests as they relate to college work. This process of verbalizing helps make clear what your values are. Such questions as the following should be covered: Are you interested in college? Why? Are you more interested in other activities? Do you understand why? What implication does this discussion of your interests have for your future plans?

Methods of Focusing Interest on College Work

Many students feel that they are quite interested in their schoolwork but find it difficult sometimes to settle down to studying. The following suggestions are some devices which will help focus one's interest in schoolwork on the immediate course or lesson.

1. Since the abstract nature of textbooks makes it difficult for them to compete in interest with football schedules, photographs, or talk sessions, one can study better if these distractions are eliminated from the immediate study environment. Methods of doing this were discussed in an earlier part of this project.

2. Students sometimes find that clarification of their vocational aims increases interest in courses related to their vocational preparation.[19] Project XI contains materials for assisting with such vocational thinking. Turn to it now if this approach seems pertinent.

3. Make practical applications of the material you are studying. Try to see the relations between the facts you study and the problems you will face in your chosen vocation. If you are not able to do this, ask your instructor for assistance in making such applications. All too often students approach courses as so much memory work rather than as being full of interesting facts. Rote memorization is rarely of interest, but understanding things is.

4. Persons who have had work experience are usually more highly motivated. Work experience apparently makes the vocational goal seem more clear cut and better understood and, therefore, more immediate. Also read all you can about your chosen vocation; it will help to focus your interests on college work.

5. Techniques of imagining more immediate goals assist in focusing interest more sharply. Studying as though there is to be a quiz in a few minutes may be hard on your blood pressure but it will arouse your interest in preparation. Setting time limits for study, as outlined earlier in this project, gives an immediate goal of completing your

---

[19] M. V. Marshall, The life career motive and its effect on college work, *J. Educ. Res.*, 1935–1936, 29:596–598; E. G. Williamson, Scholastic motivation and the choice of a vocation, *School and Soc.*, 1937, 46:353–357.

work within the time limit. This also helps resist recreational distractions since you will soon be through studying and able to relax.

6. The more one knows about a subject the more interesting the new facts will seem.

7. The story behind the discovery of facts is often as interesting as any adventure tale. Unfortunately, the stories get pretty dried out by the time they appear in a textbook, but the library contains books of real interest about the work you are doing. Often this is the purpose of collateral readings. As a rollicking example, read the story, "Turtle Eggs for Agassiz," by D. D. Sharp, which appeared in the *Atlantic Monthly* in 1932 (volume 150, pages 537–545).

8. The analysis of errors makes a problem seem much simpler and therefore easier and more interesting to overcome. For instance, it would seem more interesting and challenging to improve writing the letters *o* and *n* which accounted for 50 per cent of a person's illegibilities, than it would just to try, without such a diagnosis, to write more clearly. Thus, in this and in other courses find the cause of your difficulties and you will become more interested.

9. Knowledge of progress makes work seem much more interesting. Try to obtain even rough measures of how well you are doing and make a graph of your progress. You will probably be surprised to find out how interested you are in making the line go up. Set up a goal on the graph and move your line toward it as you complete the units.

10. The technique of asking questions, developed in Project II, arouses curiosity as you read and so makes the material seem more interesting. Another technique is to make up problems to solve; this will not only increase your interest but also insure that you comprehend the material.

Practice. Suggestions for improving motivation will not do much good unless they are tried out. Take your least interesting course and, in light of the discussion above, write out the *specific* steps which you could take to increase interest in it. Try this on an assignment and then check with your counselor.

Further information as to the factors which motivate student work will be found in the following references:

C. Bird, *Effective Study Habits*, Appleton-Century, 1931, Chap. 1.

A. W. Ham and M. D. Salter, *Doctor in the Making*, Lippincott, 1943, Chaps. 2, 3, 4, and 8. Very interesting reading.

PROJECT V

PREPARING REPORTS

Term papers are a typical part of many college courses. They should be more than a few pages of quotations copied out and fitted together, and in the upper-division courses they are supposed to be rather extensive treatises. Because instructors have to pass rapidly over many interesting points, papers and oral reports are assigned so the student can dig out the information he wants and also obtain credit for it. College reports are, therefore, real investigations of interesting topics by inquiring minds. Sometimes such papers are good enough to be published.

The expected make-up of a report varies somewhat from course to course, but three general characteristics are desired by all teachers: (a) evidence that the student has studied different sources in order to stimulate his thinking, (b) presentation in an acceptable form, and (c) evidence of original thinking. As with most activities, a report may be done the hard way or easy short cuts may be used. This project proposes to demonstrate these short cuts so better reports can be written with no greater expenditure of effort or time.

On the first of these desired characteristics, i.e., evidence of resources studied, much energy is often wasted in inefficient search. The writer has found that even in advanced classes some students work much harder at a paper than the average student but get lower grades because they do not know of the simplest library aids. The first part of this project deals with these library resources and short cuts.

On the second characteristic, i.e., correct form, students are often bothered as to the form in which a term paper should be presented and are ignorant of any peculiarities of style expected in a given subject field. The teachers, on the other hand, expect the reports to be in good form, i.e., the historians want the reports styled as historical essays and the scientists as scientific discussions. Facts presented in correct form receive higher grades than when the same facts are presented in the usual English essay form. The second part of this project indicates resources giving simple directions for report writing.

On the third characteristic, i.e., evidence of original thinking, much depends on the ability of the student. But if a student finds it easy to obtain resource material, is stimulated by it and has a plan for writing the paper, he should have the time and energy for doing some original thinking. Some suggestions will also be made which will foster such originality in papers.

A. Use of the Library

The primary resource for college work, in addition to textbooks, is more books. Because of the large number of them which have to be used, some system of cataloguing and protection is necessary; yet this very system is unfamiliar to most students and so may act as a barrier rather than a help in the use of the books. Acquaintance with library books is often limited to the reserve room where a student's request for an assigned book is all that is necessary. Such students do not know of the wealth of material which the school supplies; they do not know of one of the best and simplest ways of finding materials for term papers; and, probably worst of all, they miss interesting books on topics about which they are curious.

Concrete evidence that knowledge of the library is related to school success and that even the average senior doesn't know enough about the library is shown by a study at Ohio University.[1] The experimenters with the aid of other faculty members con-

structed a test of essential information about the library. Its items represented "beginning of a working knowledge in the use of the library." When 441 students took the test, it was found that knowledge of the library was related to grade point average even when the effect of intelligence on both scores was canceled out. The results summarized in Chart 10 also show that the average student, even among the seniors, knows only about 60 per cent of these essential items and little, if any, growth in knowledge of the library takes place during the four years in college. And the small range in scores between the first and third quartiles indicates that most of the students are about equally ignorant as to use of the library. It is evident that students need training in use of the library.

Self-Evaluation

How much do you know about the library? You may feel that you are pretty good at it since you are familiar with public and school libraries. Three tests are provided to measure your skill and also to act as training units. Each has been carefully made so as to cover the essential aspects of library service which every student ought to know. Much more technical and professional aid can be found in a library but it seems best to limit these diagnostic tests to minimal essentials. The first test covers information as to what is in the library. The second test measures your skill in the actual use of library aids. After scoring these two tests and studying up on your weak spots, you will be ready to try your skill on the third test—preparing a bibliography for an actual term paper. It will show how library aids can short-cut the writing of good term papers.

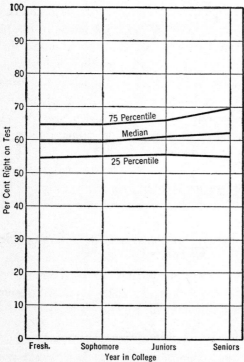

CHART 10. Success of students on a test of "beginning working knowledge in the use of the library"; the median and the range of scores for the middle 50 per cent are shown for each college year. (Adapted from Louttit and Patrick.)

[1] C. M. Louttit and J. R. Patrick, A study of students' knowledge in the use of the library, *J. Appl. Psych.*, 1932, 16:475–484.

I. *Test of Information About the Library.* This test covers the important aspects of the library which the typical student needs to know. The test is in four sections: A, Dictionary Card Catalogue; B, Parts of a book; C, Indices and Abstracts; and D, How to Use the *Reader's Guide.* The key for scoring your answers is on page 243 in Appendix II.

Place your score (No. right) in the correct box below.

Norms

Lowest Q	2nd Quarter	3rd Quarter	Top Quarter

```
|                   |                   |                   |
            44                  48                  52
            |                   |                   |
           Q₁                  Md.                 Q₃
```

A. DICTIONARY CARD CATALOGUE

What will be the alphabetic order of the following title references in the dictionary card catalogue? Indicate the proper order by numbering (1, 2, 3, 4, or 5) on the proper line to the left.

.....1. *A Manual of Determinative Mineralogy* (by J. V. Lewis).

.....2. *Social Organization and Disorganization* (by S. A. Queen).

.....3. *The American College* (by A. F. West).

.....4. *Annotated Bibliography on Adult Education* (by V. M. Proctor).

.....5. *A Syllabus on Vocational Guidance* (by V. A. Teeter).

If a statement is true, circle "T"; if it is false, circle "F."

T F   6. All classified books are listed in the dictionary card catalogue.

T F   7. The location of a book in the library is indicated by the call number on the dictionary card.

T F   8. The arrangement of the dictionary card catalogue is the same as that of books on the shelves.

T F   9. A card in the catalogue saying "Robins, *see* Birds" means that there is nothing in the library on robins.

T F   10. A student interested in the American Revolution can get started in tracing bibliography by looking up any of the following subject headings in the dictionary card catalogue: American Revolution; Revolution, American; U. S.—History—Revolution.

T F   11. A book written by Samuel Clemens should be listed in the dictionary card catalogue under the name "Mark Twain" since he is more widely known by that name.

T F   12. A book written by Zorro and translated by Kiesow would be entered in the card catalogue under both names.

T F   13. Cross reference (i.e., *see,* and *see also*) in the dictionary card catalogue and in periodical indices are for the technical use of the librarian and hence of little use to the student.

T F   14. Library books assigned by an instructor will usually be found on reserve and will always be listed in the dictionary card catalogue.

Find the best answer in the right-hand column for each statement on the left. Write the letter of that answer on the line to the left of each statement.

.....15. The card in the dictionary card catalogue on which you would find listed a book by John Ruskin.

.....16. The card in the dictionary card catalogue on which you would find a book called "The Tides of Life."

A. Author card
B. Index card
C. Title card
D. Subject card
E. Bibliography card

.....17. If you wanted information for a paper on "Indian Arrowheads," what would be the best topic to look up?

.....18. If you wanted information for a paper on "The Religious Music of Indians," what would be the best topic to look up?

.....19. If you wanted information for a paper on "Pocahontas," what would be the best topic to look up?

A. Arrowheads
B. Bow and Arrow
C. Indians of North America
D. Indians of North America—implements
E. Indians of North America—music
F. Indians of North America—religion and mythology
G. Music, sacred
H. Pocahontas

GF51
L4   **Leyburn, James Graham.**

       Frontier folkways [by] James G. Leyburn ... New Haven, Yale university press; London, H. Milford, Oxford university press, 1935.

      x, 291 p. $24\frac{1}{2}^{cm}$.

      "Published on the Louis Stern memorial fund."—p. [iii]
      Bibliography: p. [273]–288.

      1. Frontier and pioneer life.   2. Manners and customs.   3. Man—Influence and environment.   4. Sociology.   i. Title.   ii. Title: Folkways.

                                                         35–7750

      Library of Congress   GF51.L4

      —— —— Copy 2.

      Copyright   A 81816   [5]   [910]   573.4

.....20. The location of the book in the library is indicated by (1) the author's last name, (2) the number in upper left-hand corner, (3) the title, "Frontier Folkways."

T F 21. The number in the upper left-hand corner is based on the Dewey Decimal system rather than the Library of Congress system.

.....22. The book was published in what year?

T F 23. This book contains a bibliography which could be used for further reading.

.....24. In how many different places will cards for this book appear in the dictionary card catalogue of the usual library?

T F 25. A card for this book will be found if you look up the subject "Sociology."

T F 26. A card for this book will be found if you look up the subject "Pioneers."

B. PARTS OF A BOOK

Find the best answer in the right-hand column for each statement on the left. Write the letter of that answer on the line to the left of each statement.

.....27. Part which gives an outline of what the book contains.

.....28. List of references given at the end of a chapter or at the end of a book.

.....29. Page on which name of publisher appears.

.....30. Place to look up location of minor but important topics in the book.

.....31. Section which states why the author wrote the book.

.....32. Part at end of book containing additional information not in the text proper.

.....33. Statements in small print at the bottom of some pages.

A. Glossary
B. Copyright
C. Preface
D. Footnote
E. Bibliography
F. Title page
G. Index
H. Appendix
I. Table of contents

C. INDICES AND ABSTRACTS

Following are some indices, abstracts, and other bibliographical sources commonly found in college libraries.

a. *Readers' Guide to Periodical Literature*
b. *International Index to Periodicals*
c. *Agriculture Index*
d. *Art Index*
e. *Education Index*
f. *Industrial Arts Index*
g. *Science Abstracts*

h. *Psychological Abstracts*
i. *Biological Abstracts*
j. *U. S. Catalogue and Cumulative Book Index*
k. New York *Times Index*
l. *Book Review Digest*
m. Public Affairs Information Service *Bulletin*
n. Vertical File Service *Catalogue*

In answering the following questions use the list of reference works given above. Place the letter of the correct title on the line at the left of the question.

.....34. The best place to find recent articles on "intelligence testing."

.....35. Articles on "the teaching of wood work in the schools."

.....36. Articles for a paper on "mural painting."

.....37. Articles for a paper on "the divorce problem."

.....38. Articles for a paper on "testing cows."

.....39. Where find the date on which a recent major event occurred.

.....40. Where find the publisher and cost of a book not in the library.

.....41. Where find a summary of critical evaluations of a book you have not seen.

If a statement is true, circle "T"; if it is false, circle "F."

T F 42. Some books contain bibliographies; this information is listed on the dictionary card for that book.

T F 43. Bibliographies on some topics are published as separate bulletins; these are listed in the dictionary card catalogue.

T F 44. The alphabetical entries in typical periodical indices are by author and subject although both are not always included.

T F 45. *The Readers' Guide to Periodical Literature* may enter an article in its alphabetical listing by author, by subject, and by title.

T F 46. *The Readers' Guide to Periodical Literature* lists new books as well as magazine articles.

T F 47. The best way to obtain a bibliography of books from the dictionary card catalogue is to use the title cards.

T F 48. Good modern encyclopedias contain well-written articles on many topics assigned for papers or studied in college classes.

D. HOW TO USE THE READERS' GUIDE AND OTHER INDICES.

Directions: The facing page is an excerpt from the February, 1945, issue of the *Readers' Guide;* line numbers have been added to the left to help in identifying the material to be used in answering the questions below. Answer each question in terms of the line or lines referred to.

T F 49. The magazine referred to in line 31 appears once each month.

T F 50. Line 29 means that Thickstun is Blanc's real name.

T F 51. The magazine in which the story referred to in line 28 appears can be found by looking up M. Y. Lull.

T F 52. The word "Anis" in line 12 refers to a heading which will appear among the "A's" in the alphabetical listing.

.....53. The number which appears *before* the colon (:) in each listing refers to (1) the year, (2) the page the article starts on, (3) the volume number of the magazine.

.....54. The number which appears just *after* the colon (:) in each listing refers to (1) page number, (2) year, (3) volume number.

T F 55. The symbol "por" in line 26 indicates that a picture of Morgan Blake appears in the article.

T F 56. The symbol "il" in line 14 means that the article contains illustrations.

.....57. The symbol " + " in line 18 means that (1) the magazine appears late in December, (2) the article is particularly good, (3) part of the article appears on later pages in that issue, i.e., back among the advertisements.

T F 58. If interested in writing an article on the blind, some additional references might be found by looking up the heading "Sports for the blind."

T F 59. The phrase *"see also"* as in line 47 means that additional references may be listed under the topic or topics which are listed just below.

T F 60. In line 15 one finds that additional material might be found if he looked up either "Aviation" or "Physiological aspects."

.....61. How many articles are listed which deal with "Black markets"?

.....62. How many articles are listed as dealing with printing and writing systems for the blind?

.....63. In lines 20 and 21, Earl Blaik is the (1) author, or (2) subject, of the article listed.

EXCERPT FROM READERS' GUIDE (FEB. 1945)[2]

1 BLACK markets
2   Beef in trouble. tab Bsns W p 17–18 D 23 '44
3   Bootleg nylons. F. Brock. Read Digest 46:66–8 F
4   '45
5   Ceiling on hoof? Bsns W p 17–18 N 25 '44
6   Lend fleece; how American GI's and officers have
7   acted as supply agents for French black-market
8   operations. Newsweek 25:49 Ja 8 '45
9 BLACKBIRDS
10   Blackbird antics. Nature Mag 37:499 N '44
11   *See also*
12   Anis
13 BLACKMAN, Thomas M.
14   Rare goose, il Natur Hist 53:407 N '44
15 BLACKOUTS, Physiological. See Aviation—Physi-
16   ological aspects
17 BLACKSTOCK, Josephine
18   Play in battle dress. Ind Woman 23:376–7 + D '44
19 BLADES, Hacksaw. See Saws
20 BLAIK, Earl Henry
21   Biography, por Cur Biog Ja '45
22 BLAIR, Walter
23   Ugliest man in the world; story. Am Mercury
24   60:166–8 F '45
25 BLAKE, Morgan
26   Columnist-penologist. por Newsweek 24:46 D
27   18 '44
28 BLAME it on love; story. See Lull, M. Y.

29 BLANC, M. S. See Thickstun, W. R. jt. auth.
30 BLANCHARD, Janice
31   Blind street; poem. Christian Cent 61:1228 O
32   25 '44
33 BLANCHARD, Normal J.
34   Making curtains. Sch Arts 44:137 D '44
35 BLEEDERS disease. See Hemophilia
36 BLIND
37   Blind are not apart. M. M. Geffner. il Survey
38   81:14–16 Ja '45
39   Meet destiny with your head up! L. Boccelli.
40   Etude 62:621 N '44
41   My love is blind. Mrs. A Schmid. Am mag
42   138:45 + D '44
43   Scouts without sight. S. S. Jacobs. il Sat Eve Post
44   2 17:6 Ja 13 '45
45   Strictly personal; it's fun to see again. F. F. Bond.
46   Sat R Lit 28:14–15 F 3 '45
47   *See also*
48   Sports for the blind
49   *Printing and writing systems*
50   Reading for the blind: Moon system. Hygeia
51   23:140 F '45
52 BLIND, Books for the
53   *See also*
54   Books—Phonograph records
55 BLINDNESS
56   *See also*
57   Blind

II. *Laboratory Problem in the Use of Library Aids.* Your how-to-study laboratory is equipped with various sample library aids. The next step is to see if you can actually use them correctly. The second test has been prepared especially to fit the local college situation; when you are ready for it, ask your counselor for a copy. This exercise will cover the use of the dictionary card catalogue, the *Book Review Digest*, and various indices, abstracts, and encyclopedias. If any part causes trouble, the counselor will be glad to help you.

Program for Improvement

1. Did you know how to use the library? How did you compare to other college students? Even though you may have scored higher on these tests than the average student, the honor is a dubious one since it has already been shown that the average student knows little about the library. An even more realistic goal is to understand everything in these tests since each item has

been carefully selected as basic to undergraduate work.

Read up on those items which you missed. An interesting booklet entitled the *Library Key* and written by Zaidee Brown (Wilson, 1938) explains how to use the materials referred to in the above tests. The following are other excellent references:

C. Alexander, *How to Locate Educational Information and Data*, Bur. Publ., Teachers College, 1941, 2nd ed. See especially Chaps. 4, 7, and 10.

M. Hutchins, A. S. Johnson, and M. S. Williams, *Guide to the Use of Libraries*, Wilson, 1938, 5th rev. ed. An excellent book showing the best resources for different subject fields.

I. G. Mudge, *Guide to Reference Books*, American Library Assoc., 1936, 6th ed. The authoritative guide to published reference materials.

C. M. Winchell, *Reference Books of 1935–37; 1938–1940; 1941–43*, American Library Assoc. Three supplements published to bring the 6th ed. of *Guide to Reference Books* up to date.

---

[2] Used with special permission of the publishers, The H. W. Wilson Company.

2. Study a map of your library so as to familiarize yourself with the location of resources, particularly the card catalogue, indices, and general references. Take time to browse in the reference section so as actually to see where these resources are located.

3. When these two steps are done, and only then, try the following "real library project." It tests your ability to use your knowledge of the library in preparing for an actual term paper. To try this project before completely understanding the library setup will result only in confusion and waste of time. On the other hand, if you are familiar with the basic uses of libraries, this part of the project will be quite easy.

III. *Term Paper Library Project.* Parts A, B, and C can be filled out in class; Part D has to be done at the library. Do this project on your own; *do not bother the librarians.* If you need help, ask your counselor or other students (if you feel they know the answer).

Evaluation: ....

A. Select a term paper topic in an area in which you are interested. (If you have a paper to write in some course this term or if you know of a topic which can be used in a later course, use that topic.) The topic is:

....

B. Under what headings would you expect to find references to articles and books dealing with your topic?

1. .... 2. ....

3. .... 4. ....

5. .... 6. ....

C. What reference sources would it be best to use? (When this section is filled out, star the three resources which will probably be of the most value for this topic.)

1. What index or abstract journals?

....

....

....

2. Will the dictionary card catalogue be of much help?

....

3. Will an encyclopedia be of much help? If so, which one?

....

4. Will you have special problems of biographical data, current events, statistical data, small items of necessary information? If so, where should you look?

....

....

....

....

....

D. List below *at least* ten references for your topic. Use the three sources "starred" above and more if you wish; include books as well as journal articles. Do not list just any references on your topic; be selective so as to list a well-rounded selection of the best sources.

B. Writing the Paper

An early and major step has already been taken toward writing a report through completing the library projects above; you have a complete bibliography, or at least a good start on it, for a term paper. Writing the paper itself, however, also presents difficulties for many students. Some find it difficult to express their ideas in writing; some have to labor so hard over grammar and punctuation that little energy is left for creative writing. Others have trouble with organizing their ideas and others with the format expected on a term paper. Approaches to these difficulties are discussed here.

Self-Evaluation

About the only way to measure your skill and difficulties in writing term papers is actually to analyze some you have written. The following will give a basis for determining where remedial work is needed.

1. What grades have you received on past term papers? What comments were written on them?

2. If you have the opportunity, look over some term papers that have received good grades. In what ways do they differ from yours?

3. Have your counselor look over some of your former papers and make suggestions as to specific ways in which they might be improved. Old essay exams also offer a basis for constructive suggestions on writing. Primary areas of difficulty should be checked below:

...... Legibility
...... Spelling
...... Grammar
...... Punctuation
...... Capitalization
...... Sentence structure
...... Specific errors in format
...... General form
...... Length
...... Bibliography
...... Headings
...... Paragraphing
...... Organization
...... Development of ideas

Program for Improvement

With what aspects of term paper writing do you have the most difficulty? Suggestions for improvement are presented in three sections: English usage, form, and organization and writing of the paper. Emphasize those sections which are the most pertinent and then complete step 4.

1. If one of your difficulties lies in correctness of written expression, turn to Project VIII. Most persons with this difficulty have seen comments like "poor English" or "poor spelling" written so often on their papers that they feel they never will become proficient. Project VIII will show, however, that college students having such difficulties really know most of the rules of English usage but have trouble with just a few frequently recurring items. When a student sees that two or three simple rules account for over half of his errors, a remedial program seems easy and feasible.

2. Other students have difficulty in deciding what the correct form is for a term paper. Details as to length, expected divisions, use of headings, bibliographical form, use and form of quotations, use of footnotes, etc., all cause confusion and make it difficult to devote full energy to expressing one's ideas. An easy way to help with this difficulty is to study a model term paper and then refer to it as problems of form arise. One of the best sources here is a model term paper which itself tells how to write a term paper. The reference is:

C. S. Cooper and E. J. Robins, *The Term Paper, a Manual and Model*, Stanford Univ. Press, 1934.

Since the form of term papers sometimes varies from one subject field to another, one should also find out what requirements the instructor has in mind and, if available, look over former term papers in that course.

Further references on writing term papers will be found in the following:

R. W. Frederick, *How to Study Handbook*, Appleton-Century, 1938. Pages 173–180: How to gather materials for a topic; pages 181–200: How to write themes.

J. C. Hodges, *Harbrace Handbook of English*, Harcourt, Brace, 1941. Pages 376–396. Includes a specimen term paper.

3. The major difficulty for some students lies in organizing a term paper. They scarcely know where to begin or end; thus some just start writing, keep on adding this and that, and stop when the paper seems long enough. Since a job plan helps in expediting any type of work, the following plan should do much to make your approach to writing a term paper easier and more systematic:

a. Select a topic. It should be big enough to provide plenty of material for writing but not so big as to be suitable for a book. Look up several tentative topics in an index such as the *Readers' Guide* and select the one that has the best available bibliography.

b. Build your bibliography. As suggested in the first of this project, use indices, abstracts, the dictionary card catalogue, encyclopedias, etc., to obtain a select bibliography. Read these for ideas. Keep notes on your readings so that later they can be referred to, making unnecessary a return trip to the library. If these notes are kept on cards, they can later be put in some topical order and thus aid in the organization of writing.

c. Keep an idea page. A paper is usually assigned for some time before it has to be written. During this interval various ideas often come to mind which ought to be included in the paper. If these are not jotted down at once, they are often forgotten by the time you start on the paper. Use a page in your note-book to jot down these ideas; then when you are ready to write, these brief notes will serve as reminders. Instances of things to jot down are news events and stories which illustrate your points, and also new angles on your paper which occur to you. A premium is placed on originality in a paper so this device will do much to increase the quality of your paper.

d. Outline your paper in detail. In writing essay examinations it was suggested that jotting down a brief outline before starting to write would produce a bet-ter answer. This is even more true in writing term papers because the wealth of material to be covered makes it im-possible to organize as one writes. This outline should be very complete; each idea to be covered should be men-tioned in the outline. Use cue words and phrases and not complete sen-tences; as rearrangement seems neces-sary scratch out items and write them in at better locations. Finally, when the outline is completed, the organiza-tion of the paper stands out clearly. The major points in the outline repre-sent the headings for sections of your paper. With each point in its place in the outline, the job of writing merely requires that each point in turn be changed into a sentence or short paragraph.

e. Write the paper; dash it off from the outline and polish it later. It is difficult to keep many things in mind as you write. Devote your initial writing efforts to getting your ideas stated; this initial draft can be gone over later in order to correct English mistakes and to put in headings, references, and footnotes. Dashing this first version off helps a writer keep his attention on his theme rather than getting lost in details, and the sentence ideas tend to flow into each other much better. Usually all needed corrections can be inserted in this first draft, but if necessary, parts can be cut out and pasted in order.

f. Type or rewrite the paper. Legibility and good form in a paper have a great deal to do with the final grade. As was indicated in connection with writing essay examinations, papers legibly writ-ten will average 10 per cent higher grades than the same papers written somewhat illegibly. Reread this final version to be sure that a word or phrase has not been accidentally left out and to correct misspellings or illegibilities.

g. Submit the paper in an attractive form since the over-all impression also in-fluences the instructor. Put the paper in a binder. Put the title, your name and the course number or name on the front. Number the pages. And the most attractive feature of all, hand the paper in on time.

4. Do you have any papers to write this term? If so, the material on library usage earlier in this project will have given you a start. Discuss your plans for this paper with your counselor; he will be glad to assist in evaluating your outline and written report. The instructor who assigned the paper and your English instructor will also be glad to answer any questions you may have. Very often papers for your English course and for other courses can be combined.

PROJECT VI

CLASSROOM SKILLS

Because students learn through class participation and their work is evaluated from it as well, it is important that effective classroom skills be developed. Students, however, frequently feel inadequate in these skills: Many students are afraid to recite in class and are even more terrified of volunteering in discussion or of asking questions. Most students have difficulty in determining what should be learned in a lecture, and know no good way to remember what they do learn. Some students write as rapidly as they can to record what is said, but because of such a secretarial attitude scarcely understand what they have written; others write noth-

ing. Still other difficulties arise because some students do not understand that certain classroom mannerisms and practices offend the teacher and so react to the student's detriment. Principles relating to these problems will be presented under four headings: (1) Improving Ability to Handle Lectures, (2) Improving Ability to Discuss and Recite in Class, (3) Improving Class Manners, and (4) Having Conferences with the Teacher. As a preliminary step, however, answer the following questions in terms of your present classroom practices; items missed will help point up the discussion which follows:

Evaluation of Classroom Behavior   No. right out of 18......

Answer each of the following questions by writing in the word (or its number): (1) never, (2) seldom, (3) sometimes, (4) often, or (5) always.

..... 1. Do you take notes on your lecture classes?

..... 2. Do you keep your notes in one notebook at least 6 × 9 inches in size?

..... 3 Do you recopy your notes after taking them in a lecture?

..... 4 Do you write as fast and as much as you can during a lecture?

..... 5 Do you use shorthand in taking notes?

..... 6. Do you look over and edit your notes after class?

..... 7 Do you sit near the back of the classroom or near a door or window?

..... 8. Do you participate when there is classroom discussion?

..... 9 Do you feel nervous and afraid when you have to participate in class discussion?

.....10. When you don't understand something that has been explained in class, do you ask questions when given the opportunity?

.....11. When the instructor calls for volunteers, do you offer yourself?

.....12. When reviewing for a quiz, do you try to predict from your class notes what will be asked?

.....13. When having trouble in a course, do you try to talk to the instructor after class or to have a conference with him?

.....14 Do you cut classes during a school term?

.....15 Are you late to class?

.....16 Do you stack your books or put your coat on just before the bell rings?

.....17 Do you whisper to other students while the teacher is lecturing or leading a discussion?

.....18. Do you hand in term reports and other papers on or before the due date?

The questions whose numbers are followed by a period should be answered "often" or "always" and those without periods should be answered "seldom" or "never." The reasons behind these answers are presented in the following discussion.

Improving Ability to Handle Lectures

The first thing is to sit where you can easily hear the lecture. Many students gravitate toward the back of the class or sit next to a door or beside a window. In all three of these places students are subject to many distractions. Students at the back of the room have to look past all the other students in order to watch the instructor; their attention is constantly distracted from the lecturer as these intervening students squirm in their seats, whisper, or drop things. Students sitting by a door or window are also distracted by occurrences outside the classroom. Studies of students' preferences as to seat location and of the relationship between classroom position and grades show an advantage for the center of the room, toward the front.[1] Also sit where material on the blackboard can be easily seen and, if you

[1] P. R. Farnsworth, Seat preference in the classroom, *J. Soc. Psych.*, 1933, 4:373–376; C. R. Griffith, A comment upon the psychology of the audience, *Psych. Monog.*, 1921, 30:36–47.

have difficulty in hearing, sit where you can hear better and watch the speaker's lips.

Students have as much difficulty with picking out what is important and remembering it in lectures as in reading.[2] A basis for the solution of this problem can be found through appreciating the three purposes of lectures: (1) to present material not otherwise easily available to students, (2) to explain important points which might cause difficulty, and (3) to elaborate on important points through further material and explanation. Since a teacher's class time is limited, great selectivity must be used in determining what is to be discussed. Whatever is said in class should, therefore, be important. But students say, "Not with the teachers I've heard!" But even these teachers would affirm that important points were being illustrated. So the crux of the problem in learning how to listen to lectures is: How can one determine what is important and how can one remember it?

This sounds familiarly like the problem in reading textbooks. Both textbook writers and lecturers try to make only a few major points in a chapter or lecture but have to use a great deal of explanatory detail in order to make these major points clear. The problem is to learn how to spot these major points. Lectures usually contain fewer cues than textbooks and, being extemporaneously presented, the cues are not nearly so clearly emphasized. And even though such organizational cues as inflection, topic sentences, and summary statements may be skillfully presented, the average student is not trained to spot them. Just as most students pay little attention to headings in books, so most students know little about typical cues used in lecturing. To begin with, the average

[2] R. P. Larsen and D. D. Feder, Common and differential factors in reading and hearing comprehension, *J. Educ. Psych.*, 1940, 31:241–252; E. M. Spencer, Retention of orally presented materials, *J. Educ. Psych.*, 1941, 32:641–655.

student usually has a mistaken notion as to how much is covered in a lecture. He usually thinks that "lots and lots" of points are covered whereas actually they will range from a couple of major ideas to half a dozen minor ones. It is the old story of the little boy overwhelmed at the number of trees rather than seeing them as an orchard arranged in rows with these rows arranged by species of fruit.

Students usually go to one of two extremes in approaching this problem; both are bad. Some students, feeling that everything said is important, write madly trying to put everything down; those who know shorthand feel happily prepared. These persons are so busy in a stenographic way, however, that they scarcely understand a thing that is said. They may feel that they can study their notes later, but this is seldom done and if done represents double labor. At the other extreme are those students who say that it is impossible to both listen and write and anyway it is difficult to know what to write. They feel that the best approach is to listen and watch carefully so as not to miss anything; note-taking would therefore be a distraction. These individuals may understand the lecture as it is being presented but they usually do not isolate the main points and have no basis for later review.

In lectures, as with textbooks, the core ideas are important. A student needs to isolate these core ideas and to see the explanatory material as such. This is done by watching for cues which the lecturer gives. A lecturer usually starts with a topic sentence, and he may close a topic with a summary statement. He usually indicates the number of important subpoints by such cue statements as "the three parts," "the five results," etc. Lecturers may use inflection of voice to make a point stand out; they often repeat important points or pause significantly or even precede a statement by saying, "This next point is important." A student then should listen attentively and, through such cues as the above, try to determine what main point is being developed. When this is decided, he should write down a brief note summarizing the point. He then listens again until the next point is made, etc. By the end of a class hour possibly not more than a half page of notes will have been taken. The writing will not have been laborious and the several statements written will be very helpful later for review.

Insofar as possible, try to show organization in your notes. Label them as to major topic, and indent subpoints so that the major ones stand out. Since it is sometimes difficult to determine the exact organization as the lecturer proceeds, it is worth while to take a couple of minutes at the end of the class, or that evening, to glance over the class notes so as to mark important points, indent subpoints, etc. In such revising, it may also become obvious that in your haste too little has been written; therefore add further clarifying statements. Typing class notes, on the other hand, is generally a waste of time. That is, typing is hard work for most students and legibly written notes will do just as well.

Notes which show organization make major points stand out and are more easily visualized in memory. In order to make indentations which enhance this visual pattern, it is necessary to have a large notebook; such larger paper costs little more than the smaller size. Furthermore, the ideas from one or several lectures can be put on one large page so their relationship can be more easily seen. Little notebooks are cute and easy to carry but are inefficient for class notes. And probably worst of all is the use of backs of envelopes and odd sheets of paper for note-taking; these are difficult to organize and keep collected.

As was true with notes on readings (Project II), an outsider's evaluation and coaching often quickly suggest worth-while ways to simplify and improve classroom note-taking. Have your counselor check your notes against the Check List in Project II, then try to improve your technique of taking notes. Successive ratings with this Check List should show improvement in your notes, and lectures should begin to have more organization for you.

Improving Ability to Discuss and Recite in Class

Practically every teacher spends some time in class discussion and student recitation; some teachers devote most of their class time to it. There are several reasons for this. The give and take of discussion increases student interest and emphasizes understanding rather than memorization of ideas. Recitation, as was shown in Project II, tends to fix ideas in memory so they are forgotten less rapidly; class discussion plays the same role. And through listening to questions and ideas presented, the teacher can evaluate what students know. The following two experiments give an indication of how important discussion is in schoolwork: In one, an accurate count was kept of how many times each student participated in classroom recitation and discussion; this score, as well as the student's intelligence, was then compared to the grades each received at the end of the school year.[3] It was found that "test grades were influenced more by the activity of a child than by his intelligence." Of course, it may be assumed that the students who knew the most might tend to recite the most, but this is not the complete explanation. In another study, college students were measured in

[3] W. W. Carpenter and M. K. Fort, What effect do visitors have upon recitation? *J. Educ. Res.*, 1930, 22:50–53.

their ability to influence each other in discussion.[4] When this ability of students was compared to their success in class, it was found that "students able to influence their classmates most in discussion situations were also able to influence their teachers most favorably and get the highest marks" $(r = .38)$.

Yet fear of reciting or discussing in class is one of the most frequent problems mentioned by students. In a check list of 90 items in which students were to rate how they compared to other students in their class, more students put themselves in the bottom fifth on the item "speak up in class discussion" than on any other item.[5] Another indication of this same problem is obtained from the use of a "Guess Who" test. In this type of test a descriptive statement is read and the students guess who in the class it best describes. When the item "this is the student who is most afraid to discuss in class" is read, more students mention themselves than on any other item!

Why are students afraid to participate in class discussion? A large number of college students, when asked to analyze why it was difficult to obtain discussion in class, listed 25 different causes ranging from teaching procedures to student attitudes.[6] Among the most important were the four student attitudes listed in Table 4. Characteristic of all these student attitudes is a fear of appearing inferior to others. This fear is not simply limited to what the teacher may think because fear of what classmates may think is probably an even greater deterrent. For instance many students are willing to ask questions after class but not before their classmates.

TABLE 4. Student Attitudes Which Inhibit Student Questioning in Class. (Adapted from Kirkendall.)

These Attitudes Affect Recitation:	Seldom or never	Sometimes	Frequently	Very often
1. Students fear ridicule	2%	19%	46%	33%
2. Lack of preparation	2%	8%	38%	52%
3. Dislike to expose ignorance	1%	16%	41%	42%
4. Timidity	—	14%	44%	42%

Analysis of class discussions tends to indicate that students fall into three types: (1) the "off-the-beam" or "disturber" type, (2) the quiet unknown, and (3) the leader. Fear of being classed in the first of these categories inhibits many students; unluckily they then fall into the second class, unknown to teacher or students. Evidence of these student types is obtained through use of a "Guess Who" test which contains a series of items ranging from "this student can't say what he means" or "this student seems most timid in class discussions" to "this student's discussion is interesting and to the point" or "this student is easily heard and understood." The test is scored in two ways: (1) the total number of times each student's name is mentioned and (2) the number of times each student's name is mentioned on favorable items minus the number of times it is mentioned for unfavorable items. The results from administering such a test to two small classes are sum-

[4] R. H. Simpson, Those who influence and those who are influenced in discussion, *Teach. Coll. Contri. Educ.*, 1938, No. 748, 89 pp.

[5] J. A. Wright, A study of high school students' insight into their problems and resources, unpublished Master's thesis, Ohio State Univ., 1944.

[6] L. A. Kirkendall, Factors inhibiting pupil questioning in class, *J. Educ. Meth.*, 1937, 16:359–362.

marized in Chart 11. It will be noted that the distribution falls into a V shape: At the left are the individuals who received many but almost entirely negative votes. In the middle are those whom scarcely anyone remembered in thinking about the class; it is surprising to note how many "non entities" can exist even in small classes. And at the right are the accepted leaders of the groups.

What then can be done to help students participate in discussions? The primary difficulty to overcome is the fear itself. The procedures suggested below seek to give the student a feeling of assurance so he will venture a comment in class. Once started, most students have little difficulty thereafter.

1. Since it is obvious from the above results that most students feel themselves less able than others to speak up in class and secretly admire those who do, there is good reason to try it. When a student realizes that other students are not the critical judges he thought, it is less difficult to talk.

2. Since most instructors follow their textbooks rather closely, one can usually predict what will be discussed in class. Prepare yourself on a few items which will surely come up, then seize the opportunity to recite when these topics appear.

3. When class discussion emphasizes an exploration of points of view on some issue, hazard your own opinion. Such discussions move forward only as there can be differences of opinion to clarify the point at issue. In such a situation your opinion is probably as good as the next person's. The previously mentioned study on student influence on others also showed that students with definite opinions influence others more than those who aren't sure and, of course, more than those who don't speak up.

4. A good way to read is to apply what you are studying to different practical situations. A good form of class participation is to suggest such applications and if you can't think of any, ask how such material might apply in a given situation. An instructor is pleased to find students thinking rather than memorizing in a course.

5. Start participating in class discussion early in the school term. At that time the class is not yet organized so that even questions which are beside the point are ac-

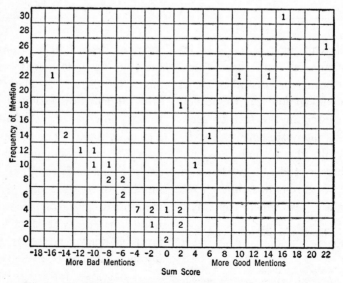

CHART 11. Distribution of frequency of mention and sum scores on a "Guess Who" test dealing with classroom behavior of students in two small classes. (Based on unpublished data of the writer.)

ceptable. And once started in a class, most students have little difficulty thereafter.

6. When something is not understood, ask questions. Instructors know that students don't understand everything in their lessons and many of them ask from time to time if there are any questions in order to clarify issues before they are included in tests. If the instructor doesn't ask for questions, he will usually be happy to help outside of class.

7. A maxim in army life is "don't volunteer!" An equally important maxim in college life, when a teacher asks for persons to work on special projects, is "volunteer"! When special projects are used in a class, it is usually planned so that all students will eventually have something to do. Those who volunteer early impress the teacher with their interest in the work; moreover, early acquaintance with the instructor actually does much to liven the work during the rest of the term.

As indicated earlier, the main problem is getting started. An analogy to the treatment of stuttering may be helpful here. Stutterers' emotional fear of stuttering, especially in social situations, increases their tension so they are even more apt to stutter. One aspect of treatment is to get them used to speaking in strange situations; many such experiences tend to reduce this emotional tension and so decrease the tendency to stutter. They also have trouble getting started; so some clinics send the stutterer out with a slip of paper and tell him not to come back until he has talked to someone and had the paper signed indicating this fact. Such drastic treatment need not be used on you, but a first step is to resolve to discuss in some class today "if it kills you."

Improving Class Manners

One approach to "how to win grades and influence teachers" is to be considerate in class. This does not mean excessive politeness but just common courtesy. Just as rules of etiquette make it easier to be comfortable and get things done at dinners and social gatherings, so the following simple rules of behavior in the classroom make it easier for students and teacher. Teachers work hard and tend to become irritated by students who constantly violate these rules.

1. Don't cut classes. The absent student misses part of his instruction and teachers occasionally react negatively toward chronic cutters. While number of absences is not highly related to grades, the data shown in Chart 12 indicate for a large number of stu-

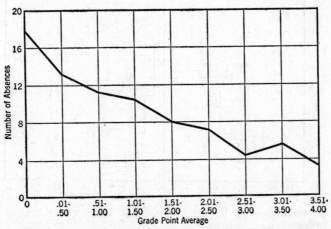

CHART 12. Relationship of class absences to grade point average. (Adapted from Jones.)

dents in a midwestern university that persons earning low grade point averages tend to cut much more than most students.[7] And not only are much cutting and low grades associated but there is a linear relationship all the way down. Merely attending class every day will not insure a B average, but conversely it can be said that cutting frequently may make it difficult to get.

2. Be on time! Some people have difficulty getting to class on time. Sometimes this is due to the preceding class being too far away; if so, be sure to tell your instructor. Others find it hard to get places on time, as for instance to an eight o'clock. In one study, a record was kept of what time students arrived at their eight o'clock classes. When the grade point average of students who were on time or even early was compared to the average of those who were late, it was found that "the early students had a grade of B, whereas the late students had a grade of C plus." [8] The following chart shows the typical distribution of time of arrival at class; most students come a few minutes early, but a minority straggle in for some time after the bell rings. They are a distraction to the class and to the instructor!

3. Carry your share in class. On a hike you wouldn't let someone else carry your pack. In class don't take the attitude of daring the instructor to try to interest you. When the instructor states an issue for discussion, don't "let George do it" but take some responsibility for moving the discussion along. The quicker it is discussed, the quicker the class can move on.

4. Classes, like many activities, sometimes get boring, but you should not show it. It is all right to look at your watch, but only occasionally, and don't check to see if it is running. Don't stack books and put your wraps on before the bell rings because the commotion will disturb the rest of the class. A coach would jerk a player who started easing up before the game was over; an instructor resents students who can't "take

[7] L. Jones, Class attendance and college marks, *School and Soc.*, 1931, 33:444–446.

[8] G. J. Dudycha, An objective study of punctuality in relation to personality and achievement, *Arch. Psych.*, 1936, No. 204, 53 pp.; also C. L. Nemzek, The value of amount of tardiness and absence for direct and differential prediction of academic success, *J. Exper. Educ.*, 1938, 7:4–10.

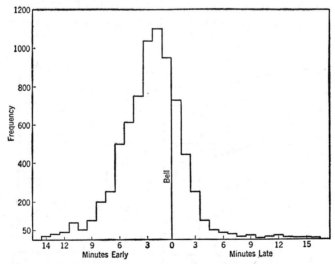

All observations to the right of the bell line represent lateness. (Adapted from Dudycha.)

CHART 13.   Distribution of time of arrival at eight o'clock classes.

it" for 50 minutes. Don't whisper to others in a lecture class; whispered comments are interesting to those about and so distract them from attending to the lecture. If you have ever talked to someone who continually looks about as if his mind is on other things, you know how instructors sometimes feel in class.

5. Get reports in on time or earlier. Most students put off writing reports until the last minute if not until a couple of days after that. But a theme takes no longer to write on time than later. Teachers appreciate getting reports on time, or even early, because they plan their work to handle these papers. Since a late paper means a special session of grading, the irritation is usually sufficient to cause a lower grade to be given.

Having Conferences with the Teacher

Many students feel that an instructor will think they are "apple polishing" if they ask for a conference. Actually most instructors enjoy the opportunity to work with and know their students individually. Part of their college job is to hold conferences with students from their classes. Certain courtesies are helpful, however.

1. If the instructor has time, questions can be asked before or after class. This informal opportunity makes it easy to have conferences without much effort.

2. If a conference has to be arranged at another time, make an appointment with the instructor and then *be sure to keep it.* It may be acceptable to "stand up" other students, but teachers' schedules are too full to be used up by missed appointments.

3. Questions can be asked in several ways, some more effective than others. In discussing a quiz, it isn't as effective to ask "How come you marked me off?" as "What type of material should I have included?" The latter will usually bring a sympathetic approach to your problem.

This project has emphasized four aspects of improving classroom skills and in each case has suggested methods of overcoming any difficulties. You should make a definite attempt then to do each of these things:

1. Take notes on lectures and have them evaluated according to the chart in Project II.

2. Make a definite effort to start participating in classroom discussions; suggestions were made to help you get started.

3. Notice what things students do in your classes which distract other students from the lecture or discussion; then make a definite effort to improve your own classroom manners.

4. If you are having trouble in any of your courses, have a conference with the instructor.

PART TWO

EDUCATIONAL DEFICIENCIES AFFECTING SCHOOLWORK

Deficiencies in the three R's affect the success of many students in college! For instance, tests show that some college freshmen read no better than the average fourth-grader, that some cannot do a single problem in long division, and that some cannot recognize pronouns in a sentence. Difficulties such as these prevent otherwise capable students from completing their lessons, from doing physics problems correctly, or from translating a foreign language easily.

Studies have shown that these difficulties are often limited to a few specific errors or bad habits and that, with individualized help, quite astounding gains can be made. For instance, rate of reading can be doubled, improving the writing of four letters will account for over 50 per cent of legibility difficulties, and learning a few specific constructions or words will eliminate a large percentage of grammatical or spelling errors.

With this in mind, it is proposed to make a survey of your basic skills (you have already completed some of the tests) in order to determine in which areas, if any, you need particular assistance. Because many of these tests are quite long in order to provide adequate diagnosis, most of the tests for Part Two are grouped together in Appendix I. Page references are made to these tests as they are needed.

PROJECT VII

READING ABILITY

Because of the great emphasis placed on long assignments in textbooks and reference books, reading ability is an important determiner of school success.[1] For this reason, higher-level skills in reading were discussed at length in Projects II and III. But some students are prevented from making full use of such higher-level skills because of deficiencies in certain aspects of basic reading skill, i.e., word-by-word reading, poor habits of comprehension accuracy, inadequate vocabularies, or inability to read graphs and tables. When deficient or lacking in such abilities, a student is like a machine with a bent wheel; he can operate only at reduced speed and with much waste of energy. The present project is devoted to the diagnosis and treatment of deficiencies in these aspects of reading skill. Tests for self-evaluation are included in this project and in Appendix I so that you can determine which sections will be of most interest.

General Characteristics of Reading

A discussion of three general characteristics of reading provides a basis for understanding the diagnostic sections into which this project is divided.

1. Various experiments show that there are many reading abilities, not just one. A person who is expert at reading fiction may not be proficient at reading non-fiction for information. Since student lessons deal primarily with the latter, reading non-fiction is emphasized here. Skill in reading different types of non-fiction may also vary because of differences in vocabulary, style of writing, and what is wanted from the selection. It is important, therefore, that reading diagnosis be carried out on textbooklike materials, e.g., non-fiction assignments which include graphs and tables and which are followed by quizzes.

2. Students show different levels of reading skill which vary not only quantitatively, as in rate, but also qualitatively. Four such levels are here described: [2]

(a) The most inefficient level is word-by-word reading. Here the reader goes at an exceedingly slow rate and makes little, if any, adjustment to the difficulty of the reading material. For instance, in one experiment with such readers in college it was found that they read a selection from an easy elementary-school reader at the same rate as one from a difficult graduate textbook.[3] Such students usually have high enough intelligence and vocabulary; their difficulty seems to lie in a carry-over from

[1] I. H. Anderson and W. F. Dearborn, Reading ability as related to college achievement, *J. Psych.*, 1941, 11:387–396; M. E. Broom, A note on silent reading comprehension and success in academic achievement in a state teachers college, *J. Appl. Psych.*, 1934, 18:561–565.

[2] F. P. Robinson and Prudence Hall, Studies of higher-level reading abilities, *J. Educ. Psych.*, 1941, 32:241–252.

[3] I. H. Anderson, Studies in the eye movements of good and poor readers, *Psych. Monog.*, 1937, 48, 1–35.

oral reading of certain perceptual-motor habits of perceiving one word at a time.[4] Students reading at this level present a special problem in rate training.

(b) Most students are at the second level of reading skill—flexible adjustment of rate to changes in difficulty and purpose. The nature of this skill is well illustrated by the bottom three lines in Chart 14. They show that

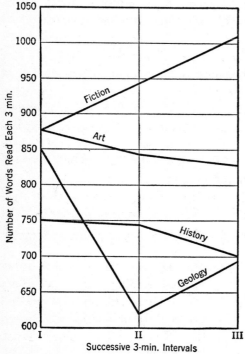

CHART 14. Change in rate of reading different subject matters during three successive three-minute intervals. (From Robinson and Hall.)

students' rate of reading over 9 minutes was adjusted to differences in difficulty in the three selections. Further, it shows that these readers start out at a good rate but gradually adjust their rate to the difficulty of the text; word-by-word readers, on

the other hand, make no such adjustment and read straight along at the same rate. The dip in the "geology" line is a further example of rate adjustment, in this case to a difficult table in the text. Not all readers have to slow down in this way on these selections; for instance, students who have a background of training in art can read the Art Reading Test straight along without slowing down. So one approach to remedial work is to increase a student's background of information, i.e., vocabulary and information in his subject fields. A second approach is to provide training in higher-level reading skills such as are described in the next two levels.

(c) The third level is the use of the context of a story to precomprehend what is coming. The "fiction" line in Chart 14 illustrates this. This fiction story is easy to comprehend so about half of readers read straight along at the same rate for the whole nine minutes; other students on catching on to the story, however, use their ability to halfway guess what is going to happen to speed up their later comprehension. Such precomprehension is very useful in reading.

(d) The fourth and highest level reading skill is the ability to benefit from typographical and writing cues in the text; the Survey Q3R Method is an example of such a skill.

Such an analysis shows the need for diagnosis of special disabilities in rate and of factors which affect comprehension ability. The use of context and typographical clues has already been discussed under the Survey Q3R Method.

[4] F. P. Robinson, The role of eye movements in reading, Univ. Iowa Studies, 1933, No. 39, 52 pp.

3. The third aspect of reading to be reviewed is an analysis of the basic factors which determine reading ability. These factors are well shown in an experiment in which 100 college students took 25 different reading and other types of tests.[5] The results on each test were correlated with every other test and these several hundred correlations were then subjected to a rather involved method of statistical treatment known as factor analysis. Through this technique of mathematical analysis, the educational psychologist is able to determine how many different, independent traits are involved in determining the scores on all of the original tests. In addition, a study of the factors which each test tends to measure enables him to describe these traits which have been isolated. The following factors were found and identified in this experiment; below each factor is listed the tests in this book which measure it.

[5] W. E. Hall and F. P. Robinson, An analytic approach to the study of reading skills, *J. Educ. Psych.* 1945, 36:429–442. See also F. B. Davis, Fundamental factors of comprehension in reading. *Psychometricka*, 1944, 9:185–197; R. S. Langsam, A factor analysis of reading ability, *J. Exper. Educ.*, 1941, 10:57–63.

1. Rate of comprehending material written in an inductive style

    Rate on Art Reading Test: words per minute.............................. ⸻

               percentile.. ⸻

2. Rate of comprehending material written in a non-inductive style

    Rate on Geology Reading Test: words per minute........................... ⸻

               percentile.................................... ⸻

3. Attitude of comprehension accuracy

    Comprehension accuracy on Art Reading Test: percentile.................... ⸻

    Comprehension accuracy on Geology Reading Test: percentile................ ⸻

4. Vocabulary

    General Vocabulary Test: percentile...................................... ⸻

    Dictionary Test: your quartile.. ⸻

5. Ability to read non-prose materials

    Table Reading Test: your quartile....................................... ⸻

    Chart Reading Test: your quartile....................................... ⸻

    Map Reading Test: your quartile.. ⸻

    Formula Reading Test: your quartile..................................... ⸻

Diagnosing Your Reading Ability

The first step in this project is to complete these tests so that you may have a profile of the abilities which determine your reading skill. Except for the General Vocabulary and the Dictionary Tests which appear later in this project, all the other tests referred to above are located in Appendix I. Directions are given with each test, although some assistance in timing will have to be given with the Art and the Geology Reading Tests. When completed, correct each test from its key in Appendix II. Norms for the Art and Geology Reading Tests are given below and norms for the other tests are included later in this project. When you have completed these tests, write your results in above as a general summary of this project and also on the Summary Sheet at the back of the book.

Some special directions are needed for scoring the Art and Geology Reading Tests. The number of the line marked at the end of the 10-minute interval gives the average number of words read per minute. Table 5 shows how well a student's rate compares with that of other college students (superior readers in the general population) in terms of percentile ranks. Thus if his words per minute on the Art Reading Test were 238, his percentile rank would be 50, or equal to that of the average college freshman. If his rate had been 285 words per minute (this number is halfway between 270 and 300 or the 80th and 90th percentiles on the table), he would interpolate and say that 285 words per minute is equal to the 85th percentile.

Comprehension accuracy in reading is determined by dividing the number of questions a student answers correctly by the number of questions asked about the material he has read. That is, if he got 10 questions right out of the 20 questions asked about the material he read on the Art Reading Test, his per cent right would be 50. (Students who wish to save themselves some work in long division will find that the table on page 213 can be used to translate fractions into per cent.) This 50 per cent right, however, does not indicate how he compares to other students, so this number is looked up in the right-hand part of Table 5 to find his percentile rank. It will be seen that 50 per cent right on the Art Reading Test is about equal to the 10th percentile.

TABLE 5. Percentile Ranks for Rate Scores and for Comprehension Accuracy Scores on the Art and the Geology Reading Tests.

Percentile	Rate in Words per Minute		Comprehension Accuracy in Per Cent Right	
	Art	Geology	Art	Geology
99	380	384	91	90
95	330	319	85	81
90	300	279	82	76
80	270	243	79	70
70	255	228	77	66
60	243	215	72	62
50	238	205	69	58
40	229	194	67	54
30	214	185	64	50
20	202	174	60	45
10	176	157	51	38
5	162	144	41	33
1	125	114	24	18

Plan of This Project

Did you have difficulty with any of these tests? What are the characteristics of your reading difficulty? You will be interested in finding the causes and methods for treating them. The subdivisions of this project are arranged to fit the above analysis, i.e., (A) Rate of Reading, (B) Comprehension Accuracy, (C) Vocabulary and Dictionary, and (D) non-prose reading skills for tables, charts, maps and formulas. If a test has shown that you have difficulty in any of these fields, you will be interested in the remedial exercises suggested in that section.

A. RATE OF READING

The two aspects of reading that show the greatest improvement during the freshman year in college are rate of reading and vocabulary. Rate of reading is intimately related to the number of fixations that the eyes make as they move across the page. A record of such eye movement patterns is shown in Chart 15. Such a record is obtained by pho-

tographing the eyes as they move across the page and then projecting the film on the original text where the location of each fixation is marked. Each line, therefore, represents a fixation; the numbers at the top of the lines indicate their sequence, and the numbers at the bottom their duration in thirtieths of a second. It will be seen that good readers make fewer fixations and regressions than poor readers do.

If conditions can be set up within the individual so that he makes fewer stops and therefore longer jumps, he will read at a much faster rate. Reading rate is primarily determined by comprehension facility which will be discussed later in this project. The present section deals with a specific condition that seems to cause a slow rate even though comprehension ability is good. That is, a carry-over of oral-reading habits into silent reading often makes an individual look at one word at a time and so develop a habit of reading slowly. This word-by-word reading was the lowest of the four levels of reading ability described above.

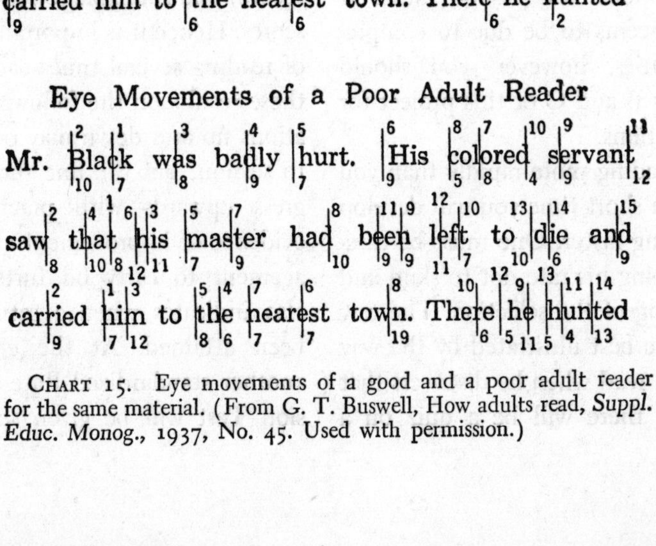

Eye Movements of a Good Adult Reader

Eye Movements of a Poor Adult Reader

CHART 15. Eye movements of a good and a poor adult reader for the same material. (From G. T. Buswell, How adults read, *Suppl. Educ. Monog.*, 1937, No. 45. Used with permission.)

Self-Evaluation

1. Are your rate percentiles consistently quite low (lowest 10 per cent)?

2. Do you tend to read the Art and Geology selections at about the same rate during each time interval? The first number marked shows the amount read during the first 3 minutes, the second number minus the first gives the amount read during the second 3 minutes, and 75 per cent of the difference between the last number and the second will give the rate for the third 3 minutes.

Tabulate these results here:

	First 3 min	Second 3 min	Third 3 min
Art			
Geology			

3. Do your lips move while reading?

Program for Improvement

If the above evaluation shows that you have a habit of reading slowly, the following remedial suggestions will be of value. If your slow rate seems to be due to comprehension difficulties, however, you should turn to Sections B and C of this project for remedial suggestions.

1. Practice reading more rapidly than you do now and in a short time you will develop a habit of reading faster. One must be careful in thus pushing his rate not to skim and miss the meaning of the selection. The way to read might be best illustrated by the way a student would read when he discovers that in ten minutes there will be a quiz on a lesson that he hasn't read. This student reads very rapidly yet gets all that he can out of the lesson. At first, reading in this way may be fatiguing—if so, take short rests to write notes on what you have read. Later, this or a faster rate will become habitual. Read all your work in this manner; halfhearted practice is of little value. Use any free time you have in this classroom for practice on rate.

The simplicity of this method of improving rate may make it appear misleadingly easy. Continued effort must be exerted, however, to produce gains. It will be difficult to remember to keep pushing your rate as you read, and the unaccustomed method will temporarily be more fatiguing and less pleasant than your usual comfortable speed. You will have to plan a definite program of practice each day and faithfully carry it out.

Since practice will be the main aid to improvement and since rate is least hampered by easy material, each person ought to do quite a bit of rapid reading of such outside material as newspapers, novels, and magazines. The form on the next page may be used for keeping a record of your outside reading; if needed, extra sheets may be obtained from the counselor.

2. It is difficult for a person to determine his improvement day by day because of the tendency for rate to fluctuate with change in difficulty of the material and, without a record, one is unable to remember his earlier scores. Hence it is important to measure rate of reading several times each week and plot these results on the following graph. Fluctuations up and down may occur from session to session, but the line should tend to progress upwards with practice. This visual evidence of improvement gives great encouragement to carry on further practice and also indicates when a satisfactory rate has been attained. At the end of the term another standardized Rate and Comprehension Test will be given so that gain from

OUTSIDE READING RECORD

Date	Pages Read	Nature of Material	Rate	Date	Pages Read	Nature of Material	Rate

practice during the term can be shown with two comparable tests.

The Rate Graph is prepared as follows: Along the left-hand edge of the paper are marked word-per-minute values in steps of 10 for each interval, e.g., 150, 160, 170, etc. Along the bottom mark the date of each test—the initial Rate and Comprehension Tests at the left-hand edge, the first weekly test on the next line, etc. As you plot each rate score, connect that dot with the previous one by a line. To minimize the fluctuations due to differences in difficulty of material read, read the same book each time. And use a book that demands "reading" (sociology, history) rather than "detailed

GRAPH OF RATE PRACTICE

Words per Minute

450

400

350

300

250

200

150

100

Date:

studying" (algebra, a foreign language). In estimating the amount read, count the words in a full page and multiply this by the number of pages read. Divide this number of words by the number of minutes it takes to read that chapter.

Care must be taken, while measuring rate, to make sure that you are comprehending as you read. This can be insured by writing a summary paragraph about what you have read when measuring rate. These summary paragraphs may also be used to evaluate your ability to summarize.

3. Lip movement, whispering, and pointing with the finger while reading all prevent rapid reading. These acts do not aid comprehension and should be eliminated.

4. Since comprehension difficulties are usually the main determinants of rate of reading, exercises to improve vocabulary, to learn to read for questions, and to improve organization will result in faster as well as better comprehension. The methods for improving these are given in the following sections of this project. Practice with the Survey Q3R Method also usually results in improved rate of reading. All these should be practiced in addition to the rate exercises.

B. Comprehension Accuracy

Students read in order to comprehend and be stimulated by the ideas in a selection; the major emphasis in training should, therefore, be on improving comprehension. The characteristics of effective comprehension vary with the requirements of the situation, so a first step is to define the nature of the undergraduate task.

Analysis of undergraduate textbooks and quizzes show that they are primarily trying to put across a limited number of basic concepts in each subject field. The great amount of detail in a text is there to elaborate and illustrate these essential concepts.

1. A first characteristic of the student task is, therefore, to select and comprehend these basic concepts.

2. A second characteristic is to complete this comprehension within a reasonable amount of time. Thus students frequently complain that their lessons take too long to read, consequently they seek ways of increasing their speed of comprehension.

3. A third characteristic of the student's reading job is the adoption of a level of comprehension accuracy which will most effectively complete the assignment. For instance, some students are capable of better comprehension but think that shallow skimming of a lesson is all that is necessary. Other students, believing that a student must know "everything," read so carefully as to have difficulty in completing their lessons and often get lost among the mass of detail they are emphasizing. These three characteristics of the student reading task are treated more fully below.

Self-Evaluation

The Art and Geology Reading Tests each provide two measures which are of interest here. The rate of reading scores, except in those instances where they are abnormally low due to word-by-word reading, are in reality measures of the speed with which you were able to comprehend the selections. That is, they provide a measure of how rapidly your background of vocabulary, knowledge of these fields, intelligence, etc., permitted you to read these selections. Is your rate of comprehension for non-fiction material at a satisfactory level for you?

While it is generally true that when a student reads more slowly and carefully his comprehension accuracy tends to increase and when he skims his accuracy score tends to go down, the Art and Geology comprehension accuracy tests actually measure an aspect of reading which is uniquely different from the factors measured by the rate tests.

The directions ask the student to read in the manner in which he normally studies his assignments. The comprehension accuracy score then represents a measure of the level of comprehension accuracy which he thinks is sufficient to answer quizzes, i.e., is a measure of his attitude toward study material. (The rate test indicates how fast he can comprehend at *that* level.) It is important that a student learn to adjust the level of comprehension accuracy with which he reads to an efficient level for college assignments.

So look over your reading rate and comprehension test scores and note below if either the rate or the comprehension accuracy scores indicate need for remedial work on this section.

1. *Selecting and Comprehending the Main Points.* Effective study consists of "reading with one's head instead of one's eyes." The student must learn to read with an active attitude of seeking what is important and subordinating what is merely explanatory. He must rise above rather passive comprehension of each succeeding sentence and paragraph. The Survey Q3R Method, which was discussed in Project II, is the main approach to this aspect of the reader's task. This material should be reread if this area is a problem for a student.

2. *Increasing Speed and Depth of Comprehension.* Students read more rapidly in those fields with which they are familiar. Although the text of the Geology Reading Test is more difficult than the text of the Art Reading Test, students of geology can usually read the former selection at the faster rate. They would, in fact, say, because of their background of vocabulary and geological concepts, that the geology selection was the easier of the two. A basic approach to improving comprehension, either in speed or depth, is to increase vocabulary and understanding of the basic ideas in a student's subject fields. (See Section C for a discussion of procedures here.) Techniques which help the reader focus his attention on the main ideas in the selection tend to keep him from becoming engrossed in detail and so speed up his reading. And techniques of using a preliminary survey and the thread of the argument thus far read to precomprehend what is coming can also help in speeding up comprehension.

3. *Developing an Effective Level of Comprehension Accuracy.* While in general the higher the level of comprehension accuracy the better, this is not always true. Obviously a person who scores very low on the comprehension accuracy tests should work to increase his accuracy in order not to miss so many essential ideas as he reads. Since the questions in the Art and Geology tests are typically based on important ideas in the selections, the student who comprehends more of them than another student is usually the better reader. Sometimes, however, students show up with a combination of extremely high comprehension accuracy with exceedingly slow rate. These students misunderstand what college studying means. Their attempts to dwell meticulously over each idea so slows them down that they waste time. While their immediate memory may be good, the large number of ideas often seem like a mass of unorganized detail and are rapidly forgotten. Thus the slow learner often tends to be the rapid forgetter. Both the inaccurate reader and the slow, meticulous reader will be discussed here.

The inaccurate reader often does not understand that a deeper comprehension is required in college work. Awareness of how his accuracy scores compare to those of other students will do much to make him read more carefully. Even more effective is adoption of a method of checking his comprehension of essential ideas after he reads each section. This can be done by changing a heading into a question, reading to answer it, then checking to see if he can answer the question from memory. If so, he can be sure he is comprehending the essential ideas. A third technique for raising comprehension accuracy is to increase a student's vocabulary and background of information so that the ideas can be comprehended more deeply and accurately. One common cause of inaccuracy and difficulty in reading is failure to understand basic material which came earlier in the book. Later parts of a textbook typically make use of basic concepts explained earlier, thus a student who doesn't get these early basic ideas is lost on the later material.

The problem of the slow, meticulous reader cannot be solved simply by way of having him speed up his reading until rate and accuracy are in better balance. Basically such a reader is going about his lessons incorrectly and a distinct shift in method may be necessary. Such students are occasionally like the apocryphal housewife who was found dusting the inside of the radio when the guests arrived; both should be admonished to keep important goals in mind. A slow reading student should turn to the material on the Survey Q3R Method and to the section above on reading to select and comprehend the main points. Much practice will be needed to develop this new skill so it can be substituted for his present method. In working on this, a student should use easy reading material such as the *Reader's Digest*. He should look at the title to orient himself, read the article rapidly, and then recite briefly on it. Such practice will gradually develop an effective substitute skill.

C. VOCABULARY

As indicated above, vocabulary is one of the most important aspects of college reading. An analysis of college quizzes, especially in freshman and sophomore courses, indicates that they frequently call for definitions of words. The vocabulary necessary for comprehending even newspapers is quite large. For instance, it is estimated that a vocabulary of 50,000 words is necessary to understand fully an edition of the New York *Times*. A large vocabulary of usable words is also an aid in making precise statements. Most students have experienced occasions when they searched rather unsuccessfully for words to express exactly what they meant.

But, as cited in Project I, few students know how good their vocabulary is in comparison to other students. Without such information a student scarcely knows how hard he should work in this area.

Self-Evaluation

A power test is provided for measuring your general vocabulary. It is based on a thorough sampling of words according to their frequency of use. You are not expected to know all the words included; but with this sampling method it can be assumed that if you know a certain percentage of these words you will also know a like percentage of all words of equivalent frequency of use. This test will be taken by everyone in the class at the same time. After you have worked 20 minutes, the counselor will read the correct answers or you may turn to pages 244–245 to score your test. Then use Table 6 to translate your score into a percentile rank. If your rank is lower than you would like, read the suggestions below for improvement. In this case, however, do not study the specific errors you made on the test.

In addition to a general vocabulary, each person has to master the basic technical vocabulary in his fields of interest. Thus, the doctor and the lawyer use many words in

TABLE 6. Percentile Ranks for Scores on Vocabulary Test

Percentiles	Scores
100	80
95	65
90	56
80	49
70	44
60	39
50	36
40	33
30	30
20	26
10	21
5	18
1	10

common, but each has a list of technical words in his own field. One of the great difficulties faced by the college student is the necessity of mastering the basic technical vocabulary in each of his courses, e.g., the terms from history, from geology, from mathematics, from social science, etc. Unless he

knows these concepts, all the explanations in text and class are "over his head."

Your competence with such technical vocabulary in your courses can most easily be measured by marking the technical words that are used in headings or that are italicized or in boldface type in the body of your textbooks. Then see if you can briefly define or explain each one. Any missed should be listed on page 125 and studied. Previous quizzes are another source of important technical terms. Whenever you find a question missed because of your not knowing the terms used, list them along with the technical terms found in your textbooks.

The dictionary is an extremely important tool in learning about concepts used by authors. Yet many students do not know how to use a dictionary effectively, nor are they in the habit of using it often. Use the Dictionary Test below to measure your skill in dictionary usage. When all of the questions have been answered, use the key on page 246 to correct your test. Place your score (the number right) in the correct box below and on the Summary Sheet at the back of the book.

Norms for Dictionary Test

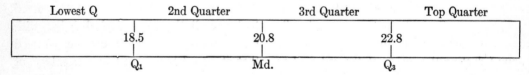

A GENERAL VOCABULARY TEST [6]

Score............. Percentile............. Date..........

In this test you are to show that you know the meaning of the following words. In the parentheses at the left, write the number of the word which means the same as the word to be defined. Note the example; then proceed at once to the test. Work rapidly.

Example:

(5) reply: (1) show (2) reason (3) call (4) rejoice (5) answer

1. ( ) illustrious: (1) clever (2) famous (3) odd (4) sensitive (5) wicked

2. ( ) confident: (1) sensible (2) confiding (3) sure (4) expectant (5) enthusiastic

3. ( ) allegiance: (1) safety (2) respect (3) loyalty (4) honesty (5) honor

4. ( ) covet: (1) hold (2) usurp (3) seize (4) refuse (5) desire

5. ( ) pensive: (1) meditative (2) quiet (3) mistaken (4) earnest (5) relieved

6. ( ) discreet: (1) secret (2) prudent (3) opposite (4) brief (5) separate

7. ( ) amiable: (1) loving (2) sad (3) satisfied (4) agreeable (5) clever

8. ( ) fatigue: (1) weariness (2) pain (3) sorrow (4) remorse (5) bitterness

9. ( ) loathe: (1) dislike (2) recall (3) hinder (4) refrain (5) detest

10. ( ) absurd: (1) peculiar (2) sick (3) ridiculous (4) laughable (5) queer

11. ( ) decade: (1) fortnight (2) a score of years (3) ten years (4) one hundred years (5) one thousand years

12. ( ) bewilder: (1) perplex (2) lose (3) soothe (4) deceive (5) chasten

13. ( ) alien: (1) opposed (2) special (3) menacing (4) foreign (5) mysterious

14. ( ) fidelity: (1) faithfulness (2) enthusiasm (3) strength (4) forbearance (5) veneration

15. ( ) dissension: (1) hypocrisy (2) elongation (3) discord (4) misery (5) discussion

16. ( ) eccentric: (1) crazy (2) odd (3) intellectual (4) sensible (5) conventional

17. ( ) latent: (1) punctual (2) late (3) dormant (4) easy (5) impossible

18. ( ) heretic: (1) communist (2) pagan (3) insane person (4) atheist (5) dissenter

19. ( ) eminence: (1) nearness (2) distance (3) greediness (4) distinction (5) generosity

20. ( ) judicious: (1) unusual (2) earnest (3) wise (4) lawful (5) bold

21. ( ) arduous: (1) endless (2) passionate (3) light (4) easy (5) difficult

22. ( ) incredulous: (1) faultless (2) surprised (3) dutiful (4) insincere (5) skeptical

23. ( ) propitious: (1) sympathetic (2) favorable (3) clever (4) odd (5) ugly

24. ( ) penury: (1) power (2) debt (3) poverty (4) graft (5) credit

25. ( ) acquit: (1) liberate (2) adjourn (3) stop (4) condemn (5) refuse

26. ( ) contentious: (1) mean (2) bitter (3) harmonious (4) mild (5) quarrelsome

27. ( ) impertinent: (1) diffident (2) modest (3) polite (4) disrespectful (5) unreasonable

28. ( ) benign: (1) aged (2) indignant (3) kindly (4) sad (5) celebrated

29. ( ) complacent: (1) snobbish (2) delighted (3) satisfied (4) dull (5) stubborn

30. ( ) ludicrous: (1) weird (2) appalling (3) weak (4) laughable (5) insane

Turn over page

[6] Devised by S. L. Pressey and used by special permission of the Ohio State Department of Education.

31. ( ) appreciable: (1) perceptible (2) welcome (3) honest (4) small (5) valuable

32. ( ) instigate: (1) sense (2) make public (3) prowl (4) start (5) find out

33. ( ) palpable: (1) readily perceived (2) safe (3) erroneous (4) fatuous (5) weak

34. ( ) adroit: (1) lucky (2) reserved (3) playful (4) deceitful (5) dexterous

35. ( ) diffident: (1) unruly (2) small (3) eager (4) silly (5) reserved

36. ( ) menial: (1) pious (2) servile (3) exalted (4) devoted (5) angry

37. ( ) candid: (1) frank (2) weak (3) clever (4) absurd (5) deceitful

38. ( ) enigma: (1) laxity (2) sentence (3) decoration (4) puzzle (5) religion

39. ( ) interim: (1) likewise (2) meantime (3) during office (4) space (5) age

40. ( ) refund: (1) guarantee (2) exchange (3) discount (4) receive (5) pay back

41. ( ) blatant: (1) evident (2) strange (3) noisy (4) wild (5) foolish

42. ( ) juvenile: (1) soft (2) weak (3) legal (4) young (5) amusing

43. ( ) anathema: (1) result (2) warning (3) blessing (4) irony (5) curse

44. ( ) contiguous: (1) smooth (2) comparable (3) distant (4) even (5) adjoining

45. ( ) adherent: (1) follower (2) cynic (3) old man (4) hermit (5) prejudiced

46. ( ) emolument: (1) flattery (2) decoration (3) theft (4) pay (5) honor

47. ( ) munificent: (1) rich (2) large (3) ideal (4) joyful (5) generous

48. ( ) litigation: (1) business organization (2) partnership (3) law suit (4) fight (5) clandestine affair

49. ( ) preamble: (1) procedure (2) introduction (3) command (4) hypothesis (5) law

50. ( ) cogent: (1) right (2) stated (3) convincing (4) absurd (5) real

51. ( ) inundate: (1) flood (2) extinguish (3) release (4) charge (5) moisten

52. ( ) veracity: (1) fear (2) wisdom (3) truth (4) courage (5) earnestness

53. ( ) abrogate: (1) annul (2) initiate (3) reduce (4) prepare (5) demur

54. ( ) dogmatic: (1) faithful (2) positive (3) religious (4) clear (5) radical

55. ( ) loquacious: (1) heavy (2) sorrowful (3) foolish (4) talkative (5) witty

56. ( ) anomalous: (1) poor (2) incognito (3) nameless (4) unimportant (5) abnormal

57. ( ) necromancer: (1) poet (2) sorcerer (3) orator (4) author (5) minister

58. ( ) soliloquy: (1) tirade (2) adage (3) conversation (4) monologue (5) cadenza

59. ( ) decorous: (1) sad (2) elegant (3) proper (4) obsequious (5) fashionable

60. ( ) mediocre: (1) good (2) odd (3) mistaken (4) ordinary (5) lax

61. ( ) comity: (1) beauty (2) humor (3) courtesy (4) godliness (5) faith

62. ( ) ascetic: (1) invalid (2) medicine (3) savior (4) athlete (5) recluse

63. ( ) nonpareil: (1) matchless (2) pacific (3) unwritten (4) foreign (5) extravagant

64. ( ) duplicity: (1) stealth (2) candor (3) deception (4) consistency (5) weakness

65. ( ) habiliment: (1) property (2) garment (3) home (4) habit (5) accessory

66. ( ) exigent: (1) departing (2) urgent (3) safe (4) timely (5) late

67. ( ) vertigo: (1) alertness (2) metamorphosis (3) action (4) speed (5) dizziness

68. ( ) charlatan: (1) prostitute (2) savior (3) servant (4) quack (5) mystic

69. ( ) amelioration: (1) calm (2) prayer (3) peace (4) penance (5) improvement

70. ( ) desiccate: (1) burn (2) cut down (3) destroy (4) remove (5) dry up

71. ( ) taciturn: (1) wise (2) loquacious (3) bashful (4) reserved (5) quarrelsome

72. ( ) chanson: (1) song (2) feat (3) noble deed (4) penalty (5) sacrifice

73. ( ) nonchalant: (1) bored (2) happy (3) indifferent (4) conceited (5) suave

74. ( ) replica: (1) antique (2) necklace (3) resemblance (4) painting (5) duplicate

75. ( ) flagitious: (1) facetious (2) villainous (3) simpering (4) repulsive (5) militant

76. ( ) recondite: (1) delinquent (2) criminal (3) pensive (4) ideal (5) profound

77. ( ) abnegation: (1) authority (2) veto (3) renunciation (4) refusal (5) surrender

78. ( ) fatuous: (1) obvious (2) celebrated (3) heavy (4) silly (5) impossible

79. ( ) amenity: (1) pleasantness (2) praise (3) correction (4) improvement (5) misunderstanding

80. ( ) ubiquitous: (1) learned (2) selfish (3) omnipresent (4) departed (5) wicked

Proper Nouns Capitalized

Vocabulary Entry

Alternative Spelling

Centered Period Between Syllables — Marks point where a word should be divided at end of a line

Hyphened Word

Geographical Label

Part of Speech

Reference Number to Pronunciation Guide

Foreign Word — indicated by prefixed parallel bars

Verb Transitive and Intransitive

Synonyms

Antonyms

Verb Phrase

Subject Label

Etymology

Usage Label

Noun Phrase

Pronunciation Key Lines

Alternative Pronunciation

Pronunciation

Obsolete Meaning

Primary Accent: '

Secondary Accent: '

Part of Pronunciation Omitted — omitted part to be supplied from the pronunciation given for the syllables identically spelled in the first preceding entry having full pronunciation

Definition

Definition with separate meanings numbered

Definition with separate meanings lettered

Variant Spelling

Cross Reference

Inflectional Forms

Pronunciation Omitted—When no pronunciation is given and vocabulary entry is spelled the same as preceding entry, the whole word is pronounced identically with the first preceding word having a pronunciation

Run-On Entry

John Bull 544 **jonquil**

Apostle, whose name is attached to the Fourth Gospel, three Epistles, and the Book of Revelation. **b** (1) The Gospel of John. (2) One of the three Epistles of John.
John Bull (bŏol). The English nation personified; the English people; also, the, or a, typical Englishman.
John Doe (dō). Law. The fictitious lessee acting as plaintiff in the common-law action of ejectment. Hence, a fictitious name for a party, real or fictitious.
John Do'ry (dō'rĭ; 70; pl. JOHN DORYS (-rĭz). Also **John Do'ree** (-rē). [John + doree, dory, the fish.] A marine fish constituting a family (Zeidae); specif., a common yellow to olive European food fish (Zeus faber), or an allied Australian fish (Zeus australis).
John Han'cock (hăn'kŏk). An autograph signature;— from the legibility of the handwriting of John Hancock.
John'ny-cake' (jŏn'ĭ-kāk'), n. [For journey cake.] U.S. A bread made of Indian meal, flour, eggs, milk, etc.
John'ny-jump'-up' n. Also Johnny jumper. a Any of several American violets, as the bird's-foot violet. b U.S. The wild pansy.
John'son-ese' (jŏn'sŭn-ēz'; -ēs') n. The diction or literary style of Dr. Samuel Johnson, or one formed in imitation of it;— used derogatorily of stilted or pompous style.
John·so'ni·an (jŏn-sō'nĭ-ăn; 58) adj. Pertaining to, or resembling, Dr. Samuel Johnson or his style; derogatorily, pompous; inflated. — n. A follower or copier of Dr. Johnson. — **John·so'ni·an·ism** (-ĭz'm), n.
∥**joie' de vi'vre** (zhwä' dĕ vē'vr'). [F.] Literally, joy in living; hence, zest; keen enjoyment of the pleasures of life.
join (join), v. t. [OF. joindre, fr. L. jungere to yoke, join.] **1.** To connect physically; to unite; to fasten or put together; to couple. **2.** To unite in association, specif., in marriage; to associate oneself with; as, to join the church. **3.** To combine or unite in time, effort, action, consideration, or other immaterial manner; as, to join prayers. **4.** To assemble in a body or group; as, to join forces. **5.** To accept, or engage in, as a contest; as, to join battle. **6.** Colloq. To be adjacent to; adjoin. **7.** Geom. To connect by a line, esp. by a straight line. — v. i. **1.** To come together; to be connected; to unite; to form a union. **2.** Now Rare. To engage; to join battle.
Syn. Join, combine, unite, consolidate, amalgamate agree in denoting the association, with varying degrees of closeness, of two or more objects. Join may express connection of any degree of closeness. Combine, rather more than unite, keeps in mind the elements associated; unite lays slightly greater emphasis on the resulting unity; as, the combined forces of the allies; the two companies united in one, a united family. Consolidate emphasizes the compactness or stability arising from the association of the parts; amalgamate emphasizes the fusion of the union; as, to consolidate two railroads; an amalgamation of races. — **Ant.** Separate, sever, disconnect, part.
join the colors. To join a service, as the army or navy. — n. Act of joining; place or point of junction.
join'der (join'dĕr), n. [F joindre, inf. as n.] **1.** Act of joining; a conjunction. **2.** Law. **a** A joining of parties as plaintiffs or defendants in a suit. **b** Acceptance of an issue tendered. **c** A joining of causes of action or defense.
join'er (join'ēr), n. **1.** One who or that which joins. **2.** One whose occupation is to construct articles by joining pieces of wood; a mechanic who does the woodwork (as doors, stairs, etc.) necessary for the finishing of buildings.
join'er·y (-ĭ), n. Also **joiner work**. Art or trade of a joiner; the work of a joiner; also, things made by a joiner.
joint (joint), n. [OF. joint, jointe, fr. L. junctus, past part. of jungere, junctum, to join.] **1.** The part, or the arrangement of the part, where two bones of an animal's body, or parts of an invertebrate's body, are joined, esp. so as to admit of motion; hence, a part in a plant where branches give off. **2.** The part or space included between two articulations, knots, or nodes. **3.** Specif., any of the large pieces of meat as cut for roasting. **4.** The place or part where two things or parts are joined or united; junction; as, a joint in a pipe. **5.** Slang. A gathering place; loosely, any establishment, resort, etc. **6.** Geol. A fracture in rock, smaller than a fault and not accompanied by dislocation.
— adj. [OF., past part. of joindre.] **1.** Joined; combined; specif., Law, of the lives of two or more persons, united in time; concurrent. **2.** Common to two or more; as: **a** Involving the united activity of two or more. **b** Shared by, or affecting, two or more; specif., in diplomacy, designating an action or expression in which two or more governments unite (dist. from identic). **3.** United, joined, or sharing with another or with others; acting together; as, joint creditor; joint debtor. **4.** Parl. Practice. Of or pertaining to the two branches of a legislative body; as, a joint committee.
— v. t. **1.** To unite by a joint or joints; to fit together. **2.** To separate the joints of; cut up into joints, as meat. **3.** To provide with a joint or joints; to articulate.
joint account. Banking. A bank deposit account owned jointly by two or more persons.
joint'ed (join'tĕd, -tĭd), adj. Having joints.
joint'er (join'tēr), n. **1.** One who or that which joints; esp., any of various tools used in making joints. **2.** Agric. Mach. A triangular-shaped edged attachment to a plow beam for covering trash in plowing.
joint'ly, adv. In a joint manner; together; unitedly.

joint'ress (join'trĕs; -trĭs) n. Law. A woman who has a jointure.
joint stock. Stock or capital held in company; capital held as a common stock or fund.
joint'–stock' com'pa·ny. Law. A company or association, consisting of a number of individuals organized to conduct a business for gain, with a joint stock, the shares owned by any member being transferable without the consent of the rest.
join'ture (join'tūr), n. [OF., fr. L. junctura, fr. jungere to join.] **1.** Obs. A joining; union. **2.** Law. The joint tenancy of an estate, or the estate so held. Obs., except specif.: Orig., an estate settled on a wife to be taken by her in lieu of dower.
joint'weed' (joint'wēd'), n. U S. An American polygonaceous herb (Polygonella articulata), with jointed, almost leafless stems, and spikelike racemes of small white flowers.
joint'worm' (-wûrm') n. The larva of any of several small chalcid flies (genus Harmolita, family Eurytomidae), which attack the stems of grain and cause gall-like swellings.
joist (joist), n. [OF. giste, fr. L. jacēre to lie] a Any of the small timbers or beams ranged parallelwise from wall to wall in a building to support the floor, or the laths or furring strips of a ceiling. b U.S. A stud or scantling about 3 by 4 inches in section.

F Floor: J, J, J Joists.

joke (jōk), n. [L. jocus joke, jest, game.] **1.** Something said or done to excite a laugh; something witty or sportive; jest; witticism. **2.** Something said or done in sport and not seriously. **3.** A laughingstock; as, he is a joke — Syn. See JEST. — v. i. To do something as a joke; to be merry; to jest. — v. t. To make merry with; to rally; banter; as, to joke a comrade. — Syn. Sport, rally, banter. — **jok'ing·ly** (jōk'ĭng-lĭ), adv.
jok'er (jōk'ēr), n. **1** One who jokes; a jester. **2** a Political Cant. An apparently harmless clause inserted in a legislative bill to render it inoperative or uncertain in some respect without arousing opposition at the time of its passage. **b** Hence, an unsuspected clause in a document, or the like, which in effect nullifies or greatly alters its apparent terms. **3.** Card Playing. An extra card now usually made to accompany the regulation pack. When used, it has special privileges; thus, in euchre it is the best trump.
jole (jōl). Var. of JOWL.
jol'li·er (jŏl'ĭ-ēr), n. Colloq. One who jollies, flatters, etc
jol'li·fi·ca'tion (jŏl'ĭ-fĭ-kā'shŭn), n. [jolly + -fication] Colloq. A merrymaking; jovial festivity.
jol'li·fy (jŏl'ĭ-fī), v. t. & i.; -FIED (-fīd); -FY'ING. Colloq. To make, or to be, jolly.
jol'li·ty (jŏl'ĭ-tĭ), n.; pl. -TIES (-tĭz). **1.** State or quality of being jolly; gaiety. **2.** Brit. A festive gathering — Syn. Mirth, joviality, hilarity.
jol'ly (jŏl'ĭ), adj.; JOL'LI·ER (-ĭ-ēr); JOL'LI·EST. [OF. joli, jolif, joyful, merry.] **1.** Full of spirits; joyful. **2.** Full of life and mirth; jovial; merry **3.** Expressing or inspiring mirth. **4.** Colloq. Splendid; pleasant; also, large; strong. — Syn See JOCULAR. — **jol'li·ly**, adv. — **jol'li·ness**, n.
jol'ly, n.; pl. JOLLIES (-ĭz). **1.** Brit. Sailors' Slang A marine. **2.** Colloq. Something said or done to keep a person or people in good humor or quiet. **3.** Slang, Eng A social meeting for mirth and good cheer. — v. t. JOL'LIED (-ĭd); JOL'LY·ING. Colloq. To encourage to feel pleasant or cheerful; — often implying a bantering spirit; hence, to poke fun at; rally. — v. i. **1.** To be or act jolly. **2.** Colloq. To jolly a person or people.
jolly boat. Naut. A boat of medium size belonging to a ship, used for general rough or small work.
jolt (jōlt), v. i. & t. To shake with short, abrupt risings and fallings, as a carriage moving on rough ground; to jar — n. A butt, knock, or blow; a sudden shock or jerk; in boxing, a jarring blow. — **jolt'er**, n.
Jo'nah (jō'nà), n. [Heb. Yōnah, lit., dove.] **1.** Bib. A Hebrew prophet, who, during a tempest sent by God because of his disobedience, was cast overboard from his ship, swallowed by a great fish, and remained in its belly three days before being cast out. **2.** The book of the Old Testament that tells his story. **3.** One who brings ill luck.
Jon'a·than (jŏn'à-thǎn), n. [Heb. Yŏnā-thǎn.] Bib. Son of Saul, and friend of David.
Jon'a·than, n. Hort. A late autumn variety of red apple.
jon'gleur' (zhôn'glûr'; jŏng'glēr), n. [F. See JUGGLER.] In medieval France and Norman England, an itinerant minstrel who recited or sang by way of entertainment, as at courts.
jon'quil (jŏng'kwĭl; jŏn'-; still by some, jŭng'kwĭl), n. [F. jonquille, fr. Sp. junquillo jonquil, reed, dim. of junco a rush, fr. L. juncus.] A bulbous plant (Narcissus jonquilla) of southern Europe and Algeria, Jonquil. (½) with long, rushlike leaves, and yellow or white, single or

(By permission. From An Outline for Dictionary Study Designed for Use with Webster's Collegiate Dictionary, Fifth Edition, Copyright, 1937, 1940, by G. & C. Merriam Co.)

TEST OF DICTIONARY USAGE

Answer the following questions by referring to the sample dictionary page printed opposite.

1. "John Dory" refers to a (1) historical character, (2) fish, (3) kind of boat. . . . .
2. "Dory" in "John Dory" is best pronounced to rhyme with (1) see, (2) may, (3) my, (4) the "i" sound in "wit." . . . .

3. The plural of John Dory is John Dories.   T   F
4. The fifth word on the page referring to a kind of bread would be spelled in what way within a sentence? (Watch capitals and the separation of words.) . . . .
5. The term referred to in question 4 originally came from the term (1) journey cake, (2) Johnny's cake, (3) indian bread. . . . .

6. The term "Johnny jump up" is written here incorrectly.   T   F
7. If it were necessary to break the word "Johnsonian" in typing near the end of a line, at what two places should this be done? Indicate answer by giving the letter just preceding each break. . . . .

8. "Joie de vivre" is an Italian word.   T   F

9. How many different meanings are given for the word "join"? . . . .

10. How many antonyms are given for the word "join"? . . . .
11. The preferred pronunciation of the word "jointed" rhymes best with the word (1) did, (2) bed, (3) bad, (4) seed. . . . .
12. The single apostrophe-like symbol which appears in most of the longer words, as after the "n" in "joinery," indicates (1) the place to divide the word at the end of a line, (2) the part preceding is spoken louder, (3) the division of syllables. . . . .

13. In terms of how many parts of speech is the word "joint" defined? . . . .

14. How many meanings are given for the word "joist"? . . . .

15. How many synonyms are given for the word "joke"? . . . .

16. How many meanings are given for the word "joker"? . . . .

17. "Jole" means (1) joke, (2) cheek, (3) pole, (4) French for "jolly." . . . .
18. The symbol *colloq.*, as used in the definition of "jollify," indicates that this word (1) should not be used in formal writing, (2) has this meaning only in certain localities, (3) was used long ago but is no longer in common use. . . . .

19. What is the past tense form of "jollify"? . . . .
20. The word "jollity," used in the sense of a festive gathering, is primarily restricted to which country? (1) Canada, (2) U.S.A., (3) Britain, (4) Scotland. . . . .

21. The plural of "jolly" is "jollies."   T   F
22. "Jonathan" apple is pronounced the same way as "Jonathan," the Biblical character.   T   F

23. A "jongleur" is a (1) juggler, (2) minstrel, (3) vein in blood system, (4) lawyer. . . . .

24. "Jonquil" has how many acceptable pronunciations? . . . .

Program for Improvement

A student should be selective in setting out to increase his vocabulary. He should learn new words which will help him the most in his schoolwork and in his daily living. The following two bases are best in making such selections: (a) He should note words and phrases used in lectures, conversations, and reading which say exceedingly well what he may have tried before somewhat ineffectually to say. List these on the page designated below. (b) Even more important for schoolwork, he should learn as early as possible the unknown words (especially the technical terminology) which occur frequently in his textbooks. A higher per cent of the running words in some science textbooks are unfamiliar to the beginning student than in some foreign language textbooks (where the vocabulary burden is more carefully controlled). However, a tabulation of the actual words used shows that the number of different unfamiliar technical terms is not particularly large. They are used frequently. Learning these words as they occur the first time saves a lot of vague comprehension later as they reappear again and again.

1. As a part of your self-evaluation, you were asked to make a list of technical terms you did not know. Make it a regular practice to mark new technical terms as you come to them in your textbooks or list them with the others on the page below. It will also be useful to take one of your courses—the one with which you are having the most difficulty if you wish, and list all the basic technical terms that have occurred (omit terms which are obviously included in the explanatory material and do not recur again). Some students may feel that such a list of technical terms in a textbook might be almost endless, but only the basic technical terms are meant here, i.e., the ones that are used again and again. Thus in one text 63 per cent of the technical terms were used only once and would not be considered in such a basic list; on the other hand, 82 words (7 per cent of the technical words) were used more than ten times in over 400 pages.[7] These words can usually be spotted rather easily from their location in headings or their being italicized in the text. Thus your list over a part of a course should turn out to be surprisingly small. Watch in your later lessons how frequently these terms recur. And if you study these terms, your new assignments should seem much easier.

2. The next step is to learn these selected words on both lists. One technique is to read down the lists or through your checkings of such terms in your texts and see if you can define each one. Look up those which cause difficulty. These words must also be made functional for you so they can be used on tests and in discussion. Try using them in discussions and explanations. There is a saying that a word used three times is yours forever. If you make a conscious effort to learn and use a few new words each week, your vocabulary will seem to develop with surprising rapidity.

3. Wide reading tends to broaden one's background so that ideas in lessons seem more familiar. Also the context of what is being read tends to develop some familiarity and understanding of new terms presented. Frequent encounters with these words will gradually build up an understanding of them. A program of regular recreational reading will do much to increase your vocabulary. It must be said, however, that while reading the sport page and comic magazines will increase your vocabulary, they do not develop an understanding of terms frequently used in college work!

4. When a new word is encountered in

[7] L. Cole, *Improvement of Reading*, Farrar & Rinehart, 1938, p. 161; F. D. Curtis, *Investigations of Vocabulary in Textbooks of Science*, Ginn, 1938.

reading, certain techniques are more helpful than others. It is a good practice not to stop reading when you come across an unknown word; finish the paragraph first. The meaning of the paragraph may be enough to indicate the meaning of the word so you won't have to look it up. If not, the word can then be looked up in the dictionary. Reading to the end of the paragraph also keeps the unfamiliar word from interrupting the main idea for which you were reading.

Several ways have been worked out which enable a reader to guess what a word means by using certain clues in the text.[8] That is, authors often accompany strange words with definitions or synonyms, or the whole context of the paragraph may indicate its meaning. Good students tend to use these clues more than poor students and any student can be helped who learns consciously to look for such clues when he has difficulty with a word. These clues, with an example of each, are as follows. Can you guess what the word omitted in each blank space means?

a. Definitions, i.e., "a ————— is a large, cat-like animal."
b. Experience, i.e., "as ————— as a boy or girl before a first date."
c. Comparison or contrast, i.e., "Eskimos have —————ing eyes like the Chinese."
d. Synonym, i.e., "When Jim heard about the trip, he was —————. He was glad there was to be no school that day."
e. Familiar expression or language experience, e.g., "harder than —————."

[8] C. M. McCullough, The recognition of context clues in reading, Elem. Engl. Rev., 1945, 22: 1–5.

f. Summary, e.g., "His knees shook and his eyes seemed to pop as he looked all around, for he was very much —————."
g. Reflection of mood or situation, e.g., "He hopped and skipped and danced about and whistled —————ly to himself."

It is interesting to analyze portions of different textbooks to see how many of these devices an author uses. Of course, the more he uses the easier it is for the trained reader.

5. If a word cannot be quickly figured out by the above techniques, look it up in a dictionary. Good readers, even the most highly educated, make very frequent use of a dictionary. In fact, the better the reader, the more apt he usually is to use the dictionary! Many students are inefficient in using a dictionary, however, and often don't know about its many values. If you missed any items on the Dictionary Test, use the keyed answers and the boxed legends at the edge of the sample dictionary page to figure out how to read a dictionary.

It may sound strange but a dictionary is an interesting book—not to read straight through but to browse in. In addition to giving the meaning of a word, a dictionary also indicates spelling, pronunciation, source, synonyms, and occasionally antonyms (words meaning the opposite). You will also be interested in the number of meanings which many words have as, for instance, over one hundred for the word "run." Pages XXII to XXV of the Fifth Edition of Webster's Collegiate Dictionary or pages XCII to XCVI of the Second Edition of Webster's New International Dictionary give further information about how to use a dictionary.

1. Everyday vocabulary

2. Technical words from your courses

Norms

Test	Lowest Q	2nd Quarter	3rd Quarter	Top Quarter
Tables	26.1	27.9	29.4	
Graphs	19.6	21.6	23.5	
Maps	18.9	21.1	22.0	
Formulae	6.0	9.0	10.7	
	Q_1	Md.	Q_3	

D. Special Reading Skills

Tables, graphs, formulae, and maps are devices that aid comprehension. Yet most poor readers skip them with a sigh of relief —"There's half a page filled by a picture I don't have to read." Tables summarize and unify a wealth of data so that you can see possible relationships and trends; graphs picture these trends even more readily for you; formulae are a shorthand method of stating involved relationships in a simple manner if you will but study them; and maps, of course, picture geographic relationships.

Difficulty with these comprehension devices springs from two causes: (1) lack of knowledge of how they are constructed and interpreted, and (2) lack of appreciation of the fact that these devices cannot be read at normal reading speed but must be studied.

Self-Evaluation

Tests of four types are included in Appendix I: reading tables, reading graphs, reading maps and reading formulae. Each test contains simple examples of the kinds of material typically found in textbooks; the questions measure your ability to get *basic* information from these materials. The norms above permit a comparison of your skill with that of other students. But since these are simple examples of basic materials, your goal should be ability to answer *all* of these questions as well as ability to understand non-prose materials which occur in your studies. The keys for correcting these tests are on pages 249–250 in Appendix II.

Program for Improvement

1. Correct and understand the test items that you miss.

2. Practice reading all graphs, maps, tables, and formulae that you find in your lessons. They emphasize and illustrate important points; effort spent on them is very worth while. Your counselor will assist you in interpreting any of these comprehension aids that give you difficulty.

Modern textbooks are using graphs and charts more and more; rather than being simply a supplement to the text they are now frequently used as the basic means of presenting ideas. During the war period, types of visual aids new to undergraduate courses have become popular, e.g., wiring diagrams, blueprints, three-dimensional drawings, weather maps, topographical maps, pictorial maps, etc. Ability to read these has become basic to schoolwork and to everyday living.

3. The following readings give further information on how to read these comprehension aids.

H. Arken and R. Colton, *Graphs, How to Make and Use Them*, Harper, 1936. Chaps. I, II, XIV.

R. W. Frederick, *How to Study Handbook*, Appleton-Century, 1938. Pages 50–64: How to read graphs and tables; pages 72–86: How to read maps.

S. L. Greitzer, *Elementary Topography and Map Reading*, McGraw-Hill, 1944.

H. P. Howland, L. L. Jarvie, and L. F. Smith, *How to Read in Science and Technology*, Harper, 1943. Pages 241–264.

E. Summary

The several sections and their interrelations indicate a need for a summary of the activities listed in this project. Look over your reading test results again and decide which areas seem most in need of remedial training. Then, in the following outline of suggested remedial activities, check those which you plan to carry out.

A. Rate
   1. Daily practice and plotting on graph
   2. Stop lip movement and line-following with finger
   3. Improve comprehension

B. Comprehension Accuracy
   1. Learn to select and comprehend main points
   2. Increase background of information and knowledge of technical terms
   3. Practice Survey Q3R Method
   4. Learn to use context of story to pre-comprehend what is being read
   5. Build an efficient attitude of comprehension accuracy

C. Vocabulary
   1. Make and study lists of technical terms and vocabulary of courses
   2. Make list of usable everyday words and use them
   3. Read widely to broaden background and vocabulary
   4. Practice techniques of figuring out meaning of unknown words
   5. Learn to use dictionary more effectively

D. Special Reading Skills
   1. Study errors made on tests
   2. Analyze tables and charts in textbooks to find any difficulties in reading
   3. Make it a practice to study all tables and charts in lessons
   4. Obtain training in reading new types of charts

Summarize briefly below further details of your proposed training program in reading.

PROJECT VIII

WRITING SKILLS

A large part of our endeavor to affect the behavior of other people is done through writing. If an account is poorly written, the reader has difficulty in comprehending it and also tends unconsciously to lower his estimation of the writer's authority. Good writing is therefore effective writing.

The essential abilities for a clear and concise written message are classified here into (1) English, (2) spelling, and (3) handwriting. A section in this project is devoted to a discussion of diagnostic and remedial procedures for each of these divisions.

A. ENGLISH

Knowledge of language form is basic to good writing. If a writer chooses effective words and presents them in correct English form, one is able to read right along. Training in this field is usually the province of English courses and taking another lesson in English may seem rather boring. The purpose of this unit, however, is to provide a description of each student's abilities. Such an analysis usually shows that a student isn't generally poor at grammar or punctuation, but rather that most of his difficulty is due to a few rather specific errors. Two or three rules do not seem difficult to master, so a student is more motivated to attack such an apparently simple problem.

Self-Evaluation

The area of English is divided into the following diagnostic divisions: grammar, cap-

italization, punctuation, and sentence structure. Tests to measure your skills in these areas are given on pages 223–232 in Appendix I. These tests do not represent a random sampling of all the many rules of English but are based on the 40 rules which research has shown are most frequently used and cause the most trouble in writing. Every item, therefore, deals with an important point.

Follow the directions printed on the tests. When these tests are completed, correct them and then translate their scores into percentile ranks by using Table 7 below.

TABLE 7. Percentile Ranks on English Survey Tests

%ile	Grammar	Capitalization	Punctuation	Sentence Structure
100	80	80	80	80
95	78	78	75	78
90	76	76	70	76
85	74	74	68	73
80	73	72	62	70
75	72	71	58	67
70	71	70	55	64
65	70	69	53	61
60	69	68	51	59
55	67	67	48	57
50	65	66	45	55
45	62	65	42	54
40	59	64	39	53
35	56	63	36	52
30	53	62	33	51
25	49	60	30	49
20	45	58	27	47
15	41	56	24	45
10	37	53	20	43
5	33	50	16	40

Write these percentiles in their respective places in the following summary list. Since choice of words is an important aspect of good writing, also write in your percentile from the General Vocabulary Test which you took in the preceding project.

Grammar   ....%ile rank.
Capitalization   ....%ile rank.
Punctuation   ....%ile rank.
Sentence
  Structure   ....%ile rank.
Vocabulary   ....%ile rank.

The percentile ranks indicate your standing relative to other students; but what is the nature of the specific errors that you make? Since a student's errors tend to "constellate" in certain areas, the extent of his remedial work may be limited. In order to find these areas, the following procedure is suggested. Each time you mark a wrong answer, copy the symbol[1] (S1, C6, etc.) which is beside the answer on the key. This symbol refers to the rule which has been violated and will expedite your looking it up in the rule section which follows. Since each of the test items, correctly written, has been placed under the rule indicated by the symbol, you can tabulate your errors quite easily. Merely check under the rule the correct form for each item you missed. When this checking is completed, a glance at the list of rules will show where the errors tend to "constellate." If you master these few rules, your performance should show marked improvement.

Organizational skill and style of writing are also important in effective writing. These were discussed in part in Project V, Preparing Reports; further help can be obtained

[1] The meaning of these symbols is as follows: G stands for grammar, C for capitalization, P for punctuation, and S for sentence structure. The numbers refer to specific rules under each of these headings. Thus G5 refers to the fifth rule under the Grammar heading which says that the verb "to be" should agree with the subject and not with the predicate noun.

from your English instructor. This project deals only with certain mechanics of English.

One further point. These tests tend to measure your peak performance, but many students do not use their full skill in everyday class work. Various essays and examinations that you have written should also be analyzed to determine the errors you make in such writing.

RULES OF ENGLISH [2]

GRAMMAR

A Verb Agrees in Number With Its Subject

1. A subject composed of two or more nouns (either singular or plural) joined by *and* requires a plural verb. A subject composed of two or more singular nouns joined by *or* or *nor* requires a singular verb.

....12. Neither Martha nor John *is* older than I.
....16. Algebra and geometry *have* been easy for me.
....28. Neither Jane nor I *was* able to play basketball.
....31. Basketball and baseball *are* what I am going to take.
....76. Either dramatics or athletics *is* going to be my specialty.

2. The number of the verb is not determined by a noun or pronoun which intervenes between the subject and the verb.

....25. The price of supplies *is* high.
....55. The price of the tickets *was* two dollars.

3. The number of the verb is not changed by adding to the subject words introduced by *with, together with, as well as, like,* etc.

....63. The referee, like the other officials, *was* dressed in white.
....69. Mary, as well as the other girls, *has* asked me to tell about the game.

[2] Adapted from the pamphlet, "Student's Handbook of Essentials," published by the Ohio State Department of Education and used with permission.

4. *There is* or *there are* should be used according to the number of the subject which follows.

....56. There were about 30,000 people there.
....72. There are several reasons.
....77. There are several things to choose from.
        Another example: There *is* a man at the door.

5. The verb *to be* should agree with its subject and not with its predicate noun.

....17. The greater part of the curriculum *is* English subjects.
....23. The weakest part of our school *is* the materials in the laboratories.
....78. Sports *are* the best part of any school.

6. The verb *does* or *doesn't* is used with a third person singular subject.

....10. Jack *doesn't* remember the other schools.
....22. Martha, . . . *doesn't* go to school.
....32. Jane *doesn't* go to school.
....75. The curriculum *doesn't* matter so much to us.

7. The pronouns *each, every, everyone, everybody, anyone, anybody, either, neither, no one, nobody* demand a singular verb. The word *most* when used in such phrases as "most of us," "most of them" demands a plural verb.

.... 2. Each of us pupils *greets* the teacher.
....15. Each of us *was* told to register.
....35. Most of us *have* a very good time playing basketball.
....51. Most of us *prefer* the schools. . . .
....71. No one in our crowd *has* seen a big game.
....79. Everybody *doesn't* agree with me.

Agreement and Case of Pronouns

8. Pronouns which refer to other nouns or pronouns should have the same number. (Note especially that the pronouns listed in No. 7 above are singular.)

.... 9. Teacher has told each one to do *his* part.
....18. The greater part of the curriculum is English subjects, which *are* very uninteresting.
....39. No one wants her on *his* (*her*) team.
....58. Everyone shouted as loud as *he* could.
....61. Each player took *his* position.

9. Pronouns have a different form when used as the subject of a clause than when used as the object of a verb or preposition. The following are some specific situations which often cause trouble:

a. When words come between the pronoun and the word which governs its case.

    ....73. Our teacher told Mary and *me*.

b. When *who* and *whom* are used in the first position in a sentence or clause.

    ....13. The teacher wanted to know *who* my father was.
    ....14. I told her . . . *whom* I was living with.

c. When the pronoun follows *as* or *than* it has the same case as the noun or pronoun with which it is compared.

    ....36. Jane is taller than *I*.
    ....37. She used to play baseball better than *I*.
         Another example: I see him more often than *her*.

d. When the pronoun follows the preposition *like* it must be in the objective case.

    ....40. She is fourteen, like Mary and *me*.
    ....80. Mary prefers athletics, like Frances and *me*.

e. When a first person pronoun stands with a noun, it has the same case as the noun.

    .... 1. Each of *us* pupils greets the teacher.
    ....45. *We* girls are going to the same college.

Tense of Verb

10. The following verbs are frequently misused, either because the wrong tense form is substituted or because a similar but unacceptable form is substituted. The past participle is used with the auxiliary verb "to have."

Present	Past	Past Part.
ask	asked	asked
attack	attacked	attacked
bear	bore	borne
begin	began	begun
blow	blew	blown
break	broke	broken
burst	burst	burst
climb	climbed	climbed
come	came	come
do	did	done
drag	dragged	dragged
draw	drew	drawn
drink	drank	drunk
drown	drowned	drowned
freeze	froze	frozen
give	gave	given
go	went	gone
grow	grew	grown
hear	heard	heard
lead	led	led
ride	rode	ridden
ring	rang	rung
run	ran	run
see	saw	seen
show	showed	shown
shrink	shrank	shrunk
sing	sang	sung
speak	spoke	spoken
swing	swung	swung
take	took	taken
tear	tore	torn
throw	threw	thrown
use	used	used
wear	wore	worn
write	wrote	written

.... 5. Sally and Richard have *asked* to occupy the seats.

.... 6. I have *climbed* into one of the seats.

....11. ... the other schools that he has *gone* to.

....21. My sister has *given* much time.

....46. We have *written* to several colleges.

....47. We have *begun* to read.

....57. I had never *seen* so many people.

....59. Our team *came* on the field.

....65. He must have *frozen*.

....67. We *sang* songs.

....68. People *threw* confetti.

....70. Mary has *asked* me to tell.

Differentiate Between Adjectives and Adverbs

11. Be careful to distinguish between adjectives and adverbs and to use the proper form. In general, adjectives may be changed to adverbs by the addition of -*ly*, although there are such exceptions as "good," an adjective, and "well," an adverb. An adverb is used if it modifies a verb, an adjective, or another adverb.

.... 4. John intends to do his work *well*.

.... 7. I can see *easily* now.

....20. I am *surely* weak in grammar.

....27. I shall consider the matter very *carefully*.

....34. I'll be able to play basketball *well*.

....38. She plays so *poorly*.

....49. There are too many nice ones to choose one very *easily*.

....60. The band played the college song very *softly*.

12. Verbs pertaining to the senses and the verbs *to grow*, *to become*, are followed by an adjective unless they indicate action.

....24. Our principal feels *bad*.

....29. We never felt *sad*.

....42. ... perfume that smells very *sweet*.
Other examples: Mary grew *hilarious*.
The flowers grow *quickly*.

Words Confused

13. The following words are commonly confused:

a. lie lay lain (to be in a stretched-out position)
lay laid laid (to be placed in a recumbent position)

He laid his hat on the table and lay
down to rest.

b. sit sat sat (to rest in a sitting position)
set set set (to place in a position of
rest)
She set the basket in a corner and sat
down to talk.

c. let let let (to permit)
leave left left (to abandon)
The police let him go, and he left the
city.

d. can could (to be able or to be possible)
may might (to be permitted)
You may go if you can find someone
to go with you.

e. a (used before words beginning with a
consonant)
an (used before words beginning with
a vowel or vowel sound)
an uncle, a hat, an onion, a cup.

f. there (adverb)
their (pronoun)
they're (contraction of they are)
They're going to buy their hats there.

g. to (preposition, or sign of infinitive)
two (adjective or noun)
too (adverb)
He was too sick to go to school for the
last two days.

h. teach (to instruct or give knowledge)
learn (to acquire knowledge)
He teaches quite effectively; as a result
his pupils learn a great deal.

.... 3. Mary, John, and Annabelle sat
in the front row.

....19. The teacher can't teach me English at all.

....26. The principal won't let me drop
chemistry.

....33. She likes to lie around.

....41. She wears such pretty clothes,
too.

....43. Mother won't let me have any
perfume.

....44. She said, though, that I might
buy some next year.

....48. There are almost too many nice
ones.

....52. Students have a better time
there.

....53. They have football games, too.

....62. The substitutes sat down on the
bench.

....74. They have interesting courses
there.

CAPITALIZATION

1. *First Words.* Capitalize the first word of
the following: (a) every sentence, (b) every
line of poetry, (c) every complete grammatical statement (independent clause)
following a colon, (d) every direct quotation. Do not capitalize the first word of a
quotation which is only a fragment of a
sentence, or the first word of an indirect
quotation.

a. This sentence illustrates the first rule.

b. My heart leaps up when I behold
A rainbow in the sky.

c. The questions were as follows: What is
an erg? What is a dyne?

d. Annie said, "I think you should go to
bed."
"I think," Annie said, "you should go to
bed."
Annie said that you should go to bed.
Stevenson called man "the disease of the
agglutinated dust."

....2. She exclaimed, "What a beautiful lake!"

2. *Names of Persons.* Capitalize the names
of persons and the titles standing for the
names of persons. Capitalize derivatives of
these names. Do not capitalize the names
of professions or professional ranks.

.... 6. "Tell me what Doctor Harris did,"
said Emily.

.... 7. "If that's all," John said, "we may as
well go."

....12. Al Smith, the Democratic candidate,
was defeated.

....21. The ring is an heirloom; it belonged
to Jenny Lind.

....23. Esther, Jane, and Mary organized a
girls' club.

....28. Sinclair Lewis wrote these books.

....34. He read Tennyson's famous poem,
"In Memoriam."

....35. A careful description of Captain Evans was given.

....42. It's too bad Gerry can't go with us.

....46. The various codes were submitted to General Johnson.

....47. He said that he saw the Prince of Wales.

....48. "Please come," she wrote, "Colonel Brown will be here."

....49. Joe is not going, nor is Sally.

....56. "You should talk to Professor Brown," she advised.

....62. "That youngster," said Coach Jones, "will be a star."

....63. It's raining hard, but Jim won't stay home.

....71. You may take this note to Mr. Adams.

....72. Joseph Conrad is the author of Lord Jim.

....73. To be frank, she doesn't like Janice very well.

....78. Mary, you may describe General Pershing's plan.

....79. . . . to see what Mrs. Jones is wearing.

....80. The play was almost over when John left.

3. Names of Places. Capitalize the names of countries, states, cities, streets, buildings, mountains, rivers, oceans, or any word designating a particular location or part of the world. Capitalize derivatives of these names. Do not capitalize the points of the compass or such terms as street, river, ocean when not part of a name.

.... 1. Are you going to Strassburg, Germany?

.... 3. The Hudson, a river in New York, is very beautiful.

.... 4. Do you expect to visit China or Ceylon?

.... 5. Three weeks from now we'll be in Kansas City.

.... 9. Why do so many people blame the Germans?

....11. She lives at 25 Whittier Street, Dolby, Kentucky.

....13. He attended Tate College; then he went to a law school.

....14. My subjects include the following: history, English, and Latin.

....17. He had started to Newberg; there was no retreat.

....18. She intended to visit Mount Baker.

....19. I think French a boring subject but like physics.

....24. The letter was sent from Detroit.

....30. If you see any American tourists, let me know.

....32. John finished his Spanish; then he worked on biology.

....37. We didn't have time to visit the Alps; still we saw almost every other part of Europe.

....39. He claims that the government is as corrupt as in the days of Rome.

....45. On Sunday we went fishing in Beaver Creek.

....55. We saw the Capitol at Washington.

....58. One of us must go to Lisbon.

....60. You'll find it easier to go by way of Athens.

....74. They went to Washington, to Oregon, and on to California.

....76. We drove to St. Louis and then took a quaint old steamer down the Mississippi River.

4. Names of Organizations. Capitalize the names of business firms, schools, societies, clubs, and other organizations. Capitalize derivatives of these names. Do not capitalize such words as company, school, society, when not part of a name.

....12. Al Smith, the Democratic candidate, was defeated.

....16. In the first place, the Ku Klux Klan was not legal.

....26. Will the Socialist Party ultimately succeed?

....38. His wife is a Presbyterian; he is a Baptist.

....40. The National Railway Association should recognize that this type of engine will not pay.

....41. The Lincoln School has been overcrowded for some time.

....50. In other words, the General Electric Company refused my offer.

....54. The Unemployed League will meet tomorrow.

....59. ... he wants to enter Harvard College next year.

....67. He told me to meet him at the Seneca Hotel.

....68. ... she was elected to the Martha Washington Club.

....69. ... we'll put the money in the Chase Bank.

....75. She resigned from the Missionary Society.

5. *Days, Weeks, Months, etc.* Capitalize the days of the week, the months of the year, holidays, and church festivals. Do not capitalize the names of the seasons unless they are personified.

.... 8. Friday, the tenth of June, was my birthday.

....10. It was the Fourth of July, a national holiday.

....24. The letter was sent from Detroit on August 8, 1933.

....25. Christmas, Memorial Day, and Thanksgiving are holidays.

....45. On Sunday we went fishing in Beaver Creek.

....57. She said she played no card games during Lent.

....64. June, July, and August are vacation months.

....79. One goes to church on Easter.

6. *Titles.* Capitalize the first word and all other important words in titles (and subtitles and headings) of themes, magazine articles, poems, books; of laws and governmental documents; of pictures, statues, musical compositions; and in trade names. Always capitalize the first and last words.

....20. This poem is called "In the Cool of the Night."

....27. I use Detoxal; it is a good toothpaste.

....28. Sinclair Lewis wrote these books: *Dodsworth, Babbitt,* and *Arrowsmith.*

....33. "By a Waterfall" is a simple little piece to play.

....34. He read Tennyson's famous poem, "In Memoriam."

....36. She recommends Gold Dust for cleaning.

....52. "I'm in a Hurry" is the name of an amusing short story.

....53. You will like these movies: *Cimarron* and *Masquerade.*

....66. ... you may have the Chevrolet.

....70. I'll send you a subscription to the *Literary Digest.*

....72. Joseph Conrad is the author of *Lord Jim;* he also wrote *Victory.*

PUNCTUATION

1. Use a period, question mark, or exclamation point at the end of a sentence.

.... 1. Are you going to Strassburg, Germany?

.... 2. She exclaimed, "What a beautiful lake!"

.... 4. Do you expect to visit China and Ceylon?

.... 9. Why do so many people blame the Germans?

....26. Will the Socialist Party ultimately succeed?

....58. One of us must go to Lisbon; which will it be?

2. Use a period after an abbreviation and after each initial.

....71. You may take this note to Mr. Adams.

....76. We drove to St. Louis.

....79. ... to see what Mrs. Jones is wearing.

3. Use commas to set off parenthetic words, phrases, and clauses. That is, set off such elements as interrupt the sequence of the thought or do not form an essential part of the sentence. Among these are introductory words and phrases, interjections, words of address, appositives, loosely modifying phrases and clauses, and the like. Do not use superfluous commas. If in doubt, leave the comma out.

.... 3. The Hudson, a river in New York, is very beautiful.

.... 8. Friday, the tenth of June, was my birthday.

....10. It was the Fourth of July, a national holiday.

....12. Al Smith, the Democratic candidate, was defeated.

....22. The captain, our old friend, met us at the dock.

....34. He read Tennyson's poem, "In Memoriam."

....78. Mary, you may describe General Pershing's plan.

4. Use a comma to set off clearly introductory ideas at the beginning of a sentence or obviously added elements at the end.

....16. In the first place, the Ku Klux Klan was not legal.

....30. If you see any American tourists, let me know.

....36. She recommends Gold Dust for cleaning, since it is cheaper.

....50. In other words, the General Electric Company refused my offer.

....66. If it's really necessary, you may have the Chevrolet.

....68. Being capable and socially prominent, she was elected.

....70. I'll send you a subscription to the *Literary Digest*, if you want it.

....73. To be frank, she doesn't like Janice very well.

....75. She resigned from the Missionary Society, thus losing many friends.

5. Use commas to separate a series of words, phrases, or clauses. In a series of more than two parts, grammarians usually ask that a comma precede the conjunction, although some style books suggest that the comma before the conjunction be omitted.

....14. My subjects include the following: history, English and Latin.

....23. Esther, Jane and Mary organized a girl's club.

....25. Christmas, Memorial Day and Thanksgiving are holidays.

....28. Sinclair Lewis wrote these books: *Dodsworth*, *Babbitt* and *Arrowsmith*.

....39. He claims that the government is as corrupt as in the days of Rome, that there is no place for an honest man in politics, and that there is little hope for reform.

...43. Oranges, lemons and grapefruit are citrus fruits.

....64. June, July and August are vacation months.

....65. He wants someone who is quick, who is ambitious, and who has had experience.

....74. They went to Washington, to Oregon and on to California.

....79. One goes to church on Easter to ease one's conscience, to wear one's new clothes, or to see what Mrs. Jones is wearing.

6. Ordinarily use a comma to separate clauses joined by the conjunctions *and*, *but*, *for*, *or*, *nor* if a change in subject takes place or if the clauses are long. Do not use a comma, however, if the subject is not changed or if it is not a clause that is joined.

....15. They're ready, but we'll have to wait awhile.

....19. I think French a boring subject but like physics.

....31. He hurried on to the bank and asked for the president.

....35. A careful description of Captain Evans was given, for he was an important witness in the trial.

....47. He said that he saw the Prince of Wales, but no one believed him.

....49. Joe is not going, nor is Sally.

....55. We saw the Capitol at Washington, and then the driver took us home.

....63. It's raining hard, but Jim won't stay at home.

....67. He told me to meet him at the Seneca Hotel but he didn't appear.

....76. We drove to St. Louis and then took a quaint old steamer down the Mississippi River.

7. Use commas to separate expressions like "he said" from a direct quotation. Indirect quotations should not be so separated.

.... 2. She exclaimed, "What a beautiful lake!"

.... 6. "Tell me what Doctor Harris did," said Emily.

.... 7. "If that's all," John said, "we may as well go."

....18. She said that she intended to visit Mount Baker.

....29. "We are," said the speaker, "at the dawn of a new era."

....44. She said that he would be glad to see you.

....47. He said that he saw the Prince of Wales, but no one believed him.

....48. "Please come," she wrote, "Colonel Brown will be here."

....56. "You should talk to Professor Brown," she advised.

....62. "That youngster," said Coach Jones, "will be a star next year."

....69. "All right," he said, "we'll put the money in the Chase Bank."

8. Use commas to separate the parts of a date or an address.

.... 1. Are you going to Strassburg, Germany?

....11. She lives at 25 Whittier Street, Dolby, Kentucky.

....24. The letter was sent from Detroit on August 8, 1933.

9. Use a semicolon between the clauses of a compound sentence when the clauses are closely related in thought and not joined by a conjunction. A semicolon is usually used where a period might be used, that is, between independent clauses.

....17. He started to Newburg; there was no retreat.

....21. The ring is an heirloom; it belonged to Jenny Lind.

....27. I use Detoxal; it is a good tooth paste.

....38. His wife is a Presbyterian; he is a Baptist.

....40. The National Railway Association should recognize that this type of engine will not pay; it is out of date.

....51. Its hair is fine and soft; it's still just a puppy.

....58. One of us must go to Lisbon; which will it be?

....59. John makes high grades in mathematics; he wants to enter Harvard College next year.

....60. You'll find it easier to go by way of Athens; you'll save twenty miles.

....72. Joseph Conrad is the author of Lord Jim; he also wrote Victory.

10. Use a semicolon between clauses of a compound sentence when the second clause is introduced by so, then, however, thus, hence, therefore, also, moreover, still, otherwise, nevertheless, accordingly, besides.

....13. He attended Tate College; then he went to a law school.

....32. John finished his Spanish; then he worked on biology.

....37. We didn't have time to visit the Alps; still we saw almost every other part of Europe.

....61. I'm too tired to go out tonight; besides it's too cold.

....71. You may take this note to Mr. Adams; then drop these letters in the mailbox.

....77. I'll take you in the car; otherwise you'll be late.

11. Use a colon after a complete independent clause which formally introduces one of the following: a list or enumeration, a statement or question, or a long quotation.

....14. My subjects include the following: history, English and Latin.

....28. Sinclair Lewis wrote these books: Dodsworth, Babbitt, and Arrowsmith.

....53. You will like these movies: Cimarron and Masquerade.

12. Use quotation marks to enclose all direct quotations and all parts of direct quotations that are divided.

.... 2. She exclaimed, "What a beautiful lake!"

.... 6. "Tell me what Doctor Harris did," said Emily.

.... 7. "If that's all," John said, "we may as well go."

....29. "We are," said the speaker, "at the dawn of a new era."

....48. "Please come," she wrote, "Colonel Brown will be here."

....56. "You should talk to Professor Brown," she advised.

....62. "That youngster," said Coach Jones, "will be a star next year."

....69. "All right," he said, "we'll put the money in the Chase Bank."

13. Use quotation marks to enclose the titles of poems, short stories, essays, chapters in books, or other parts of books, musical compositions, pictures, statues. Titles of books, movies, newspapers, pamphlets, periodicals, and poems of book length should only be underlined or italicized.

....20. This poem is called "In the Cool of the Night."

....28. Sinclair Lewis wrote these books: *Dodsworth, Babbitt,* and *Arrowsmith.*

....33. "By a Waterfall" is a simple little piece to play.

....34. He read Tennyson's poem, "In Memoriam."

....52. "I'm in a Hurry" is the name of an amusing short story.

....53. You will like these movies: *Cimarron* and *Masquerade.*

....70. I'll send you a subscription to the *Literary Digest.*

....72. Joseph Conrad is the author of *Lord Jim;* he also wrote *Victory.*

14. Use an apostrophe in contractions to indicate omitted letters.

.... 5. . . . we'll . . .
.... 7. . . . that's . . .
....15. They're . . . we'll . . .
....37. . . . didn't . . .
....42. It's . . . can't . . .
....51. . . . it's . . .
....52. I'm . . .
....54. . . . o'clock . . .
....60. You'll . . . you'll . . .
....61. I'm . . . it's . . .
....63. It's . . . won't . . .
....66. . . . it's . . .
....67. . . . didn't . . .
....69. . . . we'll . . .
....70. I'll . . .
....73. . . . doesn't . . .
....77. I'll . . . you'll . . .

15. Use an apostrophe to indicate the possessive. When the singular or plural form does not end in s, add 's. When these end in s, place an apostrophe after the s if there is no new syllable in pronunciation. If a new syllable occurs, add 's. Possessive pronouns, *its, hers, his, yours, ours, theirs,* do not require the apostrophe.

....23. Esther, Jane, and Mary organized a *girl's* club.

....34. He read *Tennyson's* famous poem, "In Memoriam."

....38. *His* wife is a Presbyterian; he is a Baptist.

....51. *Its* hair is fine and soft; it's still just a puppy.

....78. Mary, you may describe General *Pershing's* plan.

....79. One goes to church on Easter to ease *one's* conscience, to wear *one's* new spring clothes, or to see what Mrs. Jones is wearing.

         Other examples: Dickens' works
                          Jones's house

SENTENCE STRUCTURE

1. A sentence should express a complete and independent thought. Do not write as a sentence a group of words which are only part of a sentence.

Which of the following examples in the test did you miss? 6, 12, 21, 25, 26, 28, 33, 36, 39.

2. A sentence should not contain superfluous words which make the sentence cumbersome.

Which of the following examples in the test did you miss? 1, 13, 38.

3. A series of thoughts loosely strung together by conjunctions is weak and ineffective. Also avoid a series of short choppy sentences when expressing a closely unified idea.

Which of the following examples in the test did you miss? 3, 9, 16, 19.

4. The reference of phrases and modifiers should be unmistakably and immediately clear. Normally they should be next to the part modified.

Which of the following examples in the test did you miss? 4, 7, 8, 17, 22, 27, 30, 35.

5. The reference of a pronoun to its antecedent should be unmistakably and immediately clear. Pronouns should be close enough to their antecedents so that there is no possibility of misunderstanding.

Which of the following examples in the test did you miss? 2, 5, 10, 18, 20, 29, 37, 40.

6. Give parallel structure to those parts of a sentence which are parallel in thought.

Which of the following examples in the test did you miss? 11, 14, 15, 23, 24, 31, 32, 34.

Summary of Principles Violated Most Often

List below, as a series of phrases, the rules which you missed most often on these tests. These should form the primary basis for your remedial efforts.

Program for Improvement

The above analysis probably shows that work on only a few rules will raise your percentile rank quite a few points. On the other hand, you have been many years building your present language habits, so it will take definite and specific practice on your part to substitute correct language habits for these few types of errors. Not only must you know a rule, but you must also practice using it.

The following remedial suggestions are made:

1. Study the rules causing you the most difficulty.

2. Substitute the correct form for each of the errors that you have made.

3. Make a special effort to practice using the correct form in your everyday writing.

4. Regularly reread what you have written and look for instances where these few rules occur; correct any errors.

5. Have your counselor and teachers indicate incorrect forms which you use in your writing, then proceed to correct them.

6. When in doubt, use a source book on grammar.

Work hard in your English courses to remedy your difficulty. If your problem is extreme, you may wish to enroll in the special remedial English section which many colleges provide.

The primary consideration in improvement, however, is your own desire to improve; only this will lead you to be careful in your writing and to seek further practice.

Useful source books on grammar include:

J. C. Hodges, *Harbrace Handbook of English*, Harcourt, Brace, 1941. A complete handbook discussing all aspects of writing.

E. S. Jones, *Practice Handbook in English*, Appleton-Century, 1935. An excellent drillbook for further practice.

P. G. Perrin, *An Index to English*, Scott, Foresman, 1939. Very good. Problems in English presented in alphabetical order for easy reference.

C. Stratton, *Handbook of English*, McGraw-Hill, 1940. Specific words, constructions, grammatical terms, idioms, etc., arranged alphabetically. Can be used as a dictionary to check on specific questions.

B. Spelling

A student's occasional misspellings are important because their odd appearance distracts the reader's attention from the message and because people tend to judge the writer's cultural training on the basis of these errors. For example, many otherwise well-trained men have failed to obtain jobs because of misspellings in letters of application. Correct spelling is a skill which should have been learned before reaching college, but many students have not—as evidenced by the norms below. Furthermore, spelling ability doesn't tend to increase during the college years unless specific remedial steps are taken.[3]

Self-Evaluation

A spelling test, based on the 228 most frequently misspelled words as determined by combining several lists of common spelling errors, will be found in Appendix I on pages 233–241. This test is difficult in the sense that it consists only of "spelling demons." On the other hand, since each word also fits the criterion of being frequently used, a student should be able to spell practically all of them correctly. (A student may well omit learning any of the 228 words which he seldom, if ever, uses—looking them up in a dictionary takes less time.) When the test is completed, the key will be found on pages 258–260. Your success on the test (number right) may be judged against the following norms for college freshmen; but more important, you should be able to spell all these words which you use frequently.

[3] G. W. Hartmann, The constancy of spelling ability among undergraduates, *J. Educ. Res.*, 1931, 24:303–305.

Norms

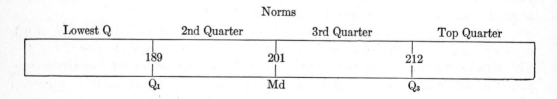

Lowest Q	2nd Quarter	3rd Quarter	Top Quarter
	189	201	212
	Q_1	Md	Q_3

To facilitate this study, use the space below to write the correct spelling of each of the words missed on this test.

You may also misspell other words which you use frequently. This is especially true of technical terms which are frequently used in your courses. Make a list below of these other words which are misspelled on your papers during the school term.

Program for Improvement

You should study the correct spelling of each of the words written in the spaces above. The most effective study method is actually to try spelling these words; don't just look at the list. Try visualizing the words (in every detail) on a flat surface in front of you, then look at the word to clear up any part that wasn't clearly visualized. Try spelling these words aloud or try writing them out. Above all, do not avoid these words in your everyday writing; make a special effort to use them correctly spelled.

Two additional ways to improve spelling have been suggested: locating the "hard spots" in words, and learning spelling rules. In many instances these methods have tended to involve more work than they were worth, but if they seem particularly applicable to many of your errors, it will be worth while for you to study this material further.

An analysis of spelling errors of college students showed that 90 per cent of the misspelled words had only one hard spot.[4] Thus a misspelled word should not be considered entirely wrong. Each of your misspellings should be analyzed to find the letter combination which needs particular attention. Furthermore, two-thirds of college students' misspellings were found to represent phonetic substitutions (other letters with the same sounds) or phonetic renditions of mispronunciations. Be sure you know the correct pronunciation of the words you misspell and pay particular attention to the places in the word which cause difficulty. Sometimes a little story or word game can be made up to help with these hard spots, e.g., remember the "sin" in "business."

The second approach is to learn spelling rules so as to have guides when spelling. The difficulty here is that most spelling rules have so many exceptions that many people feel it is easier not to bother, i.e., they just study the word in its correct form. The following seven rules, however, cover many spelling demons and have few exceptions.[5] Many "spelling errors" are actually failures to follow rules of capitalization (see Section A of this project). If many of your spelling errors are examples for some of these rules, these particular rules are well worth further study.

1. Most nouns form their plurals by adding s or es to the singular. Es is added to make the word easier to pronounce.

    Examples: *car, cars*

    pass, passes

    push, pushes

    porch, porches

2. Drop the final e before adding a suffix beginning with a vowel.

    Examples: *ride, riding*

    believe, believing

3. When final y is preceded by a consonant, change y to i before adding any suffix that does not begin with i.

    Examples: *satisfy, satisfied, satisfying*

    enjoy, enjoyable

4. Q is always followed by u

    Examples: *quiet, quick, quiver, quail*

5. *I* before *e*

    Except after *c*

    Or when sounded as $\bar{a}$

    As in *neighbor* and *weigh*

    Examples: *diet, receive, neigh*

6. The sound of i at the end of a word is usually spelled by the letter y.

    Examples: *many, very, heavy, steady*

7. With words of one syllable and with words accenting the last syllable and ending in one consonant preceded by one vowel, you double the final consonant

[4] T. G. Alper, A diagnostic spelling scale for the college level; its construction and use, *J. Educ. Psych.*, 1942, 33:273–290.

[5] T. G. Foran, *The Psychology and Teaching of Spelling*, Catholic Education Press, 1934; I. C. Sartorius, Generalization in spelling, *Teach. Coll. Contri. Educ.*, 1931, No. 472.

when adding a suffix beginning with a vowel.

Examples: *fun, funny*
omit, omitted

Many words are so infrequently used that it is not worth while to learn to spell them. And a student may occasionally experience a block in spelling words which he usually knows. In such instances, reach for a dictionary or ask a friend. For further information on use of the dictionary, see Section C of Project VII.

Additional information on learning to spell, e.g., the value of other rules and of knowledge of word roots, can be found in the following references:

> J. C. Hodges, *Harbrace Handbook of English*, Harcourt, Brace, 1941. Pages 176–190.
> E. S. Jones, *Practice Handbook in English*, Appleton-Century, 1940. Pages 163–174.
> F. Triggs and E. W. Robbins, *Improve Your Spelling*, Farrar & Rinehart, 1944.

C. HANDWRITING [6]

Experimental studies have shown that even though a teacher may endeavor not to count legibility of handwriting in his grading he actually will give higher marks for the more legible writing.[7] Legible handwriting makes for easier and more pleasant reading and is more convincing to the reader.

Many college students write so poorly (especially under pressure of speed in writing notes or quizzes) that instructors have difficulty in grading the papers. Two studies show that the average quality or legibility of college seniors' handwriting is *below* that of the average eighth-grader.[8]

Indeed, a student may occasionally even be unable to read his own writing. The purpose of the following exercise is to show how you may locate your most serious writing faults and deal with them. It will demonstrate how the difficulties of a particular individual usually center around a few recurring errors.

Writing is intended to be read. In considering the quality of a piece of handwriting, and still more in considering what faults in it may be serious and need attention, the practical approach is to determine what features of that writing interfere with ease and accuracy in reading it.

The chart below shows the result of research along this line. A large number of samples of handwriting of children, college students, and adults were gone over, the readers checking every place where they had any difficulty (even though only momentary) in reading what had been written. The places checked were then returned to, and the illegibilities analyzed and classified. These results were then brought together, and the most common illegibilities thus determined. You will notice that certain general characteristics cause trouble (such as crowding words together); but most difficulties are due to writing one letter so that it looks somewhat like another—writing *d* like *cl*, *a* like *u*, or *r* like an undotted *i*. With this chart before you, you can, much more easily than otherwise, locate and classify troublesome points in any piece of writing. Further experiment has shown that when such highly specific difficulties are located and effort is directed specifically toward the elimination of the few most common illegibilities, improvement in handwriting is relatively easily achieved.[9]

---

[6] With slight modification, from S. L. Pressey and M. E. Troyer, *Laboratory Workbook in Applied Educational Psychology*, Harper, 1945. Used with permission.

[7] H. W. James, The effect of handwriting upon grading, *Engl. J.*, 1927, 16:180–185.

[8] G. E. Hill, The handwriting of college seniors, *J. Educ. Res.*, 1943, 37:118–126; W. G. Wixted

and P. R. V. Curoe, How well do college seniors write? *School and Soc.*, 1941, 54:505–508.

[9] H. Lehman and L. C. Pressey, The effectiveness of drill in handwriting to remove specific illegibilities, *School and Soc.*, 1928, 27:546–548; W. S. Guiler, Improving handwriting ability, *Elem. Sch. J.*, 1930, 30:56–62.

ERROR ANALYSIS CHART

Illegibility	*Frequency*
Words crowded	
Too angular	
Rewriting	
Words broken	
Loops long	
a like u	
a ” o	
a ” ci	
b ” li	
c ” e	
c ” i	
d ” cl	
e closed	
e too high	
g like y	
h ” li	
h ” p	
h ” b	
h ” l	
i ” e	
Dot misplaced	
k like h	
l closed	
l too short	
m like w	
n ” u	
n ” v	
o ” a	
o ” r	
o closed	
r like i	
r ” s	
r half n	
r half u	
s indistinct	
s like r	
t ” l	
Cross omitted	
Cross misplaced	
M like N	
W like U	
l like cl	
Other illegibilities	

Total	
Two most common	

Explanations

Words crowded—too little space between words, so that word divisions are not readily seen.

Words broken—Breaks between parts of words so that word and syllable divisions are confused.

Loops long—such letters as *y* and *g* reach down into the line below or *h* and *l* into the line above.

e closed—*e* like undotted *i*.

l closed—*l* like uncrossed *t*.

h like *p*—the main difficulty here is a prolongation of the main down-stroke of the *h*.

r like half *n*—most likely in such combinations as *rr* like *n*.

r like undotted *i*—especially in such combinations as *ri* like *u*.

s indistinct—incomplete forms coming at the end of a word.

t like *l*—involves also omission or misplacement of cross bar.

Self-Evaluation

Self-evaluation procedure is simple.

1. Bring to class some sample of your handwriting at least 500 words long, written under ordinary conditions or under pressure of speed, as in writing a quiz or taking notes. Count the number of words from the beginning until you have 500; make a heavy cross after the five-hundredth word. Then have some other student who is not familiar with your writing read quickly over the material up to the cross; tell him to underline (not mark over) any letter, combination of letters, or place which caused even *momentary difficulty* in reading. (This project will be done in class.) The grader should keep in mind, however, that he is not to mark angularities, irregularities, or peculiarities, or writing which makes the appearance unattractive or unusual as long as they do not interfere with reading. The analysis is for illegibility, not beauty. In case of doubt a place should not be marked. The marked places should represent real hindrances to easy reading.

2. In consultation with the reader, so that you may know what his difficulties in reading were, go over these marked places, and determine in each instance what specific feature of your writing caused trouble. As you proceed, make a tabulation mark on the error analysis chart. Thus if the first difficulty was a like u, put a mark beside this item; if the next illegibility was due to crowding words together at the end of a line, put a tally mark after "words crowded"; if the next was another a like u, put another mark after this item. If you find an illegibility not listed in the chart, write it on one of the lines at the bottom of the chart, and put a tally mark after it.

3. Count the number of marks after each item and write these numbers to the right. Then add, giving the total number of your illegibilities, and write this figure in the "total" row.

4. Draw a circle around the figures for your two most common illegibilities. How many of your total illegibilities are due to these two? Write the number in the row marked "two most common." If you were to cure yourself of these two most common faults, what proportion of the total number of your illegibilities would you dispose of?

5. In actual practice the handwriting of the average student will receive about 27 checks per 500 words. Student scribbling, however, is not a high standard toward which to aim. A much better goal is to try to write so that your handwriting causes little or no difficulty in reading. Illegibilities should be reduced to a minimum.

Program for Improvement

Have you found that only a few letter forms are causing most of the difficulty? If so, a little care in forming these few letters will do a great deal toward improving your handwriting. You will have to try this in all writing situations, however, if you are to expect improvement in your everyday writing. Make it a regular practice to proofread your writing in order to correct illegibilities. And finally, have another person check later samples of your handwriting for illegibilities so that you may have a measure of improvement and a further indication of remaining errors.

To facilitate your remembering to be careful in your writing, indicate below which letters you will try to improve.

PROJECT IX

MATHEMATICS

Mathematical operations are basic in solving problems and doing laboratory work in most subjects. Many students, however, are not proficient even in some of the most elementary skills. Thus Arnold found that 10 per cent of entering freshmen were unable to do a single one of twenty problems in long division, 18 per cent could not multiply common fractions, and 20 per cent could not divide decimal fractions.[1]

Self-Evaluation

If there is a need for mathematics in any of your courses, the following test should be taken to point out places needing remediation. This test is based on analyses of the mathematical skills which are most frequently used in college subjects and which teachers consider essential for work in these fields. Because of the bases used for selecting the test items, a student should get every one correct. If a student misses both examples of a given process, he should give

[1] H. J. Arnold, The standing of college students in two elementary school subjects, *Research Adventures in University Teaching*, Public School Publ. Co., 1929, pp. 107–112; see also G. M. Wilson and M. B. Kite, Arithmetic deficiencies, *J. Higher Educ.*, 1943, 14:321–322.

definite remedial attention to it. The key for this test is on page 246 in Appendix II.

Number right ....

Program for Improvement

Any error made represents an item that you should know. Rather than being "altogether poor" in mathematics you have probably found that just a few processes are giving you difficulty. With such specific diagnostic information, your remedial efforts can be effectively focused on particular difficulties. If you have great difficulty with this test or with other aspects of mathematics and these areas are necessary in your work, you probably ought to enroll in a basic mathematics course in order to obtain this background.

Since elementary chemistry is one of the common places where students have difficulty because of mathematics, the following reference may be of help in explaining the necessary mathematics for chemistry problems.

P. R. Frey, *An Outline of Mathematics for General Chemistry*, Barnes and Noble, 1944, 3rd ed., 143 pp.

BASIC SKILLS IN MATHEMATICS

(1) 448	(2) 484	(3) 27831	(4) 73821	(5) 2784	(6) 4287
372	273	− 9246	− 6249	× 385	× 379
981	189				
365	563				

(7) $17157 \div 86$ ....

(8) $22989 \div 79$ ....

(9) $\frac{5}{8} + \frac{1}{5}$ ....

(10) $\frac{4}{5} + \frac{3}{4}$ ....

(11) $\frac{5}{7} - \frac{2}{3}$ ....   (14) $\frac{2}{5} \times \frac{3}{4}$ ....

(12) $\frac{5}{6} - \frac{3}{4}$ ....   (15) $\frac{1}{3} \div \frac{4}{7}$ ....

(13) $\frac{4}{7} \times \frac{3}{4}$ ....   (16) $\frac{3}{5} \div \frac{3}{4}$ ....

(17) $9.20 + 16. + .0071 + 1.275 + .7265$ ....

(18) $.0026 + 1.89 + .2478 + 86. + 1.002$ ....

(19) $3. - 1.8306$ ....   (21) $3.702 \times .207$ ....

(20) $2. - 1.7058$ ....   (22) $1.008 \times .074$ ....

(23) $.0036 \div 1.2$ ....   (25) What % is 5 of 8? ....

(24) $3.05 \div .61$ ....   (26) What % is 12 of 17? ....

(27) How is 20% written as a common fraction? ....

(28) How is 50% written as a common fraction? ....

(29) How is 20% written as a decimal fraction? ....

(30) How is 50% written as a decimal fraction? ....

(31–35) Write the squares of the following numbers from memory:

      7 .... 8 .... 9 .... 11 ....12 ....

(36) $1\frac{3}{4} \times 8 =$ ....   (37) $2\frac{1}{2} \times 16 =$ ....
(38) 20% of 50 = ...   (39) 110% of 10 = ...

Reduce these expressions to their simplest forms by cancellation and then express their answers as decimals to two places:

(40) $\dfrac{5 \times 7 \times 44}{50 \times 77} =$ ....   (41) $\dfrac{35}{560} \times \dfrac{48}{54} \times 20 =$ ....

(42) $\dfrac{.28 \times 5.6 \times 0.77}{1.1 \times 1.12 \times 140} =$ ....   (43) $\dfrac{0.45}{9} \times \dfrac{108}{1.05} \times \dfrac{.07}{1.2} =$ ....

In the following proportions, fill in the missing terms:

(44) $\frac{3}{6} = \frac{?}{10}$ ....   (45) $\frac{4}{?} = \frac{6}{12}$ ....

(46) $\frac{4}{2} = \frac{12}{?}$ ....   (47) $\frac{?}{15} = \frac{12}{36}$ ....

The next three problems deal with simple relations in chemistry for which the following sample can act as a model. These are problems in proportion just like the ones above.

$C +$ O_2 $\longrightarrow$ CO_2
12    $2 \times 16 = 32$ $12 + 32 = 44$ (These numbers underneath show the atomic weights and resulting molecular weight of CO_2. The ratio of carbon entering CO_2 to the total weight produced is $\frac{12}{44}$; that of O is $\frac{32}{44}$.)

(48) If the reaction is begun with 36 grams of C, how much CO_2 will be produced?

    That is, $\dfrac{12 \text{ g}}{44 \text{ g}} = \dfrac{36 \text{ g}}{? \text{ g}}$ $? =$ ....g

(49) How many g of O will be used to produce this?   ....g

(50) If it is desired to produce 88 g of CO_2, how much C will be needed?   ....g

PART THREE

PROBLEM AREAS INDIRECTLY AFFECTING EFFECTIVE STUDY

The problems discussed in the following projects, while not directly related to study skills, tend to decrease college efficiency by lowering general efficiency or by distracting the student from his work. Students whose health is poor work less efficiently and are distraught by worries concerning their physical condition. Students who have not made a definite vocational decision may not be highly motivated; they often worry lest, when they do make this decision, their present effort will have been wasted. Students who fear they lack social status among their fellows, or who are worried about more personal problems, are usually so upset that their work suffers. The solution of these problems is worth while in itself, and it will also permit more effective study. These problem areas are therefore the topics of projects in this section.

PROJECT X

HEALTH AND HEALTH HABITS

The value of good health is recognized by everyone. Poor health can be the basis for inefficiency or outright failure in college. Without good health one may lose that zest for living which makes for success, personal happiness, and social adjustment; and one may have in its place only discomfort and inertia.

Surveys of the population indicate that many people have health problems for which little has been done because of indifference or lack of awareness of the problems. Because of this, your college maintains a well-organized health service for your benefit— to point out your problems and to give corrective aid. You should make use of it. This project will not attempt to suggest remedial health procedures to you; that advice should come from health authorities. However, this project does include several means of aiding you in thinking about your health problems; the counselor will assist you in arranging for conferences with any of the health services.

Health Status

1. Do you know the results of your physical examination on entering college? Were any suggestions made at that time? You can find out by inquiring at the college's health service. Do you know the results of your other health examinations such as hearing and posture tests?

2. Have you had a complete physical examination lately? Every person should have such a checkup at regular intervals no matter how well he feels—potential causes of ill health may be detected and cured. If you have not, it would be well to see your family physician for a checkup. The cost is usually not very great.

3. The Betts or Snellen Vision Tests are general tests for finding those people who may need further examination by an eye specialist. Recommendations for glasses cannot be made on the basis of these tests, but they are a means of determining quickly whether you ought to have further testing. If you want to take such a test, ask the counselor to give it to you.

4. The following health questionnaire is useful in directing your thinking about health problems that you have had. Check it according to the directions. It is "normal" to check several, and interpretation should be made only in consultation with your counselor.

HEALTH QUESTIONNAIRE[1]

by

S. L. Pressey and M. E. Troyer
Ohio State University.

Total Crosses............

Name................................. Sex: M F............ Date....................

Directions: Below is a list of common ailments and symptoms, physical handicaps, undesirable health habits, or conditions affecting health. For your convenience in considering them, the items have been roughly grouped. You are to put a cross before each symptom, ailment, habit, or handicap you have had within the past twelve months. Put two crosses before each one which has been acute or caused you much concern. Begin at once. Be as accurate as you can. If you are uncertain about a symptom, do not mark it.

Symptoms, Diseases, and Handicaps

Sensory

...... 1. pain in the eyes

...... 2. headache after reading

...... 3. watering of the eyes

...... 4. difficulty in seeing clearly at a distance

...... 5. blurring or moving of letters when reading

...... 6. spots before eyes

...... 7. deafness

...... 8. earache or pain back of ears

...... 9. discharging ears

Respiratory

......10. frequent or continuing colds

......11. chronic cough

......12. nosebleed

......13. tonsillitis

......14. bronchitis

......15. frequent discharge in throat

......16. sinus trouble

......17. hay fever

......18. asthma

Digestive

......19. chronic or frequent indigestion

......20. poor appetite

......21. coated tongue

......22. bad breath

......23. gas in stomach

......24. pain or burning sensations in stomach

......25. attacks of nausea

......26. attacks of vomiting

......27. intestinal cramps

......28. diarrhea

......29. constipation

......30. piles or hemorrhoids

......31. appendicitis

Do not stop. Turn over the page and continue work.

[1] From S. L. Pressey and M. E. Troyer, *Laboratory Workbook in Applied Educational Psychology,* **Harper,** **1945,** used with permission.

Nervous

......32. chorea or St. Vitus's dance

......33. slowness and sluggishness

......34. chronic fatigue

......35. moodiness or depression

......36. tenseness, inability to relax

......37. difficulty in concentration

......38. restlessness

......39. nervousness and jumpiness

......40. habitual daydreaming

......41. stuttering or stammering

......42. marked forgetfulness

......43. fainting

......44. fearfulness or phobia

......45. twitching of face or eyelids

......46. dizziness

......47. attacks of laughter or crying

......48. attacks of excitement

Health Habits

......49. no fruit or vegetable daily

......50. less than eight glasses of water, milk, or other liquid daily

......51. fried food daily

......52. frequent eating between meals

......53. irregular or omitted meals

......54. over-exercise

......55. lack of exercise

......56. insomnia—sleeplessness

......57. restless sleep

......58. inadequate or irregular sleep

......59. going to sleep at work or school

......60. heavy smoking

......61. heavy coffee drinking

......62. use of alcoholic drinks

......63. poor ventilation in bedroom or study room

......64. poor lighting in study room

Miscellaneous

......65. decayed teeth

......66. rheumatism

......67. pain in joints

......68. mastoid

......69. backache

......70. cramps, numbness, or swelling in hands or feet

......71. pimples or eruptions

......72. goiter or enlargement of neck

......73. "palpitation of the heart"

......74. hammering in throat or head

......75. pain over the heart

......76. shortness of breath

......77. severe headaches

......78. overweight

......79. underweight

......80. injuries or lameness due to accident or illness

......81. night sweats

......82. tendency toward tuberculosis

......83. kidney trouble

......84. bladder trouble

......85. hernia (rupture)

......86. painful or irregular menses

1. List below any symptoms, ailments, undesirable health habits, or handicaps not included in the list above, with which you have been troubled during the past twelve months.

. . . .

. . . .

2. Is there anything important not mentioned above, in your "health history"? If so, please mention it briefly below. Have you had any accidents, any operations? Any severe illnesses prior to the past twelve months and so not mentioned above? Have you any physical handicap? If so, what is the nature of it?

. . . .

. . . .

. . . .

. . . .

. . . .

3. Symptoms may be due to various causes. For example, dizziness or fainting may be due to indigestion; or indigestion may be due to emotional excitement (the grouping of items given above is thus very rough). What is your understanding of the nature and causes of any symptoms you may have?

. . . .

. . . .

. . . .

. . . .

4. If you have any "health problem," what have you done about it? Thus if you have trouble with your eyes, have you had them examined recently? By whom? Have you recently had a thorough physical examination by a physician? By whom? What were the findings? What was recommended? Have you followed these recommendations?

. . . .

. . . .

. . . .

. . . .

. . . .

What to Do About Health Problems

1. See a health specialist competent to advise you on your problem. It may be your family physician, a member of the staff of the college health service, or some other specialist.

2. A person can rarely obtain enough information from reading for self-treatment but the following are interesting readings on health habits and on the importance of health.

Health Problems in College:

   H. S. Diehl, *The Health of College Students,* Amer. Council on Educ., 1939. Pages 95–103. Tables of health problems in college.

Posture:

   J. Lane, *Your Carriage, Madam!* Wiley, 1934. An interesting book on posture.

Relaxation:

   E. Jacobson, *You Must Relax,* McGraw-Hill, 1934. A short readable book on the effect of being nervous and tense, with practical suggestions on how to overcome these tendencies.
   J. L. Rathbone, *Relaxation,* Teachers College, 1944. Chaps. 1–4.

Health Habits:

   H. S. Diehl, *Healthful Living,* McGraw-Hill, 1941.
   W. R. P. Emerson, *Health for the Having,* Macmillan, 1944.
   J. F. Williams, *Personal Hygiene Applied,* Saunders, 1941, 7th ed.

3. In consultation with your counselor, list below the steps that you are taking to acquire better health.

PROJECT XI

VOCATIONAL ORIENTATION

Students may work inefficiently in college because they worry over what vocation to prepare for or because they are poorly motivated without a definite vocational goal. Assistance with your vocational planning may remove this as a distraction and increase your motivation for study.

Psychologists cannot determine the specific vocation which a person should enter, but they can help the student to see his abilities, knowledge, and interests and the demands of various occupations. Further, they can assist him to clarify his thinking in terms of these two fields of knowledge and can show him job-hunting techniques. The final decision of job selection, however, must be left to the student. That many students do not know their own abilities or the demands of various occupations is shown by the following facts: many high-school students with quite low intellectual ability want to prepare for professions requiring high intelligence, and about 40 per cent of high-school seniors indicate a desire to enter professions which can absorb only about 3 per cent of the population.

Sometimes students who do not have the pattern of abilities demanded by a given occupation persist in seeking an impossible goal and find only unhappiness and failure. If such a student feels that to alter his vocational choice at his age is a sign of poor planning on his part, it need only be pointed out that to change vocational choice is typical of the student age. Studies of several thousand high-school students show that over half of them change their vocational choice sometime during their four years in high school.[1] A study at the University of Minnesota showed that about 24 per cent of the freshmen felt "uncertain" or "very uncertain" of their vocational choice.[2] And a study of persons listed in *Who's Who in America* showed that 16 per cent had changed their vocations at least twice.[3]

Colleges maintain machinery for assisting students to change majors with the least loss, and, if the students have abilities in non-academic lines, to take up training outside of college. It is a mistaken notion to believe that it is a disgrace not to attend college or to leave when not doing well. The intelligent person, in this case, will realize that the college may not be able to give him what he needs and he will seek a better source of preparation for his preferred occupation.

Self-Evaluation

This project is a means of studying your abilities and the characteristics of various occupations. Its purpose is to assist you in coordinating the two in the best possible way.

1. What is your scholastic ability? ......
.........percentile. Your Scholastic Apti-

[1] A. R. Crathorne, Changes of mind between high school and college as to life work, *Educ. Adm. and Superv.*, 1920, 6:274–284; A. A. Douglass, Vocational interest of high school seniors, *School and Soc.*, 1922, 16:79–84.
[2] E. G. Williamson, *How to Counsel Students*, McGraw-Hill, 1939, p. 409.
[3] H. D. Kitson and L. Culbertson, The vocational changes of one thousand eminent Americans, *Nat. Voc. Guid. Bull.*, 1923, 1:128–130.

tude Examination ranking can be obtained from the counselor.

This test is especially constructed for predicting college success. Tables 8 and 9 illustrate to what degree these test results actually are related to college success at Ohio State University. Table 8 shows that brighter students are more apt to stay in school and to get better grades, but over two-thirds of the lowest group stay in school and some of them make outstanding grades. Similarly Table 9 shows that graduating students are about five times as apt to come from the top fifth as from the bottom fifth, but many in the bottom fifth do graduate.

TABLE 8.   The Per Cent of University Freshmen in Each Third (Approximate) on the Ohio State Psychological Examination That Made Various Grade Records at the End of One Year's Residence [4]

O.S.P.E. Percentile	Grade Point Average				
	Drop Out	0.0–.99	1.00–1.99	2.00–2.99	3.00–3.99
66–100	21%	2%	17%	41%	19%
30–65	24%	4%	36%	32%	14%
1–29	39%	3%	42%	15%	1%

TABLE 9.   Level of Intelligence of Students Getting Degrees from a Large University Over a Ten-Year Period. The Per Cents Indicate the Proportion of the Graduating Class in That Fifth. (Based on Unpublished Data of H. A. Toops and R. H. Bittner.)

Graduates' Level of Intelligence on Entrance to University	Degrees Earned				
	B. Arts	B.S. in Educ.	B. Engin.	B. Laws	M.D.
Top fifth	39%	31%	32%	41%	32%
Fourth fifth	25	25	24	23	27
Middle fifth	17	21	21	15	19
Second fifth	12	17	13	14	15
Bottom fifth	7	6	10	7	7
	100%	100%	100%	100%	100%

Another way of indicating the degree of relationship between scholastic ability and grades is to say that if one knows a student's score on such an ability test, he can predict the student's grades with about 20 per cent less error than just guessing. There are, therefore, many other factors affecting grades. Students with high ability scores tend to make good grades, but if such students do not work efficiently they may receive quite low grades. Students with low ability scores tend to have more difficulty with school work but with efficient study skills and hard work many of them succeed quite well.

Such an ability test will not indicate whether or not you will succeed in your chosen field. Its results only indicate the probabilities of success or failure. But such information is useful since a student will not want to spend years in struggling

[4] H. A. Edgerton, A study of elimination of O. S. U. students in relation to intelligence, *Ohio College Assoc. Bull.,* "S," p. 107.

preparation where there may be only a slim chance of success.

A person with a low percentile should realize two other points: (a) College students in the lowest deciles tend to be above the average of the general population in the ability to do scholastic work but they are in competition with a highly selected group in college. And (b) a low percentile on such a test is not necessarily a measure of other important abilities, such as running a business, making friends, etc.

If you are interested in other types of ability tests, ask your counselor about them, i.e., tests of mechanical, musical, and artistic ability.

2. Interests are a second factor which should be considered in choosing a vocation. Do you know what fields are of greatest interest to you? Do you know what occupational group your pattern of interests most resembles? The evidence indicates that a person will be most successful in the occupation where his interests and outlook on life coincide with those of active members of that occupation. The Strong Vocational Interest Test indicates which occupational groups a person's interests tend to resemble the most. The Kudor Preference Record also indicates a person's profile of interests. If you would like to take either of these tests, ask your counselor for a copy. Other rough measures of your interests include the courses in high school and college which you have liked best and least.

On the basis of these different measures, list here the occupational areas which are of primary interest to you:

3. Previous work and hobby experiences not only provide a basis for deciding whether or not you like a field of work, but the actual experience provides a head start if a related occupation is taken up. For instance, a person who has lived on a farm has such a fund of knowledge that many Colleges of Veterinary Medicine give prime emphasis to such previous experience in their entrance requirements.

Make a list here of *all* the previous work (paid and unpaid) and hobby experiences you have had which might contribute to an appreciation of, and a preparation for, a field of work.

Which Job Is Best? The above information provides some bases for choosing a vocation. The next step is to integrate these data so that the relative suitability of different types of jobs can be more easily seen. Most students usually have several occupations in mind which they feel more or less fit their abilities, interests, and previous experiences. They often wonder, however, for which one they are best suited or if there might be another, as yet unconsidered, job which would be best. The following work sheets can help answer this problem just as putting down numbers on paper helps in solving a mathematical problem. This exercise is not a magic formula; it only helps marshal the evidence so that you can think about it more clearly.

THINKING ABOUT JOBS

This exercise falls into three steps: First, you briefly appraise your background of abilities, skills, interests, and opportunities; the questions for this are on the left-hand side of the page. Second, you compare these appraisals with the demands of the jobs of the most interest to you. And third, you analyze these results.

Step 1. Answer each question on the left-hand side of the page with brief cue phrases which will act as reminders in *Step 2.* Some of the questions merely refer to material you have already filled out in this project.

Step 2. Write the names of the two or three jobs in which you are most interested at the top of the columns on the right below. Put one job name in each column. Now read how you have rated yourself on each trait at the left and judge whether it will be important in determining your success for each of the three jobs listed. If the trait is of no importance for a given job, i.e., "physical strength and size" would not be important for becoming an "accountant," mark a zero (0) in that job column opposite the trait. If the trait is of some importance in a given job, then judge whether your relative proficiency in it will be an asset or a liability. If you are above average in such an important trait, put a plus (+) in the column for that job; if you are outstandingly good in that trait, put a double plus (++) in that column. If you are deficient in such an important trait, put a minus (−) in that job column, or if you are particularly deficient in that trait, put a double minus (− −) in that column. If the trait is important, but you are only about average in comparison to your probable competition, put a zero (0) in the job column. Each trait is rated in this way for each of the jobs.

Step 3. When this rating is completed, add up the number of pluses and the number of minuses which each job receives. The difference between these two sums represents a rough score for a job which can be compared to the scores for the other jobs. Additional directions are given at the end of these work sheets.

STEP 1. HOW DO I RATE?	STEP 2. HOW IS MY RATING RELATED TO EACH OF THESE JOBS?		
	Job #1	Job #2	Job #3
Personal characteristics (answer each query relative to others entering occupations):			
Age? young ....; average ....; older			
Physical size and strength?			
Motor skill and coordination?			
Physical appearance and "looks"?			
Intelligence?			
School marks?			
Skill in making friends?			
Skill in speaking and writing?			
Pattern of interests (refer above to analysis made of vocational interests)?			
Special abilities and skills? Write them down:			
Personal attitudes (check the one phrase in each series which best describes you):			
Like to work: with people ....; around people ....; alone			
Like: outdoor work ....; industrial work ....; clerical work ....; professional work			
Prefer: job security ....; chance to make high income even though success is a gamble			
Interested more in: amount earned ....; service to society			
Want to be: near home town ....; don't care where			
Want to live in: country ....; small town ....; city			
Want to: make own work plans ....; have jobs assigned			
Preparation:			
Amount of schooling I plan to take?			
Subjects I liked best?			
Subjects I liked least?			
Previous work experiences (refer to list made earlier)?			

Present and past hobbies (refer to list made earlier)?

Other types of training? List them here:

Social situation and opportunities:

Family status (any dependents)?

Prejudice against race or religion?

Relative frequency with which you are chosen for positions of leadership?

Are there special job opportunities where you live or are well acquainted?

Do you have good "connections" to help you get started in any occupation?

Do you have enough money for further training?

Are these jobs overcrowded? Are any related jobs less crowded?

Do the opportunities for advancement in these jobs suit you?

       Total number of pluses

       Total number of minuses

          Sum

Step 3. Does one of these jobs receive a particularly high "sum score" in comparison to the others? This would tend to indicate that that particular job is the best of the three. Does the high-scoring job have quite a few minuses marked? If so, another job might be better suited to you. Go back to the place where various types of work experience and opportunities are listed and see if some other job is suggested.

List here the one or two occupations of most interest to you. Is your present college program suited for preparing you for these occupations?

Do You Know Much About Your Chosen Occupation? Most students know very little about the jobs they are considering for their future vocation! Students typically overestimate the average income in their chosen field by 100 per cent to 200 per cent; they know little about the actual activities demanded on the job, and they have scant knowledge of the factors leading to promotion and the speed with which it takes place. (Table 14 and Chart 18 in the Special Reading Skills Test in Appendix I provide some related information of interest here.) Can you answer the following questions concerning your top-scoring job?

1. What is the average income five years after entering?

2. What steps have to be taken or what jobs held before you get to the job you want?

3. How crowded is the field in your chosen occupation?

4. How much training does it take?

5. How much money does it take to get started?

6. What are the opportunities for further advancement?

7. Is the occupation stable, growing, seasonal, or on the decline?

8. What are the duties of this job? Which are the hardest to perform?

9. What are the hazards of the job?

10. What is a person's status on the job when he reaches forty or fifty years of age? Increased opportunities? Little change? Decreased opportunities?

Specific information concerning occupations of interest can be obtained from the occupational bibliography at the end of this project. The following general references on the whole field of work may also be of interest:

H. D. Anderson and P. E. Davidson, *American Job Trends*, Occupational Monograph No. 22, Science Research Associates, 1941.

H. M. Bell, *Matching Youth and Jobs*, Amer. Council on Educ., 1940.

H. F. Clark, *Life Earnings*, Harper, 1937.

Getting the Job and Getting Ahead. Vocational guidance includes more than helping a student decide what occupation he wants to enter. He also needs to know about job hunting techniques and some of the factors which make for success.

Even when jobs are plentiful and workers scarce, there is competition for the best jobs. Knowledge of how to go about finding good jobs and applying for them gives a person a decided edge over others not prepared. An excellent and practical discussion of this problem will be found in I. M. Dreese, *How to Get THE Job*, Occupational Monograph #19, Science Research Associates, 1941.

Once on the job, a person wants to make good. Almost everyone realizes that he must understand the business so as to be prepared for greater responsibilities, but most people do not realize that managers consider certain personality traits by far the most important! This is illustrated by several studies. In the first, the American Council on Education asked the personnel and employment officers of some of America's largest business and industrial concerns to list the ten traits most needed for job success.[5] They listed the following:

> *Character:* marked by honesty, dependability, and courage. A square shooter.
> *Enjoyment of work:* gets satisfaction from digging in and doing a task. Begins with vigor and continues until a task is done. Enthusiasm for job.
> *Initiative:* awareness and imagination in seeing things to do.
> *Mental alertness:* intelligence, inquiring mind, ability to think.
> *Judgment:* ability to make wise decisions, people have confidence in judgment.

[5] From *Wanted: A Job*, Amer. Council on Educ., 1939.

> *Getting along with people:* enjoys being with people, sense of humor, able to obtain willing cooperation, liked by people.
> *Health:* vitality, energy, enthusiasm for work and play. Not ill.
> *Appearance and manner:* creates a good impression, neat, expresses self well.
> *Ambition and objectives:* knows the type of job he wants and will be able to fill. Desire to advance.
> *Social and community responsibilities:* participates in group and community activities, attempts to improve community.

In other studies, analyses have been made of the reasons why some people are not promoted and others are fired.[6] They show that two-thirds or more of the instances of non-promotion or firing a worker were due to problems of personality and social adjustment; only for about one-third were lack of technical skill and background the causes. The following are typical of the personality difficulties found: insubordination, unreliability, absenteeism, laziness, troublemaking, and carelessness.

On the positive side of building helpful personal characteristics, the following readings are interesting:

A. Buchanan, *Lady Means Business*, Simon & Schuster, 1943.
P. W. Chapman, *Your Personality and Your Job*, Occupational Monographs No. 31, Science Research Associates, 1942.
F. Maule, *Girl with a Pay Check*, Harper, 1942.

Your counselor will be glad to assist you with any aspect of the problem of vocational guidance.

[6] J. M. Brewer, Causes for discharge, *Personnel J.*, 1927, 6:171–172; J. J. Gibson, Purchasing power of personality, *J. Bus. Educ.*, 1938, 14:9–10.

BIBLIOGRAPHY OF RECENT VOCATIONAL INFORMATION

Occupations are arranged below in alphabetical order. The letters and numbers which follow each title have the following significance: The letters "A" through "H" stand for different monographs and the letters "J" through "Q" stand for different books to which frequent reference is made.[7] A number following a symbol for a monograph series stands for the number or issue which deals with that occupation. The number following a symbol for a book indicates the page on which the discussion of that occupation begins. In instances where good books on an occupation have recently been published, these are also listed directly.

The several references for a given occupation tend to duplicate each other; the reader should select the one or two which seem best and which are available.

[7] The key to the symbols used is as follows:

A. Science Research Associates, *American Job Series, Occupational Monographs*, 1939–. Each about 50 pp. long.

B. Science Research Associates, *Occupational Outlines on America's Major Occupations*, 1940–. Each 4 pp. long.

C. Science Research Associates, *Occupational Briefs of Postwar Job Fields*, 1943–. Each 4 pp. long.

D. Institute for Research, *Careers, Research Monographs*, 1930–. Each about 25 pp. long.

E. U. S. Office of Education, *Guidance Leaflets*, 1932–. Each about 15 pp. long.

F. Occupational Index, Inc., *Occupational Abstracts*, 1936–. Each about 6 pp. long.

G. Western Personnel Service, *Occupational Briefs*, 1939–. Each about 12 pp. long.

H. Bellman Publ. Co., *Vocational and Professional Monographs*. Each 16 or more pp. long.

J. J. Brewer and E. Landy, *Occupations Today*, Ginn, 1943.

K. W. Campbell and J. Bedford, *You and Your Future Job*, Soc. Occup. Research, 1944.

L. M. Davey, E. Smith, and T. Myers, *Everyday Occupations*, Heath, 1941.

M. F. Maule, *Careers for the Home Economist*, Funk, 1943.

N. P. Pollock, *Careers in Science*, Dutton, 1945.

P. E. Steele, *Careers for Girls in Science and Engineering*, Dutton, 1943.

Q. D. Huff and F. Huff, *Twenty Careers of Tomorrow*, McGraw-Hill, 1945.

Accounting: B 29, 31; C 6; D 4, 98, 103; F; G; H 7; J 120; K 93; L 357.
T. W. Byrnes and K. L. Baker, *Do You Want to Be an Accountant?* Stokes, 1940.
L. W. Scudder, *Accountancy as a Career*, Funk, 1941, rev. ed.

Advertising: A 9; C 129; D 17, 133, 134; H 10, 24; J 130; K 118.
A. Broughton, *Careers in Public Relations*, Dutton, 1943.
B. Clair and D. Dignam, *Advertising Careers for Women*, Harper, 1939.
D. De Schweinitz, *Occupations in Retail Stores*, International, 1941.
W. A. Lowen and L. E. Watson, *How to Get a Job and Win Success in Advertising*, Prentice-Hall, 1941.

Agents and Credit Workers: B 30; C 72; D 95.

Agriculture: A 15, 18; B 21, 22, 23, 24, 25, 94; C 30, 31, 32, 33, 34, 108; D 20, 21, 22, 53, 63, 79, 80; F; H 11; J 17, 138; K 16, 31, 320; L 13, 25; Q.
H. P. Anderson, *Your Career in Agriculture*, Dutton, 1940.

Air Conditioning: C 122; D 67; F 17; H 33.
N. V. Carlisle, *Your Career in Engineering*, Dutton, 1942. Page 164.
L. K. Wright, *The Next Great Industry*, Funk, 1939.

Architecture; General: C 58; D 12; F 34; J 201.
Landscape: C 60; D 13; F.

Armed Services: B 85; C 1, 2, 3, 5; D 123, 124, 128, 129, 130, 131; J 251.

Art; General: B 2; C 132; D 97; H 36; J 231.
Industrial and Commercial: D 14, 107, 119, 134.
Interior Decoration: C 59; D 5; F 64; H 31.
J. I. Biegeleison, *Careers in Commercial Art*, Dutton, 1944.
D. De Schweinitz, *Occupations in Retail Stores*, International, 1941. Page 247.
M. Downer, *Be an Artist*, Lothrop, 1941.
M. Price, *So You're Going to Be an Artist*, Watson-Guptill, 1939.

Aviation: A 33; B 49; C 16, 68; D 39, 77, 122, 137; J 155, 186; L 13, 30, 165; P 128; Q.
Gen. H. H. Arnold and Lt. Gen. I. C. Eaker, *This Flying Game*, Funk, 1942, rev. ed.
C. Hall and R. Merkle, *The Sky's the Limit*, Funk, 1943.

Editor: Careers for Women, Dutton, 1941.

N. MacNeil, *How to Be a Newspaperman,* Harper, 1942.

Laboratory Technician: C 63; D 68; F; L 317; N; P.

Land Transportation: A 2, 8; B 64, 71, 79, 98; C 22, 46, 116; D 56; F; H 43; J 187; L 140; Q.

N. V. Carlisle, *Your Career in Transportation,* Dutton, 1942.

B. W. Leyson, *Automotive Occupations,* Dutton, 1941.

Language Workers: C 144.

Law: B 13; C 135; D 7; H 21, 56; J 214; K 298.

E. L. Brown, *Lawyers and the Promotion of Justice,* Russell Sage Foundation, 1938.

Librarian: C 115; D 8; F; G; H 1; J 216; K 249.

M. Lingenfelter, *Books on Wheels: Opportunities in Library Work,* Funk, 1938.

Classification and Pay Plans for Libraries in Institutions of Higher Education, Amer. Library Assoc., 1943.

B. S. Rossell, *Public Libraries in the Life of the Nation,* Amer. Library Assoc., 1943.

Manufacturing; Management: B 56; C 21, 73; D 32, 35; H 40.

Workers: A 32; B 76; C 17, 78, 80, 82, 84, 85; D 127.

Mechanics: B 48, 57; C 48; D 122.

B. W. Leyson, *Automotive Occupations,* Dutton, 1941.

Medicine: B 16; C 36; D 26, 29, 104, 105, 110, 116; E 6; F; H 4; J 204; L 280, 316; Q.

E. L. Brown, *Physicians and Medical Care,* Russell Sage Foundation, 1937.

L. M. Klinefelter, *Medical Occupations for Boys,* Dutton, 1938.

L. M. Klinefelter, *Medical Occupations for Girls,* Dutton, 1939.

Metal Trades: A 13, 27, 34; B 58, 59, 68, 69, 81; C 14, 39, 40, 41, 42, 43, 87; F; H 26, 33; J 155; K 46; L 80; Q.

B. W. Leyson, *Careers in the Steel Industry,* Dutton, 1945.

Meteorology: D 84; K 176.

Mining and Oil: B 72, 75; C 15, 125, 126; D 62, 76, 92; G; H 23, 35; J 177; K 44, 254; L 62, 71.

Modeling: H 39.

O. Malcova, *Wanted: Girl with Glamour,* Duell, Sloan, & Pearce, 1941.

C. M. Dessner, *So You Want to Be a Model!* Morgan-Dillon, 1943.

Motion Picture Workers (see Dramatics for actors): C 120; G; H 52.

Museum: D 91.

Music: A 12; B 14; C 131; D 11, 88, 93, 121; F; H 6; J 71.

H. Johnson, *Your Career in Music,* Dutton, 1944.

G. Moore, *The Unashamed Accompanist,* Macmillan, 1944.

Nursing: A 35; B 19, 92; C 37, 98; D 25, 105; F; H 41; J 208; L 298.

E. L. Brown, *Nursing as a Profession,* Russell Sage Foundation, 1940, 2nd ed.

L. M. Klinefelter, *Medical Occupations for Girls,* Dutton, 1939.

C. Schulz, *Your Career in Nursing,* McGraw-Hill, 1941.

D. Sutherland, *Do You Want to Be a Nurse?* Doubleday, Doran, 1942.

Office Machine Operation: A 11; B 41; C 7; F; H 25; K 293.

Optometry: C 114; D 27; J 233.

Osteopathy: C 147; D 28; E 23; H 20.

Pharmacy: C 101; D 44; E 14; H 51; L 317.

Photography: A 24; B 15; C 50; D 47; G; H 52, 55; J 230; K 295.

B. W. Leyson, *Photographic Occupations,* Dutton, 1940.

Physicist: J 68; N; P 50.

Psychology: C 104; K 271.

Public Relations: C 88; D 136.

A. Broughton, *Careers in Public Relations,* Dutton, 1943.

Publishing and Printing: A 6; B 8, 54; C 110, 134, 137; D 9, 118; J 158; Q.

Purchasing Agent: C 76; D 78, 94.

Radio: A 12; B 63; C 24, 117; D 59, 121; F 74; H 44; K 182, 228; L 168, 174; Q.

N. V. Carlisle and C. C. Rice, *Your Career in Radio,* Dutton, 1941.

R. DeHaven and H. Kahm, *How to Break into Radio,* Harper, 1941.

J. L. Hornung, *Radio as a Career,* Funk, 1940.

J. J. Floherty, *Behind the Microphone,* Lippincott, 1944.

F. M. Reck, *Radio from Start to Finish,* Crowell, 1942.

Real Estate: B 27; C 142; D 74; F 78; J 130.

Religious Work: B 4; C 91; H 18; K 262.

    W. A. Brown, *The Minister: His World and His Work,* Cokesbury, 1937.

    Vocations in the Church, The National Council, 1944.

Restaurant Operator: C 137, 138; D 69; H 15, 37.

Retail Store Work and Management: B 26, 33, 35, 36, 37, 38, 43, 47; C 70, 71, 77, 143; D 48, 55, 56, 65, 75, 78, 87, 90, 101, 117, 121; H 22; L 213, 232.

    N. A. Brisco and L. Arnowitt, *Introduction to Modern Retailing,* Prentice-Hall, 1942.

    D. De Schweinitz, *Occupations in Retail Stores,* International, 1941.

    D. McFerran, *Careers in Retailing for Young Women,* Dutton, 1943.

    C. G. Woodhouse, *The Big Store: Opportunities in Department Store Work,* Funk, 1943.

Salesmanship: B 34, 43; C 74, 75; D 33; J 118; K 108.

    F. Maule, *Selling—A Job That's Always Open,* Funk, 1940.

Schools and Colleges: A 5; B 5, 18; C 65, 66; D 6, 52, 88, 100, 106; F; H 12, 29; K 244; M 92; Q.

    Teachers for Our Times, Amer. Council on Educ., 1944.

    L. Cole, *The Background for College Teaching,* Farrar & Rinehart, 1940.

    L. J. Nuttall, *Teacher,* Macmillan, 1941.

    R. C. Woellner and M. A. Wood, *Requirements for Certification of Teachers and Administrators,* Univ. Chicago Press, 1944, 8th ed.

Secretarial and Stenographic Work: A 11; B 44; C 8; D 64, 66, 135; F; H 50; J 119; K 87, L 348.

    F. Maule, *The Road to Anywhere: Opportunities in Secretarial Work,* Funk, 1941.

    L. Scott and E. C. Belcher, *How to Get a Secretarial Job,* Harper, 1942.

Social, Police, and Public Service Work: A 3, 23, 32, 35; B 17, 83, 84; C 38, 90, 127, 136; D 42, 43, 50, 125; H 19, 57; J 220, 238; K 271; L 253.

    E. L. Brown, *Social Work as a Profession,* Russell Sage Foundation, 1942, 4th rev. ed.

    A. C. Klein, *Civil Service in Public Welfare,* Russell Sage Foundation, 1940.

    A. E. Fink, *The Field of Social Work,* Holt, 1942.

    L. M. French, *Psychiatric Social Work,* Commonwealth Fund, 1940.

Statistical Work: A 1; D 45.

Telegraph and Telephone Service: B 45, 46, 80; C 9, 45; H 30; J 121; K 180.

Textiles: C 81, 83; D 112; L 114; M 182; Q.

Therapists: C 62; D 102, 109; F 71, 72; H 17.

Traffic Management: A 2, 8; D 60; G.

Veterinary Medicine: C 148; D 71; E 18; F; K 152.

Water Transportation: B 77, 96; C 4, 13, 23; D 132; Q.

    N. V. Carlisle, *Your Career in Transportation,* Dutton, 1942.

PROJECT XII

SOCIAL ADJUSTMENT

Ability to get along with others is important in our crowded world. And every person wants to be liked, to become a member of some group, and to be selected for positions of leadership. With the adult world eager to have students socially adjusted and with the students themselves striving to be accepted, it would seem that little difficulty should occur, but the evidence is otherwise. Worries about not being liked or not being popular are among those frequently mentioned by college students.

As a high-school senior, the average student usually feels socially secure with his friends and his gang, but when he goes away to college, he has to work hard to make new social contacts on the campus. If he becomes unhappy over a lack of dates and congenial friends (and is a little homesick), he may make frequent trips home where he knows he is accepted. Some students, on finding it difficult to make friends, even quit school, unhappy and disappointed in their college experiences.

While a person must adjust to many types of groups, the adjustment that presents the most problems at the time of entering college is acceptance by fellow students. That is, being included as a member of some congenial group of his own age, having a few close friends, and being liked by the opposite sex. At this time some students are also going through the last stages of emancipation or becoming independent of the home. If a student feels secure in all of these social relationships, he feels free to devote a large part of his efforts to study. If not, he is apt to be distracted from his studies.

The social structure on a campus (the pattern of who is liked or not and the degree of such feeling) is much different than most persons suppose. The actual pattern is well illustrated by the results of administering a sociometry test in a girls' dormitory.[1] In this simple test the students were asked to list the two or three persons they would like as partners in several everyday campus activities such as double dating, eating, and studying. When the number of choices that each person received was tabulated, the distribution in Chart 16 was obtained. That is, most students receive less than the average number of votes and many receive almost no votes! While each one would like to be the person at the right-hand end of the distribution—the popular individual—most students are actually at the stage of feeling "when a feller needs a friend." Furthermore, an analysis of those whom the low-score persons picked in their nominations indicated to some extent how strongly such isolates feel about their position of isolation. While most of the students tended to pick individuals for desired associates who were somewhere near their own level of popularity, the isolates and near isolates picked not those who picked them but the most popular individuals (as symbols of their frustrated desires)!

In this same experiment an analysis of

[1] Jean Waid Reilly, *Correlation Between Factors in Girls' Background and Their Popularity in a College Dormitory*, unpublished Master's thesis, Ohio State Univ., 1942.

the factors related to popularity indicated that differences were not due to accidents of location in the dormitory nor particularly to family status; differences seemed in great part to spring from the personality characteristics of the individuals themselves. What then were these characteristics? Surprisingly enough, intelligence was not related to popularity in college; that is, everyone was bright enough not to be offensive to at least some other people. The factors which were related seemed to be of two types: the external niceties of behavior which make a person easy to get along with, and the worth of the person as an individual. This project deals primarily with the first of these under the following three headings: (1) Etiquette, (2) Participation Skills, and (3) Appearance and Manner. Although the other area, the worth of the individual, is on the whole very difficult to tackle through reading, the following books on the subject may be of interest and some assistance, and the next project on "personal problems" also touches on it.

L. Cole, *Attaining Maturity*, Farrar & Rinehart, 1944.

H. E. Fosdick, *On Being a Real Person*, Harper, 1943.

E. Lloyd-Jones and R. Fedder, *Coming of Age*, Whittlesey House, 1941.

F. McKinney, *Psychology of Personal Adjustment*, Wiley, 1941. Chaps. 9–11.

P. E. Osgood, *Say I to Myself*, Harvard Univ. Press, 1944.

Before discussing the different divisions in this project, a review of one further study provides an orientation to the total area of social effectiveness.[2] This author, on the basis of a thorough review of many studies of social intelligence, found that eleven characteristics could be isolated. That is, the socially effective person is one who:

a. Takes people as they are
b. Inflates the ego of others
c. Is considerate of others
d. Is adaptable to changing circumstances
e. Is careful of personal appearance
f. Displays good manners
g. Has a normal degree of functional intelligence
h. Has a normal amount of emotional maturity

[2] V. D. Jackson, Measurement of social proficiency, *J. Exper. Educ.*, 1940, 8:422–474.

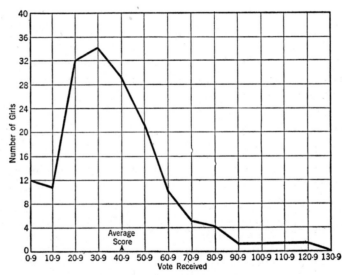

CHART 16. Distribution of popularity (sociometry) scores of 162 girls in a college dormitory. (Based on unpublished data of J. W. Reilly.)

i. Is able and willing to assume leadership when group consensus calls for such leadership

j. Possesses a high character without attitudes of reform and holiness

k. Has certain similarities to the group in which he is participating

These characteristics are covered in the sections which follow.

1. *Etiquette.* A knowledge of the accepted campus ways of behaving when with others makes one feel at ease among people and also makes one's behavior more predictable and therefore easier for others to adjust to. A list of situations which occur frequently and which give students the most trouble has been obtained through the co-operation of Mortar Board chapters from over the country. Campus leaders were also asked to state what they felt was acceptable behavior in these situations. This material is summarized in the book, *Your Best Foot Forward,* by D. C. Stratton and H. B. Schleman, McGraw-Hill, 1940.

Do you know the forms of behavior most acceptable to college students? The following etiquette test which is based on the findings of the above study will test your general proficiency in this area. When the test is completed, its key will be found on page 247 in Appendix II. While it might be said that a student ought to know all of the items on this test since the topics were selected by college students, most students are not sticklers for such form. You may, therefore, like to see how you compare to students in a large university through use of the norms below. These and your interest in etiquette can provide a basis for setting your goal of proficiency in this area. (A local campus custom may occasionally disagree with an answer on the key but be sure that this is true and doesn't merely represent an indifference among your friends to certain aspects of correct etiquette.)

Norms on Etiquette Test (No. right)

Lowest Quarter	Second Quarter	Third Quarter	Top Quarter
27	30	33	
Q₁	Md.	Q₃	

TEST OF SOCIAL USAGE

1. In making introductions, the man should be presented to the woman.   T F

2. (for men) On being introduced to another man, a man may stand or not as he chooses, *or* (for women) Women never rise for introductions.   T F

3. If no one has introduced you to a member of a social gathering, you may introduce yourself.   T F

4. In introducing a guest to a roomful of people, the guest's name should be mentioned first.   T F

5. Being in the same class with someone serves as sufficient introduction for conversation.   T F

6. A guest should always be introduced to the housemother.   T F

7. At a house dance, it is not necessary that all guests meet the chaperons.   T F

8. A girl student is introduced to a professor, and not vice versa; for instance, one might say "Professor Jones, may I present Miss Smith."   T F

9. It is customary to arrive a few minutes before the hour set for a dinner party.   T F

10. At a large banquet, one may begin to eat after those near-by have been served.   T F

11. A salad may be cut with a knife. T F

12. A good rule to follow at a dinner is to use your silver in its order of arrangement, beginning with the piece nearest your plate. T F

13. When passing your plate for a second helping, you should remove your knife and fork out of consideration for the server. T F

14. You may eat the following foods with your fingers: radishes, olives, dry crisp bacon, shoe-string potatoes, and corn on the cob. T F

15. It is all right to drink your soup if it is served in a cup. T F

16. You may use your fingers for lump sugar even though tongs are provided. T F

17. Fish bones and fresh-fruit pits should be removed from the mouth with the fingers. T F

18. It is no longer considered necessary to leave any food on your plate. T F

19. In a college dining room it is all right to help yourself to a dish which is being passed even though you have some of that type of food on your plate. T F

20. On a dinner date the man should take the initiative in ordering dinner, suggesting items he feels that he can afford. T F

21. If a man is having a dinner date and a girl stops at his table to speak to his girl, he may remain seated. T F

22. On a double date for dinner the girls sit facing their dates across the table. T F

23. The usual tip is 5 per cent of the bill. T F

24. A man should alight from a bus or streetcar first and then assist the woman with him. T F

25. The woman precedes the man into a row of seats. T F

26. It is better for a man to say, "Will you go to the Thanksgiving dance with me Saturday night?" than "May I have a date Saturday night?" T F

27. In all ordinary situations, the woman has the responsibility for suggesting the time for starting home. T F

28. A man may assume the privilege of "coming in for a few minutes" after bringing his date home. T F

29. A man should invite a woman to a dance two or three weeks early. T F

30. A man never leaves a woman alone on a dance floor. T F

31. When there is no one to serve punch, the woman should serve her partner and herself. T F

32. When a man and woman are talking on the telephone, she should be responsible for closing the conversation. T F

33. Today it is acceptable for women to telephone men when they feel like it. T F

34. The man takes the initiative in beginning correspondence with a woman. T F

35. You are expected to write a thank you note if you have been an overnight guest. T F

36. An R.S.V.P. demands that you accept or decline an offered invitation as soon as possible. T F

37. You should speak to your professors or the college president whether they know you personally or not. T F

38. A man should remove his hat when riding in *any* elevator in which women are present. T F

39. In a household where the hostess does not have a maid, the guest should offer to assist in some of the household duties. T F

40. (for men) For a spring formal, either the man's trousers or jacket should be of a light color. *or* (for women) It is not acceptable for a college woman to wear a sorority or fraternity pin to a formal dance. T F

If interested in further reading about etiquette, you will find the above-mentioned book, *Your Best Foot Forward*, by D. C. Stratton and H. B. Schleman is an excellent source. Other useful source books for college students are as follows:

B. Allen and M. P. Briggs, *If You Please!*, Lippincott, 1942.
M. Banning and M. L. Culkin, *Conduct Yourself Accordingly*, Harper, 1944.
M. E. Curdy and B. Wheeler, *Manners for Moderns*, Dutton, 1942.

2. *Participation Skills*. In order to fit in with a college group, one needs to know its meeting places, traditions, current language idioms, and how to participate in its activities. So much of the pattern of living on a given campus is specific to that locality that self-evaluation tests cannot be included here. But if you feel somewhat isolated on the campus, some thought should be given to the question: Is it because I don't know the local ways, rather than because the other students are aloof and cold?

Activities which youth participate in, however, are pretty much the same over the country. Some evaluation is possible here although the interpretation of results is difficult. For one thing, a student doesn't need to know how to participate in *all* campus activities; people have individual preferences as to what they like to do. On the other hand, inability to participate in such a universal activity as dancing may be the basis for a student's exclusion from a group of friends whom he would like to have. Further evidence of the type of problem here discussed is the finding at the University of Minnesota that 17 per cent of the men and 12 per cent of the women participated in no organized activities on or off the campus and many of the others only listed church attendance.[3]

The basis adopted here for evaluating activities is threefold: (a) Are enough activities participated in to give many social contacts? (b) Is this range of activities sufficient to permit a variety of contacts? And (c) are there enough personal hobbies and interests to act as a counterbalance to these social pursuits and to lead to the development of an interesting individuality? Thus one becomes acceptable (and also grows in personal happiness) as he can do the things that others do and is individualistic enough to be an interesting companion.

One basis for evaluation is to compare your pattern of out-of-school activities with that of other students. As noted above, it is not intended that every student should have an identical pattern but neither should a student limit his activities to lonely pursuits and hobbies. The first step then is to fill out the following Activity Questionnaire so that you will have some concrete data with which to work.

[3] C. M. Brown, Social activities survey, *J. Higher Educ.*, 1936, 8:257–264.

ACTIVITY QUESTIONNAIRE

For each of the following activity areas, list how many different kinds you participated in during the past *year*, i.e., how many different sports?

1. Different kinds of sports.. ....

2. Different kinds of card games... ....

3. Different kinds of social groups, i.e., fraternity, student government, Y.M.C.A. ....

4. Different kinds of hobbies.. ....

For each of the following activity areas, list how many times you have participated in each in the past *month*.

5. Concerts... ....

6. Movies.. ....

7. Dances.. ....

8. Dates... ....

9. Parties.. ....

10. Bull sessions... ....

For the following two activity areas, list how many hours you spend a *month* on each.

11. Leisure Reading.. ....

12. Radio.. ....

Your results on this questionnaire can be compared to those of other students through use of Table 10. It shows the results on a similar questionnaire for typical midwestern college freshmen and college seniors. For each group is shown the number checked by the median student and also the scores for the first and third quartiles. To compare your results, find the group row which best describes you and then for each type of activity mark above, below, or on the one of the three numbers which is closest to your score.

These data have to be used with some caution, however. The season of the year (spring in this case), the ratio of men to women, and the climate, all affect what is checked. And as indicated before, there is no best end to these norms; the value of this table lies in permitting a student to see if he deviates extremely in his amount of participation and in the balance of his distribution.

Another basis for evaluation, as well as an indication of a problem which faces the college graduate, is given in Chart 19 in Appendix I (see page 218). This chart shows the degree to which 13,000 youth (ages 16–24) in Maryland participated in club activities when in school and after graduation. It is startling to find that so many students do not belong to any clubs. Another important finding in this chart, and corroborated by other studies, is that on leaving school with its many social opportunities, youth show a marked drop in the amount of participation in group activities, i.e., only 21 per cent belong to clubs. In another study 38 per cent of the women who had graduated from small high schools in Ohio

TABLE 10. Extent to Which Different Groups of Students Participate in Different Types of Activities.[4]

		Number in Past Year				Times in Past Month						Hours per Month	
		Sports	Games	Social	Hobbies	Concerts	Movie	Dance	Date	Party	Bull Sessions	Reading	Radio
Males													
College freshmen	75 %	8	7	3	5	2	5	3	6	3	10	21	34
	mdn	6	4	1	3	1	5	2	4	1	5	13	21
	25 %	3	1	1	2	0	3	1	2	1	2	7	8
College seniors	75 %	9	6	3	6	2	7	3	8	3	10	33	33
	mdn	5	4	2	3	1	5	1	5	2	5	19	19
	25 %	2	1	1	2	0	3	1	2	1	2	12	10
Females													
College freshmen	75 %	7	6	3	5	2	6	5	10	4	8	18	40
	mdn	4	3	2	3	2	5	3	8	2	4	13	20
	25 %	2	1	1	1	1	3	2	5	1	1	7	10
College seniors	75 %	7	5	3	5	2	6	4	11	4	4	28	32
	mdn	4	2	2	3	1	4	2	7	2	2	15	20
	25 %	2	2	1	2	1	3	1	4	1	1	9	11

belonged to no organizations although all of them had been active in high school. Similar declines occur in other types of activities, e.g., a study of 5,000 teachers showed that 42 per cent had no hobbies and 36 per cent took no systematic exercise. Some interesting data as to how college graduates spend their free time once they are out of college is given in Table 13 on page 214 in Appendix I. In general, however, students who have an active program in school are more apt to continue it into adult life than are students with a narrow and limited program.

What a person does with his free time is in a major sense his own business; that is, he should be allowed to decide if he does not want to participate in activities or hobbies, or wishes to drop them as he leaves school. But the following studies indicate that such a pattern has its dangers and a

[4] Based on the norms for the *Recreation Inquiry* by R. Wilkinson and S. L. Pressey.

fair warning should at least be given. In one study it was found that only 19 per cent of teachers judged to be "unusually stable" had no hobbies but 39 per cent of those judged "unduly nervous" had no hobbies. Another study showed that the top fifth in personality adjustment participated four times as often in "active, outdoor, social" activities as the bottom fifth in adjustment. These two extreme groups did not differ in their number of activities which were solitary and sedentary, but the best adjusted participated only one-sixth as often in hobbies similar to their work as the least well-adjusted. Another study showed that the major characteristic of teachers admitted to state hospitals for the insane was a lack of a well-rounded interest pattern. Still other experiments have shown that persons who have friends near by are better able to withstand the effects of frustration than persons without such friends. It seems obvious that while almost any recreation is fun, a balanced recreational program is fundamental to later happy adjustment.[5]

The following questions provide a basis for integrating and further clarifying your thinking in this area. Answer each in light of the results above and your other evaluations.

  a. In what activities currently much emphasized in campus life do you have trouble participating?

  b. What means are available in college or in town for learning about these activities, i.e., classes, handbooks, activities, i.e., etc.?

  c. List specific activities that you plan to participate in during this and the next term.

The following references will also be of some assistance.

H. M. Bell, *Youth Tell Their Story*, Amer. Council on Educ., 1938. Chap. 5: How 13,000 youth (16–24) spent their time.

M. M. Crawford, *Student Folkways and Spending*, Columbia Univ. Press, 1943.

M. L. Greenbie, *The Arts of Leisure*, McGraw-Hill, 1936.

M. L. Greenbie, *Art of Living in War-time*, McGraw-Hill, 1943.

A. H. Morehead, *Modern Hoyle*, Winston, 1945.

Pocket Book of Games, Pocket Books, 1944, No. 260.

G. E. Snavely, *Choose and Use Your College*, Harper, 1941.

D. E. Super, *Avocational Interest Patterns*, Stanford Univ. Press, 1940.

C. G. Wren and D. L. Harley, *Time on Their Hands*, Amer. Youth Comm., 1941.

---

[5] The discussion in the last two paragraphs has been based on the following studies. Although many of them deal with teachers, the findings are representative for other adults. H. M. Bell, *Youth Tell Their Story*, Amer. Council on Educ., 1938, 273 pp.; F. S. Chapin, Extracurricular activities of college students; a study in college leadership, *School and Soc.*, 1926, 26:212–216; S. L. Pressey, Outstanding problems of emergency junior college students, *School and Soc.*, 1936, 43:743–747; *Fit to Teach*, Ninth Yearbook, National Education Association, Department of Classroom Teachers, 1938, 276 pp.; W. S. Phillips and J. E. Greene, Preliminary study of relationship of age, hobbies, and civil status to neuroticism among women teachers, *J. Educ. Psych.*, 1939, 30:440–444; F. V. Mason, A study of 700 maladjusted teachers, *Mental Hygiene*, 1931, 15:576–600; J. R. P. French, Jr., The disruption and cohesion of groups, *J. Abn. & Soc. Psych.*, 1941, 36:361–378; W. C. Reavis and G. E. Van Dyke, Non-athletic extra-curriculum activities, U. S. Office of Educ., Bull. No. 17, Monog. No. 26, 1932, 149 pp.

3. *Appearance and Manner.* The gist of this section may be stated simply as good taste in appearance and sincerity in manner; the very worst thing to do is to appear to be "putting on" in order to influence other people. On the other hand, students have questions as to what constitutes good taste in clothes, which mannerisms are offensive, and how one's attempts to affect other persons may be made more effective.

Something as to the importance of appearance and manner, on first meeting a person, is indicated by an experiment at one

TABLE 11. The Most Frequent of 49 Areas in Which Students Make Comments About Other Students Whom They Are Seeing for the First Time. (Adapted from Jacobson.)

Rank Order	Area	Per Cent of Comments in This Area	Positive	Neutral	Negative
1.	Grooming—general remarks	13.5	82%	4%	14%
2.5	Grooming—hair dress	10.2	47	10	43
2.5	Posture	10.2	51	14	35
4.	Emotions	8.8	64	9	27
5.	Self assurance—self distrust	6.4	13	27	60
6.	Altruism—self seeking	5.8	89	3	8
7.	Gregariousness—solitariness	5.6	81	6	13
8.	Taste in dress	4.8	87	6	7
9.	General characteristics—physical	4.6	88	7	5
10.	Grooming—make-up	4.2	17	12	71
11.	Clothing—suitability to occasion	2.6	72	3	25
12.	Clothing—harmony of color	2.6	57	4	39
13.	Physical characteristics—hair	2.5	97	1	2
14.	Suitability of clothes to person	2.1	41	5	54
15.	Physical complexion	2.0	74	10	16
16.	Eyes	1.6	95	0	5
17.	Clothing—harmony of parts	1.5	31	5	64
18.	Remarks about clothing	1.3	83	8	9

university.[6] Over 250 entering freshman girls, divided into groups of 24 each, wrote down their reactions concerning 23 other students as each in turn stood in front of the class. The several thousand offhand reactions were then analyzed and classified by judges under 49 subtopics. Table 11 summarizes the results for the top 18 of these (which accounted for 90 per cent of all the comments). Grooming and posture are mentioned the most often. Standing thus in front of 23 strangers would be more embarrassing than the usual situation, so several aspects of behavior also rank high. The right-hand side of the table shows how these comments are distributed according to categories of favorable, neutral, and unfavorable. Most comments were favorable, but it is interesting to note that several items tended toward particularly heavy negative votes, i.e., grooming (make-up), clothing (harmony of parts), self-distrust, suitability of clothes to person, grooming (hair dress),

clothing (harmony of color), and posture. When the experimenter analyzed the reactions of other students who knew each other, she found that reactions to personality traits moved up to first place, and grooming, for instance, moved down to third. Characteristics of appearance are therefore especially important for a first impression.

A person's manner, as well as his appearance, is important in dealing with other individuals. When one thinks of how different individuals influence the behavior of others, it is apparent that some seem to do it with effective skill and others "put their foot in it." A person who is pleasant and friendly is more apt to be liked and effective than one who is reserved and dour. Courtesy, honesty, interest in others, and a sense of humor are other traits which characteristically differentiate liked from disliked people in college.[7] On the other hand one often

[6] W. E. Jacobson, First impressions of classmates, J. Appl. Psych., 1945, 29:142–155.

[7] F. W. Burks, Some factors related to social success in college, J. Soc. Psych., 1938, 9:125–140; W. G. Mather, Courtship ideals of high school youth, Sociol. and Soc. Res., 1934, 19:166–172.

finds that certain mannerisms are sources of annoyance to others. Attempts to improve one's social presence and skill are worth while.

Books on how to win friends and influence people are popular, more than three million copies of one such book having been published. But you can probably recall some people who, having read such books, overdid it when they tried the techniques. To appear to be "putting on" such techniques is offensive to others; any manner of behaving must appear to be natural. Some idea as to the nature of these effective social skills can be found in the following readings, but you will do well to have a "best friend" or your counselor help you analyze what mannerisms and characteristics in your present behavior are not pleasing.

The following readings deal with both appearance and social behavior:

G. F. Alsop and M. F. McBride, She's Off to College, Vanguard, 1940.
D. Carnegie, How to Win Friends and Influence People, Pocket Books, No. 68.
V. Dengel, Personality Unlimited, Winston, 1943.
R. B. Hamrick, How to Make Good in College, Association Press, 1940. Chaps. 5–8.
E. Hawes, Fashion Is Spinach, Random House, 1938.
W. White, Psychology in Living, Macmillan, 1944.
M. Wilson, Woman You Want to Be, Lippincott, 1942.

The college years are often the time when one finds his best friends and even the person he later marries. Because the entering student wants to do whatever he can to be good at such selection, he often spends much thought on two decision areas: (a) What campus groups should I join? (b) Should I get married—and to whom? Such decisions are the person's own, but the following readings may be of interest and some assistance in clarifying these problems:

Campus Groups:

G. F. Alsop and M. F. McBride, She's Off to College, Vanguard, 1940. Chap. 10.
H. C. Hand, Campus Activities, McGraw-Hill, 1938. Chap. 9.
E. Lloyd-Jones and R. Fedder, Coming of Age, Whittlesey House, 1941. Pages 226–233.
M. McConn, Planning for College, Stokes, 1937. Pages 199–234.
R. B. Hamrick, How to Make Good in College, Association Press, 1940. Pages 28–30.

Marriage:

H. A. Bowman, Marriage for Moderns, McGraw-Hill, 1942.
D. D. Bromley and F. H. Britton, Youth and Sex, Harper, 1938.
J. K. Folsom, Plan for Marriage, Harper, 1938.
R. G. Foster, Marriage and Family Relationships, Macmillan, 1944.
E. R. Groves, Marriage, Holt, 1942.
H. M. Jordan, You and Marriage, Wiley, 1942.
P. Popenoe, Modern Marriage, Macmillan, 1942.
F. B. Strain, Love at the Threshold, Appleton-Century, 1941.

PROJECT XIII

PERSONAL PROBLEMS

Probably almost every one of us has personal problems. These worries make us inefficient by distracting our attention, preventing normal healthful habits of living, and giving us a dour outlook on life. Quite often, in spite of our resolve to stop thinking about them, they keep plaguing us.

Worries and fears can be dealt with so that either they are eliminated or adjustments are made to them. Psychologists have found that if a person talks over his problems with some adequately trained individual, he will be benefited in two ways. First, just talking over a problem with another person tends to "get it out of one's system," with quite beneficial results to his peace of mind. Second, in spite of the common belief that each person's problems are unique, psychologists have found that most problems have certain common characteristics and that people tend to react in certain regular ways to them. With this understanding of problems and of their good and poor solutions, psychologists are able to assist people in analyzing the nature of their worries and in handling them better.

The counselor in charge of this course is available for consultation concerning any personal problems you may wish to discuss with him. Many colleges also have on their staff other trained people who specialize in this personal counseling. Your counselor can tell you who these guidance specialists are. Because almost everyone is reticent about having his personal affairs and problems generally known, these specialists keep all information given them strictly confidential.

Self-Evaluation

There is no particular need to make a catalogue of all your worries. In a way, your checking on the Problem Check List in Project I represents such a listing. Each student knows his own worries; he should feel free to ask for a conference with a counselor in order to talk over any of them that he wishes.

Often if a student has difficulty in discussing a problem directly with another person, he will find that writing out a description of it for the counselor to read confidentially will enable him to present it more easily.

Program for Improvement

Your talks with your counselor (either the guidance specialist or your course counselor) will be the key aspect of this project. Some useful readings are listed among the following, although you must realize that mere reading is not a complete answer to many problems.

Finances in College:

W. J. Greenleaf, *Working Your Way Through College*, U. S. Office of Educ. V. D. Bull. No. 210, 1940, 175 pages.

W. J. Greenleaf, *Student Loan Funds*, U. S. Office of Educ., 1940, Misc. No. 2141, 19 pages.

F. J. Kelley and E. B. Ratcliffe, *Financial Aid for College Students*, U. S. Office of Educ., Bull. No. 11, 1940.

C. E. Lovejoy, *So You're Going to College*, Simon & Schuster, 1940.

M. McConn, *Planning for College*, Stokes, 1937. Pages 102–165, 261–263.

G. E. Snavely, *Choose and Use Your College*, Harper, 1941.

Home Relationships:

C. C. Fry and E. G. Rostow, *Mental Health in College*, Commonwealth Fund, 1943. Chap. 3.

E. A. Leonard, *Problems of Freshmen College Girls*, Teachers College, Child Dev. Monog., No. 9, 1932.

E. Lloyd-Jones and R. Fedder, *Coming of Age*, Whittlesey House, 1941. Chap. 3.

K. W. Taylor, *Do Adolescents Need Parents?* Appleton-Century, 1938.

Organic Factors and Personality Development:

A. V. Keliher, *Life and Growth*, Appleton-Century, 1938.

W. V. Richmond, *Personality, Its Development and Hygiene*, Farrar & Rinehart, 1937. Pages 192–200, 261–265.

A. Scheinfeld, *You and Heredity*, Stokes, 1939.

L. F. Shaffer, *Psychology of Adjustment*, Houghton Mifflin, 1936. Chap. 12.

Philosophy of Life; Religious Development:

M. E. Bennett, *College and Life*, McGraw-Hill, 1941, rev. ed.

H. E. Fosdick, *On Being a Real Person*, Harper, 1943.

L. B. Hale, *From School to College*, Yale Univ. Press, 1939.

D. B. Klein, *Mental Hygiene*, Holt, 1944. Chap. 11. On dynamics of conscience.

J. H. Miller, *Take a Look at Yourself*, Cokesbury, 1944.

Emotional Problems:

D. D. Bromley and F. H. Britton, *Youth and Sex*, Harper, 1938.

O. M. Butterfield, *Love Problems of Adolescents*, Teach. Coll. Contri. Educ., 1939, No. 798.

L. Cole, *Attaining Maturity*, Farrar & Rinehart, 1944.

C. C. Fry and E. G. Rostow, *Mental Health in College*, Commonwealth Fund, 1943.

W. Johnson, *People in Quandaries*, Harper, 1946.

F. McKinney, *Psychology of Personal Adjustment*, Wiley, 1941. Chaps. 13–16.

W. Richmond, *Making the Most of Your Personality*, Farrar & Rinehart, 1942.

L. F. Shaffer, *Psychology of Adjustment*, Houghton Mifflin, 1936. Chaps. 5–10.

E. A. Strecker, K. E. Appel, and J. W. Appel, *Discovering Ourselves*, Macmillan, 1944, 2nd ed.

L. E. Travis and D. W. Baruch, *Personal Problems of Everyday Life*, Appleton-Century, 1941.

W. White, *Psychology in Living*, Macmillan, 1944.

LOOKING AHEAD

The purpose of this final project is to make an inventory of your progress and to plan for whatever future work seems necessary. This cannot be a final closing of your record or of your efforts since a single course cannot be expected completely to remedy the deficient attitudes, skills, and knowledge you may have developed over a period of many years. Thus far, you have had the following purposes in this course: (1) the development of an awareness of your various abilities and problems, (2) training in higher-level work skills, and (3) an initial attack to remedy deficiencies in, or adjust your plans to, your profile of abilities. Now there is need for a progress report upon which you can base your future efforts. Because training in how-to-study must be done in terms of specific problems, your diagnosis at the beginning of this course must now be changed in light of the work that you have accomplished.

Note also that if your present survey indicates the solution of some problem, such as reading rate, you still have to practice further in order to make this skill habitual and lasting.

What are some of the bases by which you may evaluate your present status?

1. A retest on some of the tests that you took initially and on which you did poorly will indicate the extent of your gains and the present status of these problems. Tests comparable to some of these first ones are avail- able for retesting and may be obtained from the publishers.[1]

2. These remeasured basic skills, while important, represent only a small part of what you have been working on this term. Also measure your improvement in the quality of your notebook and class papers, in your study habits, in your use of time, in your ability "to concentrate," and in your ability to predict quiz questions and take tests.

3. You should include an evaluation of your social and vocational adjustments and the steps that you are taking toward their improvement.

4. Your conferences with your counselor about various problems also offer a good basis for the analysis of your present problems.

5. There are probably some traits on which you did not know your relative standing before taking this course. This new orientation should have assisted in your school adjustment.

Your problem in this project, then, is to (1) state your present status in terms of all these measures, (2) evaluate the gains you have made, and (3) outline the program of

[1] Rate and comprehension accuracy, "Russian History" or "Canadian History," Ohio State Univ. Press. Vocabulary, Form B (Part II of General Reading Test.), State Department of Education, State Office Building, Columbus, Ohio. English Survey, Form B, State Department of Education, State Office Building, Columbus, Ohio.

remedial work that you plan to carry on after this course. You can best do this with an informal essay covering these points; it is to be handed to the counselor not later than the last day of class before exam week.

Your counselor will be glad to go over your outline before you write this paper, and make pertinent suggestions and corrections.

If at a later time in your college program you need help with any aspect of the work that has been covered in this course, feel free to ask your present counselor for assistance.

APPENDIX I

Tests

Do not turn the page until the signal to begin reading is given.

A Test of Reading Ability for

ART

by

Francis P. Robinson and Prudence Hall
The Ohio State University

THE ARTIST'S ETERNAL QUEST OF BEAUTY[1]

Name.. Age.....................

Grade..................... School...

Directions

1   The purpose of this test is to measure your ability to read school assignments. You are to read
2   the following art selection in your usual manner of reading assignments; after ten minutes of
3   reading you will be asked to answer questions over the material read. These questions will be
4   of the type generally asked in class over such readings.
5   At the end of 3 minutes, 6 minutes, and 10 minutes of reading you will be asked to "Mark."
6   This means that you are to encircle quickly the number of the line that you are reading (num-
7   bered as in the left-hand margin here) and then go on immediately with your reading. At the
8   end of 10 minutes you will be asked to stop reading and to turn to the questions which follow.
9   Be accurate in noting the last line read for *you will be expected to answer questions* over all the
10   material that you mark as having been read.

THE ARTIST'S ETERNAL QUEST OF BEAUTY

2   What is "art"? Let us begin shaping our answer to this
3 question by going back to the original meaning of the word.
4 The two letters *ar* form a very ancient word root appearing
5 in many languages. Its meaning is to bind or join together.
6 When a man joins or binds materials together, as pieces of
7 wood in a chair, or lines and colors, as in a picture, he is
8 an artist—one who makes. An *arm*, the part so beautifully
9 joined to the human shoulder, is a work of art, "the art
10 of God." A coat of chain mail, a piece of *armor*, is made
11 of many metal rings linked ingeniously and beautifully to
12 one another. This is a work of art, the art of man. In
13 both "arm" and "armor" the *ar* appears, and both imply
14 the fundamental significance of art—joining and binding to-
15 gether. To this elementary idea let us add what the great
16 painter Walter Sargent said: "Art is not a mere skillful rep-
17 resentation of nature, but a concrete embodiment of a signifi-
18 cant range of human experience." Now we have a broad and
19 firm foundation upon which to build an understanding of
20 our subject.

CLASSES OF ART

22   The various arts are broadly divided into two classes,
23 ordinarily distinguished as the useful arts and the fine arts.
24 The meaning of the former of these terms is self-evident.
25 The fine arts begin when there is a conscious attempt to
26 express beauty in the form of the thing made, and in its
27 decoration.
28   Man exposed to rain and cold builds a roof and four
29 walls within which to be protected against the elements. His
30 building is a work of useful art. But suppose he makes his
31 roof project, so that it casts a deep shadow on the walls when
32 the sun shines, and that he makes the chimney large, so that
33 his house will not only be, but *seem* to be, a place of shelter
34 and warmth. And suppose that he sets ornamental columns
35 at either side of his door to make it at once suggestive of
36 hospitality and beauty. Then his house does more than with-
37 stand the elements; it *celebrates its triumph over them*. This
38 is the *fine art of architecture*; a form of emotional expression.
39 And this is precisely what the fine arts are.
40   This celebrating of the triumph theme is evidenced in
41 every form of fine art. From the aboriginal song and dance
42 of savage warriors after battle down to the day of Sousa
43 marches, triumph has found expression in the fine art of
44 music. Since before the time of the Greeks, it has been ex-
45 pressed in sculpture. From ancient Egyptian times it has been
46 presented in painting. In every age the fine art of poetry has
47 made triumph its theme.

48   Architecture, sculpture, painting, music, and literature
49 are not the only fine arts. Wherever there is an effort to
50 express beauty in the form and decoration of the thing made,
51 we find a fine art; and the person who seeks to create beauty
52 thus is an artist.

53   IDENTIFICATION OF ARTIST WITH OBJECT

54   The joy, pain, devotion, scorn, patriotism, or ecstasy
55 which the artist felt when he wrote the sonnet, composed the
56 funeral march, formed the vase, wrought the inimitable iron
57 hinges of the doors of Notre Dame of Paris is in turn felt
58 by the person who reads the sonnet, hears the march, or sees
59 the vase and the hinges. Art speaks a universal language—
60 a language, as Charles Reade says, "without words; unfettered
61 by the penman's limits, it can steal through the eye into
62 the heart or brain, alike of the learned and the unlearned—
63 and is at the mercy of no translator." This is seen in dancing,
64 a form of musical appreciation in which the listener becomes
65 a part of the performance, a co-worker with the composed.
66 Arthur B. Davies says: "When I paint a wave I *am* the
67 wave." True. And it is also true that when we look at his
68 painting of the wave we are that wave. When the painter
69 sweeps his brush over the canvas, he feels himself doing just
70 what the wave is doing. He becomes, as he says, a sort of
71 conscious wave; when we sweep our eyes over the lines where
72 his brush has led, we, too, become a sort of acting, conscious
73 wave.

74   ARTIST INTERESTED IN EFFECTS

75   In answer to the question: "What is a wave?" the
76 scientist with his cold analytical method will explain that
77 it is the result of certain causes and principles; he will sep-
78 arate it into its elements, and will point out the relations
79 of the wave to other things. He will always lead away from
80 the wave itself. The artist, on the other hand, forces atten-
81 tion solely to the wave. "The real work of art," it has been
82 said, "leads nowhere, and its frame ends the world." In
83 general, art may be said to show effects, not to seek their
84 causes.
85   The fine arts make us share the hope, fear, aspiration,
86 joy, and sorrow of humanity, because a work of fine art is
87 always the expression of one or the other of these. Whistler,
88 the most famous American painter, said, "The artist is to
89 arrest and typify in materials the harmonious and inter-
90 blended rhythms of nature and humanity."

91   NATURE AND FINE ARTS

92   Another way of explaining fine arts is to say that they
93 are what man makes out of the inspiration which he receives
94 from nature. He is so profoundly impressed that he must

95   give utterance to his feelings, and he does so in a hymn of
96   joy, a nobly formed statue, a perfectly proportioned vase,
97   or the pattern and colors of an oriental rug. In all art, he
98   seeks to preserve the significance of the passing moment—
99   in the joy of seeing a sea-shell or a fern frond and fixing
100 some of that joy which nature has given him in the shape
101 of a silver basin or an Ionic capital, or in the line of a
102 drawing.
103   The arts thus inspired by nature put us into a state of
104 receptive calm. They first make captive our imagination or
105 our joy in sight or sound; and then, through the unity and
106 intensity of their interest, they grip our whole consciousness
107 until, like the children and the Pied Piper, we forget all else
108 and follow. Even in this calm, however, there is a sort of
109 activity, for when we are enjoying a lyric, a musical rhap-
110 sody, a symphony of color, a bit of Roman glass, or a fine
111 fabric, we are living as intensely as at any other time, but
112 we are free of the conscious effort of living.

114   WHAT ARTISTIC "UNITY" MEANS

115   To give this feeling of calm, a work of art must have
116 but one theme; it must be free within itself from conflicting
117 attractions or suggestions; that is, it must have *unity*.
118 Whether it be sonnet, picture, vase, or cathedral, it must at
119 a glance give one unified impression. That impression may
120 be simple, as is that produced by the architecture of a Greek
121 temple; it may be as complex as is that given by the cathe-
122 dral of Amiens. But it must be *one*. It may be imposing,
123 as in Michelangelo's statue of Moses; or it may be delicate,
124 as in the carvings of the Japanese; but it must produce an
125 unconfused impression. It may be brought about by com-
126 bining many similar forms, colors, lines, or ideas until they
127 add power to one another, as in the poems of Milton and in
128 the paintings of Corot. It may be brought about by leading
129 the attention to an unlikeness in certain related things, as
130 in Keats' sonnet 'On the Grasshopper and the Cricket,' which
131 brings out a contrast. But in any case, a single impression
132 must result.
133   Nature does not always give us simple relations, and so, if
134 he would produce pictorial beauty, the artist must make many
135 changes in the "landscape with figures amid which we dwell."
136 He must select, arrange, subdue, and accent the elements
137 of his work so that they will produce the mood or set forth
138 the idea which he is endeavoring to present. He must not
139 admit confusion, the enemy of all the fine arts, unless it is
140 a part of the subject matter, as for example, the picture of a
141 volcanic eruption. It must never be a part of his technique.
142 Whistler said: "Nature contains the elements, in color and
143 form, of all pictures (of all varieties of fine art), as the

144 keyboard contains the notes of all music. But the artist is
145 born to pick and choose, and group with science, these
146 elements that the result may be beautiful."

147   THE MEANING OF "COMPOSITION"

148   This process of selection and arrangement is called "com-
149 position." For illustration we turn to painting. When, in
150 looking over the fields, we send our glance from the trees
151 to the hills beyond them; when we remove our eyes from
152 a person to whom we are speaking, to the walls just behind
153 him; when, in fact, we leave off looking at any one thing
154 and look at something either farther away or nearer than
155 that at which we were looking before, our eyes change
156 their focus in somewhat the way the focus of a camera is
157 changed to suit varying distances. Now, if the artist were
158 to try to paint in one picture the hills as he sees them
159 when looking directly at them, or the trees, or the clouds,
160 he would have a picture with as many separate interests
161 as it contained objects—a picture which would never have
162 unity or give repose of any sort. So the artist must select
163 some one thing for the main theme of his picture, and
164 to this he must subordinate all other things which occur
165 in it.
166   In nature it is sufficient if the form of a tree be
167 beautiful against the sky; in a picture the visible shapes
168 of sky seen through the tree must be equally beautiful. The
169 picture, since it is all to be seen at once, must be a beau-
170 tiful pattern in which every shape is fine. Consistency of
171 character, which has been called harmony, consistency of
172 attractions, which has been called balance, and consistency
173 of movement, which has been called rhythm, will keep all
174 elements of the work together in an integral whole. Here
175 again the artist in forming his work must exercise his aesthetic
176 judgment, varying from nature's appearances, if need be, to
177 bring finer proportion into his work, to give it more perfect
178 unity and deeper meaning.
179   Corot's landscape 'Morning' has now come to be called
180 'The Dance of the Nymphs.' Is this because there is a group
181 of tiny figures at the bottom—who in truth are scarcely
182 dancing and who may hardly be called nymphs? Or is it
183 because of the witchery of that flowing movement which
184 takes us from the bottom up into the picture, across the
185 top and down the other side, lastly circling round and round
186 the bit of sky in the center, leading us, before we know it,
187 in an airy dance through the treetops? The little figures
188 give the keynote—they form a statement of the theme,
189 Morning, Happiness, Dancing. But even if they were suddenly
190 to whisk themselves out and disappear on the other side of

191   the tangled shrubbery, the movement of the picture would
192   still go on, and it would still be a dance of the nymphs.
194   Turner's great picture 'The Fighting Temeraire' ex-
195   presses a contrasting mood. What is there about this pic-
196   ture to show that this ship is the heroine of England's
197   battles that she is—or to tell us that she is being towed
198   away for breaking up? And yet Ruskin says that of all
199   pictures not visibly involving human pain, this is the saddest.
200   What has the artist done to make us feel the solemnity of
201   this occasion? We see a sheet of still water under a
202   great bending sunset sky. On the other side a tall ship is
203   coming up, towed by a black tugboat. Long ripples are thrown
204   to left and right, and thin smoke pours back from the funnel
205   of the tug. Shadows are gathering from all sides, and there
206   are the buildings of a great city beyond in the gloom. Con-
207   sider the use of lines. Are they like those merry ones that
208   circle round the canvas of Corot's 'Morning'? Or are they
209   the lines which we see in the solemn groves of pine or
210   cypress, in the desert, and in the great cathedrals? Are
211   they like the figures in a funeral march? Has the artist
212   accepted Nature only as he found her?

214   MESSAGE OF ART IS A MOOD

215   The beauty of a picture, a piece of music, a Greek vase
216   does not lie in pleasing the emotions alone. Perhaps it is
217   impossible for the emotions to be stirred at all without the
218   mind receiving some deeper message through it. Thus, art
219   is a sort of language; but the message which that lan-
220   guage has to give is not an intellectual one. Art does not
221   exist primarily to set forth facts. The message from a
222   picture, like that of the music or from the vase, comes as
223   an experience, a mood which the work awakens within us,
224   and not as a story which the thing itself tells. A Bokhara
225   rug may be of "sleepy coloring" and give us the repose of
226   twilight as we contemplate it; a clear melody may give
227   us the same feelings as a view from a mountain top; a dash
228   of thrilling color may be to us like a battle-hymn; the
229   curve of a vase may absorb our whole being. Such, and
230   numerous others, are the artistic messages we may receive
231   if we fit ourselves to receive them, instead of the common-
232   place message that "here is a man and he is doing so and
233   so." These are the feelings which come to us straight from
234   the heart of the artist himself, even though he be cen-
235   turies in his grave. The tree, the figure, and the incident
236   are merely the words of the message. Its charm or inspira-
237   tion is something very different. We are aware of this when
238   we look at a 13th-century stained glass window, a silver
239   teapot by Paul Revere, or the spire of a great cathedral.
241   Three principal considerations compel an artist to turn

242 away from attempting to copy nature slavishly. Of these,
243 doubtless the chief is the desire for expression of emotion.
244 Intimately related to this is the second, namely absolute
245 beauty, a beauty other than that which is associated with
246 the subject as being merely one of the many things in life.
247 This is feeling for beauty which Jean Simeon Chardin (French,
248 1699–1779) or Emil Carlsen (American, 1853–1932) get into
249 a picture of such objects as a ragged book, a cut of meat, or
250 a battered copper pot. And so we see why beauty may be
251 defined as being a light which shines *about a thing* and is
252 not the thing itself. The third deals with the translation of
253 the three-dimensional aspect of nature into the two-dimen-
254 sional limits of a picture or a pure pattern. Artists whose
255 aim is merely to portray nature are busy with only the vocabu-
256 lary of art and not the ideas; with externals and not emotional
257 reactions. These three considerations give artists a working
258 grammar of art, the means, along with the vocabulary, of
260 expressing themselves; but their expression in terms of beauty
261 and permanence—be it in pottery, weaving, metal working,
262 painting, architecture, or poetry of deep human experience
263 —is the great purpose of them all. Its attainment stamps
264 the seal of success on all that can properly be called "the
265 fine arts." Without this successful expression of experience
266 or emotion, it becomes mere slavish reproduction.

266   INDUSTRIAL ARTS

267   By industrial arts, decorative arts, we understand all
268 those things which make our dwelling rooms attractive. Wil-
269 liam Morris, an Englishman (1834–1896), started a move-
270 ment to increase the beauty of common objects and to add
271 beauty to machine-made objects of daily use. This revolution
272 in taste spread over Europe and the United States. Since
273 the opening of the 20th century France has done a similar
274 thing with distinguished, far-reaching success. At present
275 the improvement of taste and the betterment of design in
276 our own country are making great headway through the in-
277 terest of educational institutions and the support of manu-
278 facturers and retail establishments. Artists are being asked
279 to bring their training and taste to bear on labels, packages,
279 and even the shapes of products.

280   CYCLES IN ART'S HISTORY

281   The story of art from ancient to present times is a record
282 of many changes, tendencies, and attainments. Once these
283 have run their course, they seem to begin all over and repeat,
284 like a wave which rises to its crest and then subsides to its
285 trough again and again. First, in every fine art, come a child-
286 like technique and strong emotion, as seen, for example, in
287 the drawings of children in Cizek's classes, or the glazed

288   pottery horses of the ancient Chinese. Later comes the stage
289   of developed technique, in which emotion is still strong, as,
290   for instance, in a Paul Potter bull, a Rembrandt landscape,
291   a statue by Michelangelo. Last comes a consuming passion
292   for realism, the effort to make everything—picture, carpet
293   or wall-paper design, sculpture—deceptively real to vie with
294   nature, not to create. In the industrial arts this tendency
295   is seen in an extreme concern for detail, as in flower-painted
296   Chinese jars as compared with Dresden ware, ornamented
297   with naturalistic flowers in relief.
298   After a period of realism, which is the siren that lures
299   all the arts to destruction, comes reaction to pure design and
300   pattern. Many believe that we are just now entering such a
301   period. They believe that modernistic art, although it is pro-
302   ductive of some absurdity, is none the less leading to better
303   things. What was considered beautiful in earlier days is still
304   a part of the beautiful, but it does not impress us today as it
305   did then. As life changes, so does beauty; and since the fine
306   arts express life, they are affected by the tempo and the spirit
307   of change and efficiency in present-day living. In general,
308   the modern tendency is toward simplicity and usefulness.

309   FINE ARTS IN THE SCHOOLS

310   There is no better witness to the fact that the fine arts
311   help to explain life and add happiness to it than the marked
312   increase of interest in them which present-day education is
313   showing. Methods of teaching focus attention on making
314   them means of self-expression. One of the world's successful
315   art teachers of children, the famous Prof. F. Cizek of Vienna,
316   assigns a subject, such as Spring, or Autumn, and leaves
317   each child to invent his own expression by using the forms
318   and facts which he has gathered from his own experience.
320   Startlingly fresh and often beautiful have been the results;
321   for example, the 'Dog and Ducks' by a 13-year-old child.
322   Opportunities are given for actual work with the materials
323   and tools of various fine arts. Through successes and failures
324   the pupils learn of the difficulties involved, and their sense of
325   appreciation and selection is thereby awakened as in no
325   other way.

325   HOW TO APPRECIATE ART

326   How can we learn to appreciate good pictures, sculpture,
327   engraving, and other forms of fine art, when there are so many
328   kinds, and so many conflicting opinions about them? There are
329   no sure rules for doing this any more than for appreciating
330   good literature; but a few suggestions have been helpful.
331   First of all, never try to force your likings. Give them
332   a chance to develop by looking at all kinds, especially heed
333   what good authorities call excellent. Second, never condemn

334   a work of fine art because its subject does not appeal, or is
335   absolutely distasteful to you. Distinguish between the picture
336   or object as an arrangement of color, shadow, line, and mass,
337   and as the portrayal of a specific subject. Look for patterns
338   as apart from the details which express them. Look for
339   rhythms. Look for deft lines that bind the parts into one
340   unified whole. Heed with utmost care the picture that at first
341   glance gives you a single clear impression. Look for strength
342   first, and admire delicacy afterward. Be neither intellectually
343   brow-beaten by a great name—the greatest have their weak
344   moments—nor contemptuous in the presence of an unknown
345   one. Use eyes and mind wherever pictures are concerned
346   and be glad when they make your heart beat rapidly. Remem-
347   ber George Meredith's words, "He who sees well is king of
348   what he sees; eyesight is having."

Do not look at the next two pages until after text is read.

QUESTIONS

for

ART READING TEST

by

Francis P. Robinson and Prudence Hall
The Ohio State University

Name.. Age.....................

Grade..................... School..

Directions I

Note the number of the last line you had read at the end of 10 minutes. Turn this page and find the number in the left-hand margin which is just equal to, or just less than, this number. Draw a line across the page *under* the question thus numbered and then answer each of the questions down to this line.

After you have answered these questions, read *Directions II* and do what it requests.

Directions II

Write in below the three numbers which you encircled in the text at the end of 3 minutes, 6 minutes, and 10 minutes of reading.

Rate of Reading.....................
- 3 minute line...............
- 6 minute line............... | percentile |
- 10 minute line [2]..............

Comprehension Accuracy: $\dfrac{\text{No. right}}{\text{No. tried}}$ .... = | % right | percentile |

[2] This value for the 10-minute interval also equals the average number of words read per minute during this time.

In the left-hand margin there is a series of "line numbers." Find the number that is equal to, or just less than, the number of the last line you read. Mark this and do not answer questions beyond this point.

line

20 What is the fundamental quality of art? (1) joining together (2) beauty (3) perspective (4) skillful representation (5) balance................ (1) ....

20 Art is a skillful representation of nature as in a photograph......... ... (2) T F

26 What are the two classes of art? (1) useful (2) practical (3) fine (4) industrial (5) literary.. (3) ....

(4) ....

40 To what class of art does a hand-tooled leather purse belong? (1) useful (2) practical (3) fine (4) industrial (5) literary...................... (5) ....

47 The theme that is celebrated in every form of fine art is (1) beauty (2) representation (3) decoration (4) triumph (5) deficiencies of world..... (6) ....

52 An artist is a person who (1) copies (2) creates what is beautiful....... (7) ....

73 The painter identifies himself with the object of his art.............. (8) T F

73 The observer identifies himself with the art object he is observing...... (9) T F

84 The artist is more concerned with causes than effects................. (10) T F

89 The fine arts deal almost entirely with the hopes and aspirations of humanity and with that which is good in life......................... (11) T F

102 Where does the artist ultimately get his inspiration? (1) himself (2) nature (3) history of race... (12) ....

113 What effect do the arts have upon one viewing them? (1) arouse him to criticism (2) free him from the conscious effort of living (3) inspire him to create a work of art (4) soothe his nerves........................ (13) ....

132 A work of art may have how many themes? (1) only one (2) related ones (3) many (4) themes within a theme............................... (14) ....

135 The artist must simplify the relationship he finds among the objects he portrays.. (15) T F

141 It would never be artistic to portray the havoc of a battlefield as it really is.. (16) T F

149 By what name is the process of selection and arrangement known? (1) composition (2) consistency (3) unity (4) subordination.............. (17) ....

165 In developing a scene depicting "Jealousy," the principle of unity would suggest the use in this picture of (1) all three people in the triangle (2) two of these people (3) the jealous person only (4) any of these or other combinations of persons that would best depict your theme........... (18) ....

165 Why should some things in a painting appear to be out of focus? (1) it is a more skillful technique (2) that is the way they look in real life (3) to give a single impression (4) the artist does not have time to concentrate on less important aspects.................................... (19) ....

line

173 Consistency of attractions in a picture is called harmony.............. (20)   T   F

178 In this process of selection and arrangement, what three things are important? (1) beauty (2) harmony (3) focus (4) curved lines (5) balance (6) perspective (7) rhythm... (21) ....

(22) ....

(23) ....

193 Why is Corot's landscape "Morning" also called the "Dance of the Nymphs"? Because of (1) the three figures (2) the movement in the painting (3) the consistency (4) the rippling water................... (24) ....

213 What is the theme of Turner's "Fighting Temeraire"? (1) bravery (2) sadness (3) glory of war (4) irony (5) sternness...................... (25) ....

213 The theme of these two pictures is produced primarily by (1) the selection of objects in the painting (2) the flow and direction of the lines (3) the titles used... (26) ....

224 The message of art is primarily (1) intellectual (2) a mood (3) emotional (4) an inspiration... (27) ....

240 The message of art is to present the beauty of the scene rather than to use a scene to present the beauty which the artist is experiencing...... (28)   T   F

255 What three considerations compel the artist to turn away from trying to copy nature slavishly? (1) artistic scruples (2) absolute beauty (3) principles of design (4) desire to improve upon nature (5) desire for expression of emotions (6) knowledge of the futility of trying to copy nature (7) translation of three-dimensional aspects to the canvas....... (29) ....

(30) ....

(31) ....

279 According to the text, the industrial arts resemble the fine arts more closely than they resemble the useful arts.......................... (32)   T   F

285 The stages of art history (1) go in cycles (2) progress with frequent regression (3) occasionally regress, by accident (4) are leading to a fifth and new stage... (33) ....

296 List the following stages of art history in chronological order: (1) realism (2) childlike technique (3) developed technique...................... (34) ....

300 What is the siren that leads all the arts to destruction? (1) surrealism (2) realism (3) simplicity (4) cubism (5) impressionism (6) classicism... (35) ....

308 In general, according to the text, the modern tendency is toward (1) realism (2) simplicity and usefulness (3) classicism.................. (36) ....

315 How is art taught in the schools? (1) self-expression (2) copying art forms (3) studying about artists..................................... (37) ....

330 Authorities are agreed upon a theory of art........................ (38)   T   F

348 To appreciate art, one should confine his study to works of great masters (39)   T   F

line

348 Which, in each of the following pairs, is more important to consider in
     judging a work of art?
     (1) subject portrayed vs. (2) arrangement of color, shadow, line and
     mass.................................. (40) ....

     (1) patterns   vs. (2) details............................... (41) ....

     (1) strength   vs. (2) delicacy............................... (42) ....

Do not turn the page until the signal to begin reading is given.

A Test of Reading Ability for

GEOLOGY

by

Francis P. Robinson and Prudence Hall
The Ohio State University

THE WONDROUS STORY WE READ IN THE ROCKS [3]

Name.. Age......................

Grade..................... School..

Directions

1   The purpose of this test is to measure your ability to read school assignments. You are to
2   read the following geology selection in your usual manner of reading assignments; after ten
3   minutes of reading you will be asked to answer questions over the material read. These questions
4   will be of the type generally asked in class over such readings.
5   At the end of 3 minutes, 6 minutes, and 10 minutes of reading you will be asked to "Mark."
6   This means that you are to encircle quickly the number of the line that you are reading (num-
7   bered as in the left-hand margin here) and then go on immediately with your reading. At the
8   end of 10 minutes you will be asked to stop reading and to turn to the questions which follow.
9   Be accurate in noting the last line read for *you will be expected to answer questions* over all the
10   material that you mark as having been read.

[3] Used with permission from Volume GH, pp. 39–45, *Compton's Pictured Encyclopedia*, Chicago: F. E. Compton and Co., 1941.

THE WONDROUS STORY WE READ IN THE ROCKS

2   Geology is the science which deals with the history of the
3 earth. It is the task of geology not simply to recite the history
4 of the earth so far as it is known, but to show how this his-
5 tory became known and how the limits of knowledge are being
6 extended. Geology is a young science, and in its study at the
7 present time it is needful to take account of the limitations
8 of present knowledge as well as of the knowledge itself.
10   Everything which throws light on the history of the earth
11 falls within the field of geology. The history of the atmosphere
12 and the history of the ocean are really parts of geology, since
13 the atmosphere and the ocean are parts of the earth. The
14 popular impression, therefore, that geology has to do only with
15 the rocks of the earth is not altogether adequate. The rocks
16 of the earth, to be sure, furnish the larger part of the data
17 for unraveling the history of the earth, though they are not
18 the only sources of information. It is to be remembered, too,
19 that when the geologist studies the rocks, he studies them for
20 the light they can be made to throw on earth-history, rather
21 than for their own sake.

23   How Earth Rehearses the Story of Her Life

24   In working out the history of the earth, so far as it has
25 been worked out, the line of approach has been through the
26 study of the changes which are now taking place on the earth's
27 surface. The rain falls on the land, and some of it gathers
28 into streams, and the streams flow into the sea. In the flow
29 of the water the substance of the land is worn away. The
30 material is carried to the sea and deposited there in the form
31 of gravel, sand, mud, etc. The sand and mud need nothing
32 but cementation to become sandstone and shale, two of the
33 commonest sorts of rocks found on the land. The process of
34 cementation is now going on by natural means in many places.
35 In the sand and the mud, as they are deposited in the sea,
36 shells of various animals are imbedded. The shale and sand-
37 stone of the land also contain shells and other traces of marine
38 animals known as fossils. Hence it is inferred that the sand-
39 stone and shale, as well as certain other sorts of rock found
40 in the land, originally were deposited as beds of sand and mud
41 in the sea, and that they have since been elevated so as
42 to become dry land.
45   The activities of other surface agencies are studied sim-
46 ilarly. The detailed study of the work now being done by
47 rain and rivers, underground water, waves and currents, the
48 atmosphere, glaciers, changes of temperature, gravity, organic
49 agencies, and all other forces and activities operative on the sur-
50 face of the earth, has taught geologists how to interpret the rocks
51 formed in ages long past. It is by the interpretation of the re-

52 corded results of the past, in the light of the processes now taking
53 place, that the science of geology has grown up. The study of
54 present processes is becoming more and more exhaustive, and the
55 application of this increased knowledge of present processes to
56 the records of the past is continually enlarging and perfecting
57 our knowledge of the earth's history.

58   THE MYSTERY IN THE WORLD'S BEGINNINGS

59   Geology really begins with the origin of the earth, and at
60 this point it touches the field of astronomy. The early ages of
61 the earth's history are as yet speculative. There seems to be good
62 reason for doubting the truth of the "nebular hypothesis," which
63 was long regarded as satisfactory. The only rival hypothesis
64 which has been framed is the "planetesimal hypothesis," which
65 supposes that the earth is made up of an aggregation of small
66 bodies comparable to the meteorites and shooting stars which
67 daily reach the earth by millions at the present time. While the
68 stages of the earth's history preceding the beginning of sedi-
69 mentation are largely conjectural, many lines of investigation
70 are being pursued which ultimately may throw much light on
71 the early and obscure stages of the earth's development. The
72 general outlines of this history since sedimentation began are
72 fairly well understood.

73   CLASSES OF ROCKS

73   The rocks of the earth which contain the principal record
74 of the earth's history are of three great classes: (1) igneous
75 rocks, or those which represent solidified lava; (2) sedimentary
76 rocks, as shale, sandstone, conglomerate, etc., most of which are
77 made up of fragments of older rocks; and (3) metamorphic
78 rocks, which may have been so far altered by various means that
79 they are now very unlike the materials from which they were
80 first made. In the metamorphism of rocks, pressure is the most
81 important agent. Chemical change, under the influence of mois-
82 ture, is probably second in importance; and heat third. A special
83 class of sedimentary rocks is due to life. Here belong most lime-
84 stones, made of shells, corals, etc.; coal, of plant origin; and a
85 number of lesser formations.
86   The composition, position, and structure of these several
87 sorts of rock and their fossil contents, so far as they contain
88 fossils, interpreted in the light of processes now taking place,
89 allow geologists to infer the conditions under which the various
90 sorts of rocks are made. When geologists are able to tell what
91 the conditions were on every part of the earth at every period
92 of the past, the science of geology will be complete.

93   ECONOMIC GEOLOGY

94   Among the many branches of the science, economic geology
95 is one of the most important. It deals with the materials of
96 the earth's crust which are commercially valuable, and has to

97   do with ores of all sorts, with coal, with building stone, with
98   clays which are valuable for the manufacture of brick and pot-
99   tery, and the like. It deals also with materials which can be
100 used for pigments; sand, used for making glass; with precious
101 stones; with abrasive materials; with asphaltum, petroleum,
102 natural gas, salt, fertilizers, etc. One function of economic geol-
103 ogy is to determine the origin of these substances and, so far as
104 possible, the laws which govern their distribution.

104   FIVE VAST CHAPTERS IN EARTH'S STORY

105   Geologic time is divided into five eras, and most of these
106 are divided into several periods, as shown in the following table
107 reading from the present to the remote past.

Eras	Periods
108 CENOZOIC	Quaternary (including glacial)
	Pliocene ⎫
	Miocene ⎬ Tertiary
	Oligocene ⎪
	Eocene ⎭
109 MESOZOIC	Upper Cretaceous
	Lower Cretaceous
	Jurassic
	Triassic
110 PALEOZOIC	Permian ⎫
	Pennsylvanian ⎬ Carboniferous
	Mississippian ⎭
	Devonian
	Ordovician (= Lower Silurian)
	Silurian (= Upper Silurian)
	Cambrian
111 PROTEROZOIC	Algonkian
111 ARCHEOZOIC	Archean

111   ARCHEOZOIC ERA: FORMATION OF OLDEST ROCKS

112   The Archeozoic era was the time occupied in the making
113 of the oldest known system of rocks. The Archean rocks are
114 mostly metamorphosed igneous rocks, though with them are
115 some metamorphic sedimentary rocks. Fossil algae have been
116 found in this system of rocks, and it is certain that life existed
117 before the close of this era.

117   PROTEROZOIC ERA: LONG PERIOD OF SEDIMENTATION

118   The Proterozoic era is the time during which were deposited
119 the greatest system of rocks lying above the Archeozoic and
120 below the oldest rocks containing abundant fossils. The rocks
121 of the Proterozoic era are mainly sedimentary, though igneous
122 rocks have great development locally. The formations of the
123 Proterozoic era are many thousands of feet thick, though con-

124 siderable portions have been removed by erosion. The Protero-
125 zoic era was perhaps as long as all subsequent time. Some forms
126 of life existed during this era, as is shown by the few fossils
127 which have been found in the rocks, and by the nature of
128 some of the formations, even where fossils are wanting. For
129 example, there are black shales and graphitic slates, the carbon
130 of which probably is of plant origin. The Proterozoic (Algon-
131 kian) rocks of the Lake Superior region contain rich deposits
132 of iron and copper.

133 PALEOZOIC ERA: THE RANGE OF LIFE AND THE ORIGIN OF COAL

134   The Paleozoic (formerly called Primary) era was the time
135 when the several systems of rocks bearing the names Cambrian,
136 Ordovician, Silurian, Devonian, Mississippian and Pennsylvanian
137 (Carboniferous), and Permian were deposited. The time occupied
138 in the deposition of each of these systems is a period. These
139 systems of rocks are mainly of sedimentary origin, and the
140 materials of which they are composed were derived from the land
141 areas existing when these systems were being laid down. Most
142 of the materials of the systems were washed down from the land
143 to the sea, and there deposited. The several systems of Paleozoic
144 rocks are distinguished from one another by their fossils. Thus,
145 the fossils of the Cambrian system of rocks are sufficiently un-
146 like those of the Ordovician system to be readily distinguished
146 by those familiar with fossils.

147   Even at the beginning of the Cambrian period *the range*
148 *of life was great*, all the great types which now live except
149 the vertebrates being represented. Even the vertebrates may
150 have lived, though relics of their existence have not been found.
151 In this period trilobites and brachiopods seem to have been
152 the most abundant and characteristic life. In the rocks of the
153 Ordovician system fish remains have been found, and also relics
154 of air-breathing life. Mollusks, orinoids, and corals lived in
155 great profusion, in addition to the types of life which pre-
156 dominated in the Cambrian period. Most of the oil and gas
157 of Ohio and Indiana has come from rocks of the Ordovician
158 age.

159   In the Silurian period the same general types of life were
160 prevalent, but the species are so unlike those of the preceding
161 period as to be readily distinguished by those familiar with
162 fossils. The Devonian period is often known as the Age of
163 Fishes, on account of the abundance of fish remains in the
164 rocks of this system. It is far from certain, however, that
165 fish were more abundant than now, and the variety of fish
166 probably was less than at the present time. The Devonian was,
167 however, the first period when fishes were abundant, so far as
168 now known. The oil of Pennsylvania and Canada is largely
169 derived from beds of Devonian age.
170   During the Mississippian period, animal life seems to have

171 become notably more abundant, and *some beds of coal were*
172 *formed*, though coal is more characteristic of the next system.
173 Much oil has been derived from the Mississippian system of
174 rocks in Illinois. During the Pennsylvanian period there were
175 extensive marshes in the United States and in some other parts
176 of the world, in which vegetable matter accumulated in great
177 quantity. These marshes (peat-bogs) subsequently were sub-
178 merged, and the vegetable matter buried by mud, sand, etc.,
179 and ultimately converted into coal. Most of the coal of the United
180 States east of the Great Plains was accumulated at this period.
181 Plant life was abundant, but the plants were largely of types
182 now extinct. Land animals of early reptilian types were common.
183 The Mississippian, Pennsylvanian and Permian periods some-
183 times are called the Carboniferous period.

184   The Permian period represents a transition stage between
185 the Paleozoic and the Mesozoic eras. In the Permian period there
186 was extensive glaciation in Australia, South Africa, India, and
186 South America.

187   The several systems of Paleozoic rocks have somewhat dif-
188 ferent distribution, and, since the area of the deposits of any
189 period corresponds approximately with the submerged area of
190 that period, the distribution of the several systems helps us to
191 understand the relations of land and water during the several
192 periods. In this way it is known that the relations of sea and
193 land were different at different times. It would appear either that
194 the continent repeatedly rose and sank, causing areas which were
195 at one time submerged to become land, and vice versa; or that
196 the sea-level itself rose and fell. If the sea-level rose, it would
197 overspread the low lands; if it were lowered, it would cause areas
198 which had been submerged to become land. How far the many
199 changes in geography during the Paleozoic era were the result
200 of land oscillations, and how far they were the result of oscilla-
201 tions of sea-level, never has been determined. So far as present
202 knowledge goes, it would appear that the deep-sea bottom has
203 at no time been land, and that the areas which were alternately
204 above and below sea-level were low when they were land, and
205 covered by shallow water only when they were submerged.

206 MESOZOIC ERA: WHEN GIANT REPTILES RULED THE LAND

207   The Mesozoic (formerly called Secondary) era, as the term
208 indicates, was the era when life intermediate between the ancient
209 and the present existed. This era is divided into several periods,
210 as indicated above. The Triassic formations of North America
211 are somewhat widespread in the western third of the continent,
212 but have but little development in the eastern part. During
213 this period reptiles perhaps were the dominant type of life. They
214 were not only numerous but the individuals attained great size.
215 The earliest known remains of mammals date from this period.

216 Marine life abounded, but departed notably from the types which
217 had prevailed in the Paleozoic era. Vegetation was abundant,
218 but of types now extinct or rare.
219   The Jurassic period followed, and the distribution of its
220 formations is similar to that of the Triassic formations. The life
221 of this period was somewhat different from that of the preceding,
222 though the same general types abounded. Reptiles were the most
223 distinctive type, and they were even larger than in the preceding
224 period. The oldest remains of birds yet found are Jurassic.
225   The Jurassic period was followed by the Cretaceous (Chalk)
226 periods. In the early part of the first period chalk was not
227 being deposited, but in the later part chalk deposits were in
228 process of formation in many parts of the earth. The chalk
229 deposits are made up, for the most part, of the shells of minute
230 marine animals. The Cretaceous formations of North America
231 are much more widespread than those of the Jurassic and
232 Triassic periods. Their distribution indicates that a large part
233 of the North American continent was submerged during part
234 of the later Cretaceous periods. It was during the Upper Cre-
235 taceous that modern types of plants and fishes made their ap-
236 pearance. During the last stages of the Cretaceous periods
237 extensive coal beds were laid down in the western United States.

238 Cenozoic Era: Exit the Monsters; Enter the Mammals

239   The Cenozoic era, or era of modern life, followed the
240 Mesozoic. Mammals, the earliest remains of which were found
241 in the rocks of the Triassic system, abounded during the
242 Cenozoic era, while the huge reptiles which had been especially
243 characteristic of the Mesozoic era had disappeared. Reptiles
244 still existed, but they were of relatively small types, and their
245 numbers appear to have been few. As the Cenozoic era pro-
246 gressed, the forms of life approached more and more closely to
247 those of the present time, and by the end of the Pliocene the
248 life was nearly the same as that which now exists.
249   One theory ascribes this change from Mesozoic to Cenozoic
250 life to a change in climate and ground surface. Before the
251 change much of the ground was marshy, and since under such
252 conditions size and power were more important than speed for
253 survival, ponderous reptile forms dominated the earth. Then
254 geologic changes drained off the water, created large areas of
255 hard ground surface suited to running, and supplanted the
256 luxurious swampy vegetation with modern "dry land" flowering
257 plants. These changes gave the running types of animal, with
258 their speed and ability to range far in search of food, an advan-
259 tage over the clumsy giant reptiles, which therefore gradually
259 became extinct.
260   The Quaternary (Pleistocene) period was a remarkable one,
261 on account of the great climatic changes which occurred at this
262 time. The result of these climatic changes brought on a glacial

263 climate, and an ice-sheet or series of ice-sheets covered some-
264 thing like 4,000,000 square miles in the northern part of North
265 America. A large ice-sheet was developed, probably contempo-
266 raneously, on the continent of Europe, affecting especially its
266 northwestern part.

266 ## AGE OF THE EARTH

268 The duration of the earth's history is a matter which has
269 received much attention, but no conclusions have been reached
270 which can be relied upon, beyond the very general one that
271 the history of the earth has been exceedingly long. Various
272 conjectures as to the number of years occupied in bringing
273 the earth to its present condition have been made. They range
274 from 25,000,000 years or so to 1,500,000,000 since the time of
275 the formation of the oldest rocks now accessible. As stated
276 above, the Archeozic era probably was longer than all subse-
277 quent time put together. The Proterozoic era was perhaps as
278 long as all that followed. The Paleozoic era was perhaps two
279 or three times as long as the Mesozoic, and the Mesozoic probably
280 longer than the Cenozoic.

280 ## GREAT CHANGES IN CLIMATE

281 The climatic changes which the earth has undergone have
282 been great, but their causes are not well understood. There
283 is little basis for the belief, formerly widespread, that the climate
284 has on the whole been growing cooler. Cold periods seem to
285 have alternated with warmer ones. There was local glaciation
286 in the Paleozoic era, and extensive glaciation at the close of
287 the Paleozoic. There was glaciation in the early Cenozoic era
288 and very extensive glaciation later in that era; and there is
289 some indication of cold periods at other times. On the other
290 hand the lands of high latitudes enjoyed genial climates during
291 some parts of the earth's history, even as late as the mid-
292 Tertiary time.
293 Volcanic activity seems to have been greater at some periods
294 than at others, but on the whole it seems to have been about as
295 great, so far as now known, in late as in early stages of the
296 earth's history, if the Archeozic era be excepted.

297 ## THE WORK AND TRAINING OF A GEOLOGIST

298 Although geology is among the youngest of the sciences it
299 is also one of the most useful. Much that is useful to mankind
300 comes out of the earth. Fuel for warmth and power, stone, clay,
301 and cement for our houses, metals for making the machines that
302 serve the modern industrial world—all these are earth products.
304 The various useful commodities are not placed within the
305 earth like plums in a pudding without law or order. Each de-
306 posit of every one of them is where it is for some good geological

307 reason.   The study of the origin, distribution, and laws of
308 occurrence of such deposits is part of the science of geology.
309   Geology has a particularly strong appeal to the man who
310 has a love for the great outdoors, "the glory of the sun and
311 streams that murmur as they run."   The earth itself is the
312 great textbook of geology, open everywhere to the one who is
313 willing and knows how to read its lesson.   To become expert in
314 his science the geologist must travel widely and often to difficult
315 and dangerous places.   He should be proficient in all manners
316 of travel—afoot, with a pack-sack, on horseback, in the canoe,
317 and by wagon—and able to camp in forests, on the plains, or
318 in the mountains.
319   Since geology is largely the application of other sciences
320 to earth problems, the geologist must have at least an elementary
321 knowledge of chemistry, physics, and mathematics.   His work
322 is largely the study of minerals, rocks, and ores and their rela-
323 tions to one another, and particularly the relations of groups of
324 rock or rock formations to each other, and the relations of
325 mineral deposits to the various rock masses in which they are
326 found.   Since a large part of his business is the making of maps,
327 he should know surveying and drafting.

Do not look at the next two pages until after text is read.

QUESTIONS

for

GEOLOGY READING TEST

by

Francis P. Robinson and Prudence Hall
The Ohio State University

Name.. Age.....................

Grade.................... School..

Directions I

Note the number of the last line you had read at the end of 10 minutes. Turn this page and find the number in the left-hand margin which is just equal to, or just less than, this number. Draw a line across the page *under* the question thus numbered and then answer each of the questions down to this line.

After you have answered these questions, read *Directions II* and do what it requests.

Directions II

Write in below the three numbers which you encircled in the text at the end of 3 minutes, 6 minutes and 10 minutes of reading.

	3 minute line...............	
Rate of Reading....................	6 minute line...............	percentile
	10 minute line [4].............	

Comprehension Accuracy: $\dfrac{\text{No. right}}{\text{No. tried}}$ .... = | % right | percentile |

---

[4] This value for the 10-minute interval also equals the average number of words read per minute during this time.

APPENDIX I

In the left-hand margin there is a series of "line numbers." Find the number that is equal to, or just less than, the number of the last line you read. Mark this and do not answer questions beyond this point.

line

9   The main object of study in geology is (1) rocks (2) the history of the earth (3) geography (4) minerals and oils . . . . (1) . . . .

22   Geology is interested in the history of the ocean and of the atmosphere, as well as of rocks . . . . (2)   T   F

44   The presence of what indicates that certain land rocks were originally in the sea? (1) sandstone (2) shale (3) marine fossils (4) cementation (5) beds of sand and mud . . . . (3) . . . .

57   The study of the recently made "dust bowl" would be of little value to geologists . . . . (4)   T   F

67   The "nebular hypothesis" says that the earth is made up of an aggregation of such things as meteorites and shooting stars . . . . (5)   T   F

72   The general outlines of the earth's history are pretty well understood from the time (1) of origin of the earth (2) of beginning of buckling and volcanic action (3) when sedimentation began . . . . (6) . . . .

75   Solidified lava is (1) sedimentary (2) metamorphic (3) igneous, rock . . . . (7) . . . .

85   List the following in order of their importance in the metamorphism of rocks: (1) chemical change (2) heat (3) pressure . . . . (8) . . . .

104   Some geologists are professionally interested in finding the best clays for making brick . . . . (9)   T   F

105   How many major eras are there in the earth's history? (1) three (2) five (3) ten (4) eighteen . . . . (10) . . . .

113   Which era constituted the time occupied in making the oldest known system of rocks? (1) Proterozoic (2) Archeozoic (3) Paleozoic . . . . (11) . . . .

122   The Proterozoic era had rocks mainly of what origin? (1) sedimentary (2) igneous (3) metamorphic . . . . (12) . . . .

127   Which one of these eras was longer than all the rest put together? (1) Cenozoic (2) Paleozoic (3) Mesozoic (4) Proterozoic . . . . (13) . . . .

130   The fossils of what indicate that there was life before the end of the Archeozoic era? (1) fish (2) trees (3) algae (4) mammals . . . . (14) . . . .

136   To what era do the Silurian and Mississippian periods belong? (1) Paleozoic (2) Proterozoic (3) Mesozoic . . . . : . . . . (15) . . . .

146   How does one distinguish between the various periods of the Paleozoic era? (1) appearance of carbon (2) levels of their rocks (3) kinds of fossils (4) geographical location of the rocks . . . . (16) . . . .

158   Which one of the following probably did not exist during the Cambrian period of the Paleozoic era? (1) Protozoa (2) algae (3) corals (4) vertebrates (5) mollusks . . . . (17) . . . .

line

165 Changes in animal life from the Cambrian period to the Silurian period consisted mainly in modification of (1) complexity (2) size (3) species (4) habitat. . . . . (18) . . . .

169 Which form of animal life was abundant in the Devonian period of the Paleozoic era? (1) amphibians (2) mammals (3) fishes (4) protozoa. . . . . (19) . . . .

175 The periods in which our coal beds were laid down generally preceded those in which fossil animals are found. . . . . (20)   T   F

183 The periods accounting for the origin of oil generally (1) precede (2) come at the same time as (3) follow, those which cause coal. . . . . (21) . . . .

186 During the Permian period (end of Paleozoic era) there was extensive glaciation in (1) southern hemisphere (2) northern hemisphere (3) both southern and northern hemispheres. . . . . (22) . . . .

200 The distribution of rocks in the Paleozoic era indicates that (1) there was considerable glaciation at this time (2) the damp land areas and those covered by water changed considerably (3) there was much bending and breaking of the earth's surface (earthquakes and volcanic activity). (23) . . . .

210 What was the era which had life intermediate between the present and the ancient? (1) Proterozoic (2) Mesozoic (3) Paleozoic (4) Archeozoic. . (24) . . . .

218 What form of life was most abundant during this era? (1) reptiles (2) mammals (3) fish (4) birds. . . . . (25) . . . .

224 Which form of life apparently made its appearance in the Jurassic period of the Mesozoic era? (1) man (2) mammals (3) insects (4) birds (5) amphibians. . . . . (26) . . . .

237 What formations were numerous in the Cretaceous period of the Mesozoic era? (1) fossils (2) sandstone (3) chalk (4) lava. . . . . (27) . . . .

242 What form of life abounded in the Cenozoic era? (1) mammals (2) reptiles (3) primates (4) birds. . . . . (28) . . . .

248 What period of the Cenozoic era marks the end of changes in animal life and had life forms similar to those today? (1) Eocene (2) Miocene (3) Pliocene. . . . . (29) . . . .

250 One theory ascribes the change in life from Mesozoic to Cenozoic to change in (1) climate (2) sea level (3) evolution. . . . . (30) . . . .

262 The outstanding feature of the Quarternary period of the Cenozoic era was changes in (1) climate (2) rock formation (3) distribution (4) forms of life. . . . . (31) . . . .

295 How closely do geologists agree as to the age of the earth? (1) they agree within a few thousand years (2) their estimates vary about 1,000,000 years (3) there are great differences (many millions of years) in their estimates (4) they find it impossible to make any estimate. . . . . (32) . . . .

280 The earliest era was longer than all the other eras put together. . . . . (33)   T   F

280 Each succeeding era is shorter than its predecessors. . . . . (34)   T   F

line

283 What is the cause of the marked changes in climate in the earth's history? (1) changes in sea level (2) cause is unknown (3) earth is farther from sun (4) earth is cooling off...................................... (35) ....

291 The earth's changes in climate are characterized by (1) increasing coldness (2) increasing heat (3) alternating hot and cold periods........... (36) ....

296 Volcanic activity has decreased a great deal during the last (Cenozoic) era as compared to the earlier ones................................. (37)   T   F

300 Geology is one of the oldest and best developed sciences.............. (38)   T   F

310 A geologist needs to know different kinds of ore when he finds them, but there is little he can do to limit the area over which he must search to find them... (39)   T   F

SPECIAL READING SKILLS

A. Reading Tables:

No. right out of 30......

Number Tried	Number Right																								
	10	11	12	13	14	15	16	17	18	19	20	21	22	23	24	25	26	27	28	29	30	31	32	33	34
10	100																								
11	91	100																							
12	83	92	100																						
13	77	85	92	100																					
14	71	79	86	93	100																				
15	67	73	80	87	93	100																			
16	63	69	75	81	88	94	100																		
17	59	65	71	76	82	88	94	100																	
18	56	61	67	72	78	83	89	94	100																
19	53	58	63	68	74	79	84	89	95	100															
20	50	55	60	65	70	75	80	85	90	95	100														
21	48	52	57	62	67	71	76	81	86	90	95	100													
22	46	50	55	59	64	68	73	77	82	86	91	95	100												
23	44	48	52	57	61	65	70	74	78	83	87	91	96	100											
24	42	46	50	54	58	63	67	71	75	79	83	88	92	96	100										
25	40	44	48	52	56	60	64	68	72	76	80	84	88	92	96	100									
26	38	42	46	50	54	58	62	65	69	73	77	81	85	88	92	96	100								
27	37	41	44	48	52	56	59	63	67	70	74	78	81	85	89	93	96	100							
28	36	39	43	46	50	54	57	61	64	68	71	75	79	82	86	89	93	96	100						
29	34	38	41	45	48	52	55	59	62	66	69	72	76	79	83	86	90	93	97	100					
30	33	37	40	43	47	50	53	57	60	63	67	70	73	77	80	83	87	90	93	97	100				
31	32	35	39	42	45	48	52	55	58	61	65	68	71	74	77	81	84	87	90	94	97	100			
32	31	34	38	41	44	47	50	53	56	59	63	66	69	72	75	78	81	84	88	91	94	97	100		
33	30	33	36	39	42	45	48	52	55	58	61	64	67	70	73	76	79	82	85	88	91	94	97	100	
34	29	32	35	38	41	44	47	50	53	56	59	62	65	68	71	74	76	79	82	85	88	91	94	97	100
	10	11	12	13	14	15	16	17	18	19	20	21	22	23	24	25	26	27	28	29	30	31	32	33	34

TABLE 12. Table for Converting the Fraction $\dfrac{\text{No. right}}{\text{No. tried}}$ into Per Cent Right.

1. If a student gets 17 out of 21 questions right, what per cent does he have right? ....

2. If a student gets 13 out of 15 questions right, what per cent does he have right? ....

3. If a student gets 19 out of 21 questions right, what per cent does he have right? ....

4. 13/23 is a larger fraction than 16/27.　　　　　　　　　T　　F

5. 17/21 is a larger fraction than 25/30.　　　　　　　　　T　　F

6. What divided by 18 equals 78 per cent? ....

7. What divided by 24 equals 71 per cent? ....

Activity	Percentage of Youth in Each Grade Group					
	6th Grade or Less	7th or 8th	9th, 10th, 11th	11th or 12th, Graduate	1, 2, or 3 Years Beyond High School	4 or More Years Beyond High School
Reading..................	11.5	17.9	23.3	32.2	42.6	42.9
Individual sports..........	12.4	13.6	15.9	15.6	15.2	18.4
Dancing, dating...........	12.6	10.9	15.5	14.0	10.4	8.3
Movies..................	9.4	12.8	13.4	10.2	8.2	7.6
Loafing..................	21.7	15.8	7.5	5.9	3.9	4.3
Hobbies.................	8.7	10.1	8.4	10.4	10.7	9.9
Team games..............	10.1	8.2	8.7	5.4	4.0	3.5
Listening to radio.........	2.8	2.4	2.3	1.8	0.9	1.0
Quiet games..............	2.2	1.8	1.0	0.7	0.9	1.8
Other activities...........	8.6	6.5	4.0	3.8	3.2	2.3
Total...............	100.0	100.0	100.0	100.0	100.0	100.0
Number of youth.....	1483	2762	2569	2885	770	396

TABLE 13. Principal Leisure-time Activities of Out-of-school Youth According to the Grades They Completed (From H. M. Bell, *Youth Tell Their Story*, American Council on Education, 1938, p. 166).

8. What per cent of college graduates say that reading is their principal leisure-time activity? . . . .

9. What per cent of out-of-school youth with less than a 6th-grade education say that loafing is their principal leisure-time activity? . . . .

10. What per cent of out-of-school youth with a 7th- or 8th-grade education say that hobbies are their principal leisure-time activity? . . . .

11. Reading is the most popular leisure-time activity with each of the educational divisions of the youth group.   T   F

12. Youth who have been to college tend to do the following things more than do youth who have not been to college:
    a. Read . . . .   T   F
    b. Dancing and dating . . . .   T   F
    c. Movies . . . .   T   F
    d. Loafing . . . .   T   F
    e. Team games . . . .   T   F

13. Youth with some college education tend to seek more social and less individual recreation than do youth without any college education.   T   F

14. Out-of-school youth with the most education tend to consider hobbies a more important activity than do any of the other groups.   T   F

15. Out-of-school youth tend to participate more in activities which do not necessitate having someone else around than in activities which do demand someone else.   T   F

School Grade Completed	Number of Youth	Median Weekly Wage	Median Weekly Hours	Percentage Stating Dead-end Job
Less than 6th grade..........................	431	$ 7.84	50.5	53.2
6th grade................................	349	8.75	44.9	50.0
7th grade................................	708	9.27	48.7	51.5
8th grade................................	586	10.89	42.3	46.5
9th grade................................	485	13.19	45.0	45.0
10th or 11th grade, not graduate............	788	14.51	42.4	44.6
11th-grade graduate......................	508	12.72	50.3	35.4
12th-grade graduate......................	1026	15.38	42.5	44.1
1 year beyond high school graduation........	198	15.71	42.0	34.1
2 or 3 years beyond graduation.............	267	19.74	42.3	23.4
4 or more years beyond graduation..........	233	22.23	41.5	17.4
All youth.............................	5579	$12.96	42.8	43.2

TABLE 14. Median Weekly Wages and Hours of Out-of-school Employed Youth by Grade Completed. (From *ibid.*, pp. 121, 128.)

16. The typical out-of-school employed youth earns how much per week? ....
17. What per cent of youth, who are college graduates and working, believe they have dead-end jobs? ....

18. This study is based on how many people? ....

19. The largest single group of students in this table are those who have graduated from 12th-year high school and have gone no further. T F
20. According to this table, the median (as many people have more, as have less, education than he) working youth has had how much education? (1) 8th grade, (2) 9th grade, (3) 10th or 11th, but not a graduate, (4) high school graduate. ....
21. Because he has had more time to advance before he is 25 years of age, the high school graduate who goes to work tends to earn more money per week before the age of 25, than the person who goes to college for a few years and then goes to work. T F
22. Typical youth (16–24) who work, earn about how much per year? (1) $675, (2) $1000, (3) $1550, (4) $2125. ....
23. College graduates (16–24) who work earn about how much per year? (1) $1150, (2) $1550, (3) $2100, (4) $2600. ....
24. Persons with less education work longer hours and earn less money than persons with more education. T F
25. The less their education, the more youth consider their jobs to have little future. T F
26. At the time of this study, most youth worked less than 40 hours a week. T F

B. Reading Charts

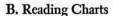

No. right out of 24......

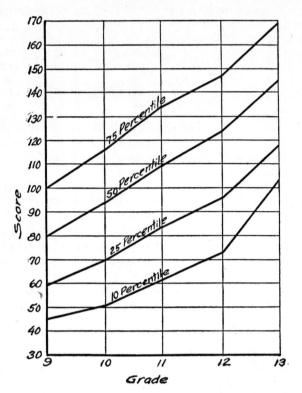

CHART 17. Increase in the Iowa Silent Reading Test norms from grade 9 through grade 13. (Based on publisher's norms.)

Use Chart 17 to answer questions 1–6:

1. The average score during the freshman year in college is: ....

2. At which grade is the most marked gain shown in reading ability? ....

3. On this test, the person at the 10th percentile of college freshmen is midway between the average student of what two grades? ....

4. Which part of the distribution of readers shows the greatest change on entering college? (1) highest quarter, (2) average, (3) lowest quarter, (4) lowest 10 per cent. ....

5. There is a greater difference within the middle 50 per cent of 12th graders (75th percentile–25th percentile) than there is between the average 12th grader and the average 9th grader.   T F

6. The most marked change in one year is made in what year at what level? ....

THE JOBS YOUTH WANT AND THE JOBS THEY GET

WHAT THEY WANT   WHAT THEY GET

PROFESSIONAL OR TECHNICAL	
MANAGERIAL	
OFFICE OR SALES	
SKILLED	
SEMI-SKILLED	
UNSKILLED	
DOMESTIC OR PERSONAL	
RELIEF PROJECT	

EACH FIGURE REPRESENTS 150 YOUTH

CHART 18.   The jobs employed youth (16–24 years of age) want, and the jobs they hold. (From Bell, op. cit., page 133.)

Use Chart 18 to answer questions 7–11:

7. The type of work youth most want to enter is: . . . .

8. The type of work these youth are most frequently employed in is: . . . .

9. How many of these youth were employed in unskilled labor?   . . . .

10. (1) More than half, (2) less than half, (3) half of these youth are employed in office or sales and semiskilled labor.   . . . .

11. How many youth are employed at skilled labor? About (1) 150, (2) 225, (3) 300, (4) 950.   . . . .

EXTENT TO WHICH STUDENTS AND NONSTUDENTS BELONGED TO CLUBS
(PERCENTAGE IN EACH SCHOOL GRADE GROUP OF OUT-OF-SCHOOL YOUTH)

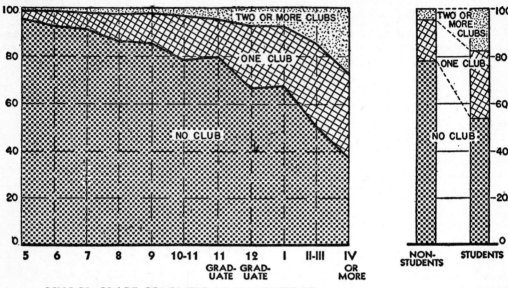

SCHOOL GRADE COMPLETED BY NONSTUDENTS

CHART 19. The extent to which students and nonstudents (aged 16–24) belonged to clubs and the relation of grade completed to belonging.

Use Chart 19 to answer questions 12–16:

12. More out-of-school youth belong, than don't belong, to clubs.   T   F

13. Out-of-school youth who have had the most schooling tend to belong to more clubs than those with less schooling.   T   F

14. Of the group who have graduated from an 11-year high school, what per cent don't belong to any clubs?   . . . .

15. Students belong to more clubs than youth who have left school.   T   F

16. Less than half of college graduates in this group belonged to clubs.   T   F

Use Chart 20 to answer questions 17–24:

17. What per cent of entering freshmen graduate in the same college?   . . . .

18. The greatest number of voluntary withdrawals takes place at the end of which quarter?   . . . .

19. There were more dismissals than there were withdrawals.   T   F

20. The time of greatest change in the original class is at the end of which quarter?   . . . .

21. The time of greatest increase in incoming transfers is at the beginning of which quarter?   . . . .

22. More students are dismissed from school at the time of their senior year than at any other year.   T   F

23. The class graduating from the college is (1) less than half as big, (2) slightly smaller, (3) larger than the class entering the college as freshmen.   . . . .

24. More than half of the class graduating from this college is made up of students who entered this college as freshmen.   T   F

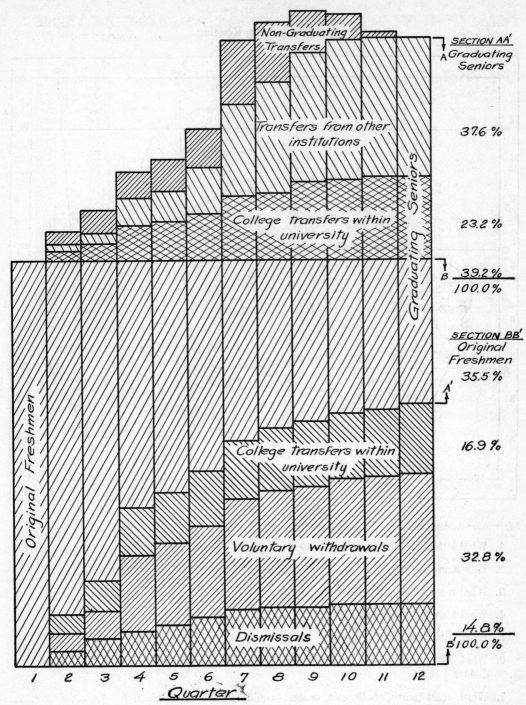

Non-Graduating Transfers

Transfers from other institutions

College transfers within university

Graduating Seniors

Original Freshmen

College transfers within university

Voluntary withdrawals

Dismissals

SECTION AA'
Graduating
Seniors

37.6 %

23.2 %

39.2 %
100.0 %

SECTION BB'
Original
Freshmen

35.5 %

16.9 %

32.8 %

14.8 %
100.0 %

Quarter

1 2 3 4 5 6 7 8 9 10 11 12

CHART 20. The academic history of students who enter and who graduate from a college in a university. (R. D. Bennett, Ohio State University, mimeographed report.)

C. Skills in Map Reading

No. right out of 22......

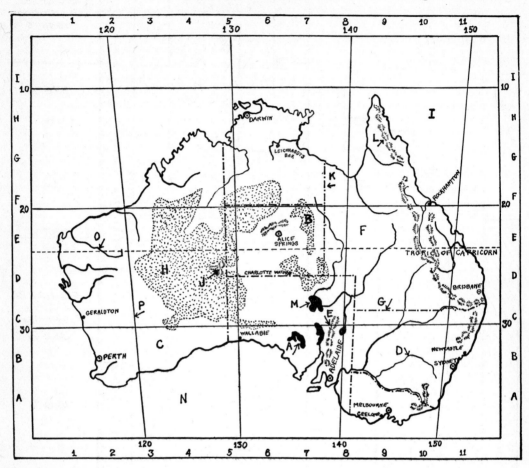

Directions: Answer each question as it tells you to do.

1. What letters indicate borders of states?

   1. ....,

2. How many capital cities are there on this map?

   2. ....

3. What town is located at 1–C?

   3. ....

4. What town is located at 6–E?

   4. ....

5. What letters represent desert?

   5. ....

6. What letter represents a group of mountains almost surrounded by desert?

   6. ....

7. Which coast (north, south, east, or west) could be called mountainous?

   7. ....

8. Is Darwin on the north, south, east, or west coast?

   8. ....

9. Is Darwin or Melbourne closer to the equator?

   9. ....

10. Is Alice Springs east or west of Wallabie?

    10. ....

11. What town is located directly on one of the latitude lines?

    11. ....

12. What town is located directly on one of the longitude lines?   12. ....

13. What letters indicate lakes?   13. ....

14. What letters indicate the ocean?   14. ....

15. What letters indicate rivers?   15. ....

16. What town is located on a river and on the coast?   16. ....

17. What direction is the equator from this country?   17. ....

18. What town is farthest south?   18. ....

19. What town is farthest west?   19. ....

20. Is Alice Springs in the torrid zone or the temperate zone?   20. ....

21. If one inch (| 1″ = 500 m. |) equals 500 miles on this map, about what is the greatest length of this country?   21. ....

22. About what distance is the greatest width?   22. ....

D. Mathematical Formulae: No. right out of 11......

Directions: Place the letter of the best answer in the space provided. (Note: The purpose of this test is to measure your ability to manipulate values in formulae. For this reason some of the formulae do not represent actual physical events; hence you cannot depend upon your knowledge of physics to answer the questions.)

1. $f = ws$ where f = force, w = weight, s = speed. In the case of a one-ounce bullet which hits an object with the same force as a two-ounce bullet, the value of s in the formula is (a) halved, (b) doubled, (c) squared, (d) equal.   1. ....

2. $d = vt$ where d = distance, v = velocity, t = time. Where the values of d and v are both doubled, the value of t (a) remains the same, (b) is also doubled, (c) is halved, (d) is squared.   2. ....

3. $rt = mv^2$ where r = radius, t = tension on string, m = mass of whirling object, v = velocity. An object at the end of a string is whirled around one's head. If the length of the string is doubled and the velocity remains the same, what happens to the value of t? (a) doubled, (b) halved, (c) quadrupled, (d) almost doubled.   3. ....

4. $V_1P_1 = V_2P_2$ where V_1 = original volume, P_1 = original pressure, V_2 = second volume, and P_2 = second pressure. If the value of P_2 is twice that of P_1, the value of V_2 is how large in relation to V_1? (a) double, (b) half, (c) quadruple, (d) squared.   4. ....

5. $P = haDg$ where P = pressure at outlet, h = height of water above outlet, a = area of outlet, D = density of liquid, and g = force of gravity. The pressure at the outlet of identical containers completely filled with different liquids will vary with (a) volume, (b) height, (c) area, (d) density.   5. ....

6. $E = vDgh$ where E = energy lost by drop of liquid, v = velocity of drop, D = density of drop, g = force of gravity, and h = height drop falls. If two drops of the same size fall under identical conditions but lose different amounts of energy, they must have differed in respect to (a) their densities, (b) the velocity of fall, (c) the height fallen, (d) the effect of gravity.   6. ....

7. $2v = gt^2$ where v = velocity, g = gravity and t = time. For the velocity of one object to be 4 times as great as that of a second object, when the effects of gravity are constant, the value of t must be (a) halved, (b) doubled, (c) quadrupled, (d) squared.   7. ....

8. $2v = gt^2$ where v = velocity, g = gravity, and t = time. Where the value of g remains constant, doubling the value of v has what effect on the value of t? (a) halved, (b) doubled, (c) about $1\frac{1}{2}$ times, (d) about quadrupled.   8. ....

9. $E = \frac{1}{2}mv^2$ where E = energy, m = mass and v = velocity. When the velocity is doubled, the value of E is (a) halved, (b) doubled, (c) squared, (d) quadrupled.   9. ....

10. $V = \sqrt{K/D}$ where V = velocity of sound, K = a constant unchanging value, and D = density of air. As the density of air is doubled, what change occurs in velocity of the sound? (a) decreases more than $\frac{1}{2}$, (b) decreases $\frac{1}{2}$, (c) decreases less than $\frac{1}{2}$, (d) stays the same.   10. ....

11. $t = \sqrt{2d/a}$ where t = time, d = distance, and a = acceleration. If the value of a remains unchanged while the value of d is doubled, what change occurs in the value of t? (a) decreases about $\frac{1}{2}$, (b) doubles in value, (c) increases about $\frac{1}{2}$, (d) decreases less than $\frac{1}{2}$.   11. ....

ENGLISH SURVEY TEST [5]—FORM A

By S. L. Pressey
Ohio State University

No. lines right.................................Percentile............Date................

Grammar Test

Directions: In each line of the passage below, four words are underlined. In most of the lines, *one* of these underlined words is grammatically incorrect. Disregard punctuation; assume that it is correct.

Make your answer to each line in one of the following ways: (1) When there is an error, write the correct form of this wrong word on the line at the left. (2) When you are sure that there is no error in the line, write a "0" to the left. (3) If you do not know what the correct form is, or if you are uncertain whether or not there is an error, leave the line at the left blank.

Look over the examples below. Then begin at once. Work rapidly. You will have 25 minutes in which to complete this section. The key for correcting this test is on pages 251–252.

Example:

.......were...... There was money, bonds, and other valuable papers

........to........ in the safe.   The boys were anxious too see the inside.

1. ....   It is the first day of school; each of we

2. .... pupils greet the teacher.   We have already taken

3. .... our seats.   Mary, John, and Annabelle set in the

4. .... front row.   John intends to do his work good this

5. .... year.   Sally and Richard have ask to occupy seats

6. .... near the window.   I have clumb into one of the seats in

7. .... the front row.   I can see easy now.

8. .... Miss McDonald, our new teacher, has told

9. .... each one to do their part.   We accomplish more if

10. .... there is co-operation between us.   Jack don't remember

11. .... the other schools that he has went to.   Mary is two

12. .... years older than I.   Neither Martha nor John are

13. .... younger than I.   The teacher wanted to know whom my

14. .... father was.   I told her his name and who I was living

15. .... with.   Each of us were told to register.   Algebra and

16. .... geometry has been easy for me; so I chose more math-

[5] Used with the permission of the Ohio State Department of Education.

17. .... ematics. The greater part of the curriculum are

18. .... English subjects, which is very uninteresting.

19. .... The teacher can't learn me English at all.

20. .... Verbs make my head ache. I am sure weak in grammar.

21. .... My sister has gave much time to her lessons. Martha,

22. .... my older sister, don't go to school. The weakest

23. .... part of our school are the materials in the labora-

24. .... tories. Our principal feels badly about the lack

25. .... of funds. The price of supplies are high. Perhaps

26. .... the principal will leave me drop chemistry. I shall

27. .... consider the matter very careful.

28. .... Neither Jane nor I were able to play basketball

29. .... last year. However, we never felt sadly

30. .... about it for we could not help it. Basket-

31. .... ball and baseball is what I am going to take this

32. .... year. Jane don't want to play games because she is

33. .... lazy. She likes to lay around and read too much to

34. .... suit me. Soon I'll be able to play basketball good

35. .... and then she will be sorry. Most of us has a very

36. .... good time playing baseball. Jane is taller than me

37. .... and she used to play baseball better than me, but

38. .... she plays so poor now that no one wants her on

39. .... their team. I wish I were as pretty as Jane, though.

40. .... She is fourteen, like Mary and I, and she has curly

41. .... black hair. She wears such pretty clothes to. She

42. .... has some perfume that smells very sweetly. Mother

43. .... won't leave me have any perfume. She said, though

44. .... that I could buy some next year.

45. .... When we graduate from high school us girls

46. .... are going to the same college. We have wrote to

47. .... several colleges and have began to read all about

48. .... the different ones. There are almost to many nice

49. .... ones to choose one very easy. A few like women's

50. .... colleges better than co-educational colleges. Most

51. .... of us prefers the schools where both boys and girls

52. .... may attend because students have a better time their.

53. .... They have football games, to. I saw a football game

54. .... once at Hopewell College. The price of the tickets

55. .... were two dollars and seventy-five cents. We surely

56. .... had a good time. There was about 30,000 people there.

57. .... I had never saw so many people in one place. Every-

58. .... one shouted as loud as they could when our team

59. .... come on the field. Between halves the band played

60. .... the college song very soft while everyone sang.

61. .... Then the teams came back and each player took their

62. .... position on the field. The substitutes set down on

63. .... the bench. The referee, like the other officials, were

64. .... dressed in white linen knickers. His sleeves

65. .... were rolled up. He must have froze because it was

66. .... very cold. Everyone was happy when our team won

67. .... the game. We sung songs and cheered as we followed

68. .... the band out of the stadium. People throwed confetti

69. .... everywhere. Mary, as well as the other girls, have

70. .... ask me to tell about this game over and over again.

71. .... No one in our crowd have seen a big game except me.

72. .... There is several reasons why we want to go to

73. .... Hopewell College. Our teacher told Mary and I

74. .... that they have interesting courses their. To tell

75. .... the truth, the curriculum don't matter so much to us.

76. .... Either dramatics or athletics are going to be my

77. .... specialty.   There <u>is</u> several things <u>to choose</u> from.

78. .... I <u>think that</u> sports <u>is</u> the best <u>part</u> of any school.

79. .... Everybody <u>don't agree</u> with <u>me, however.</u> Mary prefers

80. .... <u>athletics, like</u> Frances <u>and</u> I.

Capitalization and Punctuation Test

Capitalization: No. lines correct...............................Percentile....................

Punctuation: No. lines correct...........................Percentile.........................

Directions: All the capitals and punctuation marks have been omitted from the sentences below, except the capital at the beginning of each sentence and the period at the end.

Look over these sentences carefully. Whenever you find a word which should be capitalized, write the letter which should be a capital on the line at the left of the sentence. Sometimes several capitals are needed in one sentence; you will then write several letters on the line at the left. In some sentences no words need to be capitalized. When this is true leave the line blank. If you are uncertain, it is generally best to omit a capital.

Also, insert in the places in each sentence where they are needed such punctuation marks as you think should be added. You may change a period to an exclamation point or question mark when desirable, but do not cut a sentence into two or more short sentences. In some sentences, no punctuation marks are needed. When in doubt it is best to omit a mark. Make all marks large enough to be seen readily.

Study the examples below and then begin at once. Work rapidly. You will have 25 minutes in which to complete this section. The key for correcting these tests is on pages 252–257.

Examples:

.....S S V D..... Do you like s. s. van dine's mystery stories?

.......I....... Just imagine how frightened i was!

1. .... Are you going to strassburg germany.

2. .... She exclaimed what a beautiful lake.

3. .... The hudson a river in new york is very beautiful.

4. .... Do you expect to visit china or ceylon.

5. .... Three weeks from now well be in kansas city.

6. .... Tell me what doctor harris did said emily.

7. .... If thats all john said we may as well go.

8. .... Friday the tenth of june was my birthday.

9. .... Why do so many people blame the germans.

10. .... It was the fourth of july a national holiday.

11. .... She lives at 25 whittier street dolby kentucky.

12. .... Al smith the democratic candidate was defeated.

13. .... He attended tate college then he went to a law school.

14. .... My subjects include the following history english and latin.

15. .... Theyre ready but well have to wait awhile.

16. .... In the first place the ku klux klan was not legal.

17. .... He had started to newburg there was no retreat.

18. .... She said that she intended to visit mount baker.

19. .... I think french a boring subject but like physics.

20. .... This poem is called in the cool of the night.

21. .... The ring is an heirloom it belonged to jenny lind.

22. .... The captain our old friend met us at the dock.

23. .... Esther jane and mary organized a girls club.

24. .... The letter was sent from detroit on august 8 1933.

25. .... Christmas memorial day and thanksgiving are holidays.

26. .... Will the socialist party ultimately succeed.

27. .... I use detoxal it is a good tooth paste.

28. .... Sinclair lewis wrote these books dodsworth babbitt and arrowsmith.

29. .... We are said the speaker at the dawn of a new era.

30. .... If you see any american tourists let me know.

31. .... He hurried into the bank and asked for the president.

32. .... John finished his spanish then he worked on biology.

33. .... By a waterfall is a simple little piece to play.

34. .... He read tennysons famous poem in memoriam.

35. .... A careful description of captain evans was given for he was an important witness in the trial.

36. .... She recommends gold dust for cleaning since it is cheaper and just as good.

37. .... We didn't have time to visit the alps still we saw almost every other part of europe.

38. .... His wife is a presbyterian he is a baptist.

39. .... He claims that the government is as corrupt as in the days of rome that there is no place for an honest man in politics and that there is little hope for reform.

40. .... The national railway association should recognize that this type of engine will not pay it is out of date.

41. .... The lincoln school has been overcrowded for some time.

42. .... Its too bad that gerry cant go with us.

43. .... Oranges lemons and grapefruit are citrous fruits.

44. .... She said that he would be glad to see you.

45. .... On sunday we went fishing in beaver creek.

46. .... The various codes were submitted to general johnson.

47. .... He said that he saw the prince of wales but no one believed him.

48. .... Please come she wrote colonel brown will be here.

49. .... Joe is not going nor is sally.

50. .... In other words the general electric company refused my offer.

51. .... Its hair is fine and soft its still just a puppy.

52. .... Im in a hurry is the name of an amusing short story.

53. .... You will like these movies cimarron and masquerade.

54. .... The unemployed league will meet tomorrow at seven oclock.

55. .... We saw the capitol at washington and then the driver took us home.

56. .... You should talk to professor brown she advised.

57. .... She said she played no card games during lent.

58. .... One of us must go to lisbon which will it be.

59. .... John makes high grades in mathematics he wants to enter harvard college
next year.

60. .... Youll find it easier to go by way of athens youll save twenty miles.

61. .... Im too tired to go out tonight besides its too cold.

62. .... That youngster said coach jones will be a star next year.

63. .... Its raining hard but jim wont stay at home.

64. .... June july and august are vacation months.

65. .... He wants someone who is quick who is ambitious and who has had experience.

66. .... If its really necessary you may have the chevrolet.

67. .... He told me to meet him at the seneca hotel but he didnt appear.

68. .... Being capable and socially prominent she was elected to the martha washington club.

69. .... All right he said well put the money in the chase bank.

70. .... Ill send you a subscription to the literary digest if you want it.

71. .... You may take this note to mr adams then drop these letters in the mailbox.

72. .... Joseph conrad is the author of lord jim he also wrote victory.

73. .... To be frank she doesnt like janice very well.

74. .... They went to washington to oregon and on to california.

75. .... She resigned from the missionary society thus losing many friends.

76. .... We drove to st louis and then took a quaint old steamer down the mississippi river.

77. .... Ill take you in the car otherwise youll be late.

78. .... Mary you may describe general pershings plan.

79. .... One goes to church on easter to ease ones conscience to wear ones new spring clothes or to see what mrs jones is wearing.

80. .... The play was almost over when john left.

Test on Sentence Structure

No. right *times 2*:...Percentile......................:

Directions: Each of the following paragraphs contains three statements. One of these violates some rule of good sentence structure; it is poorly expressed or not clear. Write the number of the *wrong* statement in each paragraph, in the parentheses at the left. Do not change or mark on any sentence. Look over the example. Then begin at once. Work rapidly. You will have 15 minutes in which to complete this section. The key for this test is on page 257.

Example:

1. (1) (1) The man with the pipe sitting on the bank. (2) The man with the pipe is sitting on the bank. (3) The man sitting on the bank has a pipe.

1. (   ) (1) Where is he? (2) Where is he at? (3) Where has he gone?

2. (   ) (1) The grocer offered me a job, but I refused it. (2) The grocer said that I could work for him Saturdays, but I refused it. (3) The grocer offered me work on Saturdays, but I refused his offer.

3. (   ) (1) I saw your uncle. The one from Dayton. (2) I saw your uncle who lives in Dayton. (3) I saw your uncle, the one from Dayton.

4. (   ) (1) While reading a book, I was startled by the telephone ringing. (2) While reading a book, the telephone rang. (3) While I was reading a book, the telephone rang.

5. (   ) (1) Jane was nervous when Nancy called to her. (2) When Nancy called to Jane, she was nervous. (3) Nancy was nervous when she called to Jane.

6. (   ) (1) His brother is very strong. (2) He has a brother who is very strong. (3) He has a brother is very strong.

7. (   ) (1) Riding down the street in a car they passed John who was afoot. (2) Walking down the street we met John in a car. (3) Walking down the street John passed us in his car.

8. (   ) (1) He had a revolver in his desk, which he had carried in the army. (2) In his desk he had a revolver which he had carried in the army. (3) In the army he had carried the revolver which he now had in his desk.

9. (   ) (1) I got this book from Tom, who got it from Mary. (2) Since this book has left the store it has been first Tom's and then Mary's. (3) This is the book which I got from Tom, who secured it from Mary, who purchased it at the store.

10. (   ) (1) John raced down the field, which was 110 yards long. (2) John ran the full length of the field, which made him a hero. (3) John, who is our best player, raced down the field.

11. (   ) (1) Helen prefers Mary to Jane. (2) Helen likes Mary better than Jane does. (3) Helen likes Mary better than Jane.

12. (   ) (1) Cheering wildly as the team came on the field, all ready for the game. (2) The crowd cheered wildly as the team came on the field. (3) Cheering wildly, we rushed the bleachers.

13. (   ) (1) Chinning is when you pull yourself up to a rod. (2) Chinning is pulling yourself up to a rod. (3) Pulling yourself up to a rod is called chinning.

14. (   ) (1) I like football better than basketball. (2) A game of tennis gives more exercise than a ride in an automobile. (3) Playing tennis is better exercise than to ride in an automobile.

15. (   ) (1) It is a novel which has great merit and which should be read by all. (2) *A Tale of Two Cities* is a novel of great merit and which should be read by all. (3) *A Tale of Two Cities* is a fine novel which should be read by all.

16. (   ) (1) We went to the city and saw a show. We had a good time. (2) After going to the city and seeing a show, we came home. (3) We went to the city and we saw a show, and we came home, and we had a good time.

17. (   ) (1) We took an airplane because it was the quickest means of travel. (2) Wanting to get there quickly, an airplane was taken. (3) To get there quickly we took an airplane.

18. (   ) (1) The boys fumbled in the third quarter. This fumble caused us to lose the game. (2) The boys fumbled in the third quarter, which caused us to lose the game. (3) The game was lost when the boys fumbled in the third quarter.

19. ( ) (1) He ran home. He told his mother. She came out. We were severely scolded. (2) He ran home and told his mother. She came out and scolded us severely. (3) John having gone home and told his mother, we were severely scolded.

20. ( ) (1) John spoke to the man, and he was very cross. (2) John spoke crossly to the man. (3) John spoke to the man, who was very cross.

21. ( ) (1) A lesson which was too long and which should not have been assigned. (2) The lesson, which was too long, should not have been assigned. (3) The lesson was too long and should not have been assigned.

22. ( ) (1) He arose late and ate no breakfast. (2) Having arisen late, no breakfast was served. (3) He ate no breakfast because he had arisen late.

23. ( ) (1) The summer being very dry, and all the creeks dried up. (2) Because the summer was very dry all the creeks dried up. (3) The summer was very dry. All the creeks dried up.

24. ( ) (1) We finished the problem at noon; then we called the teacher. (2) We finished the problem at noon and called the teacher. (3) We finished the problem at noon and calling for the teacher.

25. ( ) (1) Ann is a cute child. Who is always getting into trouble. (2) Ann is a cute child, but she is always getting into trouble. (3) Ann is a cute child who is always getting into trouble.

26. ( ) (1) After the car stopped we stepped out. (2) We stepped out. The car having stopped. (3) The car stopped. We stepped out.

27. ( ) (1) She joined the party, reserved and quiet. (2) The party which she joined was a reserved and quiet affair. (3) She joined the party, but was reserved and quiet.

28. ( ) (1) Although he read everything he could, he acted as if he were compelled to do it. (2) He read everything as if he were compelled to do so. (3) Reading everything he could, as if he were compelled to do so.

29. ( ) (1) John was talking about that man. (2) That is the man whom John was discussing. (3) That is the man; he was just discussing him.

30. ( ) (1) Tom was sorry because he was too late. (2) Tom was too late, and he was sorry. (3) Tom was sorry, being too late.

31. ( ) (1) He is a student who is popular, but who is always in trouble. (2) That student is popular, but always troublesome. (3) He is a popular student, but who is always in trouble.

32. ( ) (1) Everyone is welcome, and you do not have to contribute. (2) Everyone is welcome, and no one has to contribute. (3) You are welcome; you do not have to contribute.

33. ( ) (1) She thought of only one person. Her brother, who was ill. (2) She thought of only one person, her brother. (3) Her brother, the one who was ill, is coming.

34. ( ) (1) I like a good novel—one which portrays strong characters and which thrills the reader. (2) I like a good novel—one which portrays strong characters and in reading the book you are thrilled. (3) I like novels which are thrilling and which portray strong characters.

35. ( ) (1) James, sitting on the platform, was looking at the audience. (2) There was James, looking at the audience sitting on the platform. (3) There was James, sitting on the platform and looking at the audience.

36. ( ) (1) If she is better tomorrow we will go. (2) We do not expect to go. Unless she is better tomorrow. (3) We do not expect to go unless she is better tomorrow.

37. ( ) (1) The ball which he had just purchased was thrown into the gutter. (2) He threw the ball which he had just purchased into the gutter. (3) He threw the ball into the gutter which he just purchased.

38. ( ) (1) Mother was ill. That was why I was absent. (2) The reason I was absent was because Mother was ill. (3) I was absent because Mother was ill.

39. ( ) (1) We will keep going regardless of anything. (2) Whether we win or lose, we will go on. (3) Whether we win or lose; whether we fail or succeed.

40. ( ) (1) A long lesson was assigned before Christmas, which made us angry. (2) A long lesson assigned before Christmas made us angry. (3) A long lesson was assigned before Christmas. This assignment made us angry.

TEST OF WORDS COMMONLY SPELLED INCORRECTLY

No. right out of 228: ....Date....................

This is a self-administering test of spelling and has no time limit. You are to write out the spelling of each of the words listed below.

The sound of each word is indicated at the left by a crude phonetic method (exactly correct pronunciations are not always indicated and a few times the correct spelling is used to indicate how the word sounds); the middle column gives a definition of each word; and you are to write the correct spelling of each word, thus sounded and defined, in the space at the right-hand side.

A good way "to take" this test is to decide what the word is in terms of the first two columns and then, disregarding the first two columns, sound the word as you spell it. A dash over a letter, e.g., "ā," indicates that it has a "long" sound, i.e., sounded as in saying the alphabet.

The key for correcting this test is on pages 258–260.

How word sounds	*Definition*	*Spelling*
1. ab sense	to be away	....
2. āk	to pain	....
3. all together	without exception	....
4. a fect	to influence	....
5. ak si dent ily	without intention	....
6. ak sept	to approve	....
7. a cross	on the other side of	....
8. add vize	to warn	....
9. a comma date	to adapt to	....
10. all red i	previously	....
11. ā n jell	celestial being	....
12. a mung	in the midst of	....
13. all ways	at all times	....
14. all most	nearly	....
15. ang gull	sharp corner	....
16. a per ate us	machine	....
17. auks ill er i	helping	....
18. ath let ick	good at sports	....
19. are gu ment	dispute	....

APPENDIX I

How word sounds	Definition	Spelling
20. a tack t	assaulted	....
21. a pier unce	external show	....
22. ath leet	football player	....
23. be leave	to accept as true	....
24. ba lense	equilibrium	....
25. be gin ing	at the start	....
26. biz nes	commercial enterprise	....
27. ben i fit	for the sake of	....
28. by sickle	vehicle with two wheels	....
29. come er shell	related to industry	....
30. ch owes	to have selected in the past	....
31. care actor	reputation, sum of one's characteristics	....
32. chain ja bull	varying	....
33. kal end er	table of days and months	....
34. care actor i stick	typical, distinctive	....
35. kol ledge	university, school	....
36. ch ooze	to select	....
37. chēf	leader	....
38. sir ten	sure	....
39. cap ten	officer in army	....
40. come ing	approaching	....
41. krit i size	to find fault	....
42. korse	school subject	....
43. kon vēn yent	near at hand	....
44. komp li ment air i	given to flattering remarks	....
45. komp li ment	flattering remark	....
46. come pair i tiv lee	relatively	....
47. come it ē	group of people	....
48. kon shence	feeling of obligation to do right	....

How word sounds	*Definition*	*Spelling*
49. kon she en chus	faithful, exact	....
50. kon troll	govern, direct	....
51. kon shus	aware of	....
52. kon spick you us	prominent, easily seen	....
53. de sēēve	mislead	....
54. dē side	to conclude	....
55. deaf a nit	limited, fixed	....
56. duz	form of verb "to do"	....
57. dis a point	to not fulfill expectation	....
58. dis a pier	to go from sight	....
59. de vel up	to form, expand	....
60. de vel up ment	formation, expansion	....
61. de scribe	to relate, depict	....
62. des send	to go down	....
63. die ning	eating	....
64. dis sip lin	to punish	....
65. dock ter	medical person	....
66. de pen dunt	not self-sustaining	....
67. doe nt	contracted form of "do not"	....
68. eks is tense	to be	....
69. eks pier ē ense	to live through an event	....
70. eks er size	exertion, to run, play games	....
71. eks ek ū tiv	administrator	....
72. eks sept	to leave out	....
73. ē nuff	adequate	....
74. ē quip t	furnished	....
75. em a grunt	person from a country	....
76. em bear us ment	to feel uncomfortable	....
77. em bear us	to make uncomfortable	....

How word sounds	*Definition*	*Spelling*
78. e fekt	result of a cause	. . . .
79. el ij a bull	qualified to be chosen	. . . .
80. fas sin ate	to hold attention	. . . .
81. feb you wary	second month of the year	. . . .
82. fine ul ē	at last	. . . .
83. four mer li	previously	. . . .
84.	spell "40"	. . . .
85. full fill	to satisfy, to carry out	. . . .
86. frend	person that likes you	. . . .
87. great full	to have gratitude	. . . .
88. grēv us	heavy, distressing	. . . .
89. gram er	language form	. . . .
90. guv urn er	head of a state	. . . .
91. ges	to judge at random	. . . .
92. hugh mer us	funny	. . . .
93. hope ing	desire for something	. . . .
94. hear	at this place	. . . .
95. hear	to sense sounds	. . . .
96. hair us	to worry by repeated attacks	. . . .
97. ear resist a bull	overpowering	. . . .
98. its	contracted form of "it is"	. . . .
99. i me grunt	person coming into a country	. . . .
100. i mēd i et li	right away	. . . .
101. i maj in	to form a mental image	. . . .
102. in deep end ent	free from external control	. . . .
103. in ti rest ing	exciting	. . . .
104. judge ment	belief, opinion	. . . .
105. jew dish al	pertaining to a court	. . . .

How word sounds	Definition	Spelling
106. new	past tense of verb meaning to **have** information about	. . . .
107. lab ra tor i	place for experiments	. . . .
108. lād	past tense of verb meaning "to place upon"	. . . .
109. led	past tense of verb meaning "to show the way"	. . . .
110. lee zure	time outside of work	. . . .
111. lie berry	place for books	. . . .
112. lew z	not to win	. . . .
113. lew se	to be free from	. . . .
114. litter a ture	books, writing	. . . .
115. lie sense	official permit	. . . .
116. man age ment	those in charge	. . . .
117. ment	past tense of "to mean"	. . . .
118. miss spell	to spell incorrectly	. . . .
119. miss cheev us	to cause annoyance	. . . .
120. more gage	a debt on property	. . . .
121. mi nut	1/60th of an hour	. . . .
122. nessy sary	something that must be	. . . .
123. notice a bull	conspicuous	. . . .
124.	spell "19"	. . . .
125.	spell "20"	. . . .
126. knee se	daughter of one's sister or brother	. . . .
127. O.K. shun	the time for	. . . .
128. O.K. shun a lee	now and then	. . . .
129. aw per toon i ti	chance	. . . .
130. ō mish un	left out	. . . .
131. offen	happen frequently	. . . .
132. ō clock	time of day	. . . .
133. ō mit ed	left out	. . . .

APPENDIX I

How word sounds	Definition	Spelling
134. ō cur d	happened	. . . .
135. pair a lel	extending in same direction	. . . .
136. prob bub lee	likely	. . . .
137. pro seed	to begin or go forward	. . . .
138. pro fes er	college teacher	. . . .
139. praw fess i	prediction (noun)	. . . .
140. purr man ent	continue without change	. . . .
141. purr miss a bull	allowable	. . . .
142. percy vear	to keep trying at something	. . . .
143. pick nick ing	lunch outdoors	. . . .
144. pre seed	to go ahead of	. . . .
145. pose esh un	to have with one	. . . .
146. plan ing	scheming, devising	. . . .
147. plan d	schemed, devised	. . . .
148. peace	a part of	. . . .
149. preh fur unce	greater liking for	. . . .
150. pre fur d	had greater liking for	. . . .
151. priv i ledge	a right or immunity	. . . .
152. preh purr ā shun	state of readiness	. . . .
153. prince a pull	head of a school	. . . .
154. prince a pull	fundamental truth	. . . .
155. preh jew dis	opinion against	. . . .
156. par la ment	governing body	. . . .
157. part ner	associate	. . . .
158. purr form	to do, accomplish	. . . .
159. purr haps	possibly	. . . .
160. kwan ti tea	amount, sum	. . . .
161. kwī et	without noise	. . . .

How word sounds	Definition	Spelling
162. kwīt	entirely, positively	. . . .
163. rē a li	actually	. . . .
164. re seat	acknowledgment of payment	. . . .
165. ri them	movement marked by regular re-currence	. . . .
166. rye m	poetry	. . . .
167. re spon sa bull	trustworthy	. . . .
168. re speck full lee	regardful for	. . . .
169. rep i ti shun	repeating	. . . .
170. rē lij us	godly, pious	. . . .
171. rē leave	to free from burden	. . . .
172. wreck ō mend āshun	good suggestion	. . . .
173. wreck ō mend	to suggest as good	. . . .
174. wreck og nīz	identify, to know	. . . .
175. rē sēv	to accept	. . . .
176. sal ar i	wage	. . . .
177. se purr ate	to divide, take away	. . . .
178. seas	to take, grab	. . . .
179. sek ri tary	stenographer	. . . .
180. sked yule	time table, catalogue	. . . .
181. seen	view, part of a play	. . . .
182. sin sear lee	genuinely, honestly	. . . .
183. shine ing	reflecting light	. . . .
184. sim i ler	being alike	. . . .
185. shep urd	a tender of sheep	. . . .
186. s peach	talk, oration	. . . .
187. sof a more	2nd year in college	. . . .
188. skill full	expert	. . . .
189. stay shun ery	writing material	. . . .

How word sounds	Definition	Spelling
190. stay shun ery	stay in one place	. . . .
191. sh your	with certainty	. . . .
192. stop ing	ceasing of movement	. . . .
193. stud ē ing	to read lessons	. . . .
194. suck ses	to attain a goal	. . . .
195. sue purr seed	to be in place of	. . . .
196. sue purr in ten dent	head of school system	. . . .
197. stop t	to have ceased moving	. . . .
198. sir prize	unexpected	. . . .
199. sill i bull	part of a word	. . . .
200. tare if	tax on imports	. . . .
201. th air	opposite of here	. . . .
202. th air	belonging to them	. . . .
203. th air	contraction of "they are"	. . . .
204. th air four	for that reason	. . . .
205. threw	to be done with	. . . .
206. to	also	. . . .
207. two gether	in company with	. . . .
208. tra jed i	fatal or mournful event	. . . .
209.	spell "2"	. . . .
210.	spell "12th"	. . . .
211. try z	he attempts	. . . .
212. true lee	genuinely, honestly	. . . .
213. un nessy sary	useless, needless	. . . .
214. un till	to the time that	. . . .
215. use ing	employing	. . . .
216. witch	interrogative or relative pronoun	. . . .
217. hole	all of	. . . .

How word sounds	Definition	Spelling
218. wi men	persons of female sex	. . . .
219. weth er	state of the atmosphere	. . . .
220. Wens day	4th day of week	. . . .
221. wear	at or in what place	. . . .
222. wry ting	what one has composed	. . . .
223. use you lee	commonly, ordinarily	. . . .
224. vil un	scoundrel	. . . .
225. vil edge	small town	. . . .
226. woe nt	contraction of "will not"	. . . .
227. wood	form of verb "will"	. . . .
228. rīt	to compose a letter	. . . .

APPENDIX II

KEYS

LIBRARY INFORMATION
(pages 83–86)

1. 3
2. 4
3. 1
4. 2
5. 5

6. T
7. T

8. F

9. F

10. T

11. F

12. T

13. F

14. T

LIBRARY INFORM. (*Cont.*)

15. A
16. C

17. A

18. E

19. H

20. 2

21. F

22. 1935
23. T
24. 7

25. T
26. F

LIBRARY INFORM. (*Cont.*)

27. I
28. E

29. F
30. G
31. C
32. H

33. D

34. h
35. f
36. d
37. a
38. c
39. k
40. j
41. l

42. T

43. T

44. T

45. T

LIBRARY INFORM. (*Cont.*)	GENERAL VOCABULARY TEST	GEN. VOCAB. (*Cont.*)
	(pages 117–119)	
	Score Rights (80)	
46. F		
47. F	1. (2)	15. (3)
48. T	2. (3)	16. (2)
	3. (3)	17. (3)
	4. (5)	18. (5)
49. F	5. (1)	19. (4)
50. F		
51. T	6. (2)	20. (3)
52. T	7. (4)	21. (5)
53. 3		
54. 1	8. (1)	22. (5)
55. T	9. (5)	23. (2)
56. T	10. (3)	24. (3)
57. 3	11. (3)	25. (1)
58. T	12. (1)	26. (5)
59. T		27. (4)
60. F	13. (4)	28. (3)
61. 4	14. (1)	
62. 1		29. (3)
63. 2		30. (4)

31. (1)
32. (4)
33. (1)
34. (5)
35. (5)
36. (2)
37. (1)
38. (4)
39. (2)
40. (5)
41. (3)
42. (4)
43. (5)
44. (5)
45. (1)
46. (4)
47. (5)
48. (3)
49. (2)
50. (3)

51. (1)
52. (3)
53. (1)
54. (2)
55. (4)
56. (5)
57. (2)
58. (4)
59. (3)
60. (4)
61. (3)
62. (5)
63. (1)
64. (3)
65. (2)
66. (2)
67. (5)
68. (4)
69. (5)
70. (5)

71. (4)
72. (1)
73. (3)
74. (5)
75. (2)
76. (5)
77. (3)
78. (4)
79. (1)
80. (3)

DICTIONARY USAGE (page 121)	MATHEMATICS (pages 147–148)	MATHEMATICS (*Cont.*)
1. (2)	1. 2,166	27. 1/5
2. (4)	2. 1,509	28. 1/2
3. F	3. 18,585	29. .20
4. johnnycake	4. 67,572	30. .50
5. (1)	5. 1,071,840	31. 49
6. T	6. 1,624,773	32. 64
	7. 199.5	33. 81
7. n i	8. 291.00	34. 121
8. F		35. 144
9. (9)	9. 33/40	
10. (4)	10. 1 11/20	36. 14
11. (2)	11. 1/21	37. 40
	12. 1/12	38. 10
12. (2)	13. 3/7	39. 11
13. (3)	14. 3/10	
14. (2)	15. 7/12	40. .40
15. (3)	16. 4/5	41. 1.11
16. (4)	17. 27.2086	42. .007
17. (2)	18. 89.1424	43. .30
	19. 1.1694	44. 5
18. (1)	20. .2942	45. 8
19. jollified	21. .766314	46. 6
20. (3)	22. .074592	47. 5
21. T	23. .003	48. 132
22. T	24. 5.	49. 96
23. (2)	25. 62.5%	50. 24
24. (3)	26. 70.59%	

Test of Social Usage (pages 171–172)	Social Usage (Cont.)	Art Reading (pages 196–198)
1. T	22. F	1. (1)
	23. F	2. (F)
2. F	24. T	
	25. T	3. (1)
3. T		4. (3)
4. T	26. T	
5. T		5. (3)
6. T	27. T	
7. F		6. (4)
	28. F	7. (2)
8. T	29. T	
9. T	30. T	8. (T)
10. T	31. F	9. (T)
	32. F	10. (F)
	33. F	
	34. T	11. (F)
11. T	35. T	
	36. T	12. (2)
12. F		
	37. T	13. (2)
13. F	38. F	
14. T	39. T	14. (1)
15. T		
16. T		15. (T)
17. T	40. T	
18. T		16. (F)
19. T		17. (1)
20. T		
21. F		18. (4)
		19. (3)

Art (*Cont.*)	Art (*Cont.*)	Geology Reading (pages 210–212)
20. (F)	40. (2)	1. (2)
	41. (1)	
21. (2)	42. (1)	2. (T)
22. (5)		
23. (7)		3. (3)
24. (2)		4. (F)
25. (2)		5. (F)
26. (2)		6. (3)
		7. (3)
27. (2)		
		8. (3, 1, 2)
28. (F)		
		9. (T)
		10. (2)
29. (2)		
30. (5)		11. (2)
31. (7)		
		12. (1)
32. (T)		
		13. (4)
		14. (3)
33. (1)		
		15. (1)
34. (2, 3, 1)		
		16. (3)
35. (2)		
36. (2)		17. (4)
37. (1)		
38. (F)		
39. (F)		

18. (3)

19. (3)

20. (F)

21. (1)

22. (1)

23. (2)

24. (2)

25. (1)

26. (4)

27. (3)

28. (1)

29. (3)

30. (1)

31. (1)

32. (3)

33. (T)

34. (T)

35. (2)

36. (3)

37. (F)

38. (F)

39. (F)

A. READING TABLES
(pages 213–215)

1. 81%

2. 87%

3. 90%

4. F
5. F

6. 14

7. 17

8. 42.9%

9. 21.7%

10. 10.1%

11. F

12a. T
b. F
c. F
d. F
e. F

13. F

14. F

15. T

16. $12.96

17. 17.4

18. 5579

19. T

20. 3

21. F

22. 1

23. 1

24. T
25. T
26. F

CHARTS (pages 216–218)	C. SKILLS IN MAP READING (pages 220–221)	D. MATHEMATICAL FORMULAE (page 222)
1. 145	1. GK	1. (b)
2. 13	2. 7	
3. 10 & 11	3. Geraldton	2. (a)
	4. Alice Springs	
	5. BH	
4. 4	6. J	3. (b)
	7. East	
5. T	8. North	4. (b)
6. 13, 10th %ile	9. Darwin	
	10. East	
7. Professional	11. Rockhampton	5. (d)
8. Office or sales		
9. 750		
10. 1		6. (a)
	12. Wallabie	
11. 225	13. AM	7. (b)
	14. IN	
12. F	15. DO	8. (c)
13. T	16. Rockhampton	9. (d)
	17. North	
14. 80%	18. Geelong	
15. T	19. Geraldton	10. (c)
16. F	20. Torrid zone	
17. 35.5%	21. about 2300 mi.	11. (c)
18. 3rd	22. about 1750 mi.	
19. F		
20. 3rd		
21. 7th		
22. F		
23. 2		
24. F		

GRAMMAR (pages 223–226)

Rule   Answer

1. (9)   us

2. (7)   greets

3. (13) sit

4. (11) well

5. (10) asked

6. (10) climbed

7. (11) easily

8.   0

9. (8)   his

10. (6) doesn't *or* does not

11. (10) gone

12. (1) is

13. (9) who

14. (9) whom

15. (7) was

16. (1) have (had)

GRAMMAR (*Cont.*)

17. (5) is

18. (8) are

19. (13) teach

20. (11) surely

21. (10) given

22. (6) doesn't *or* does not

23. (5) is

24. (12) bad

25. (2) is

26. (13) let

27. (11) carefully

28. (1) was

29. (12) sad

30.   0

31. (1) are

32. (6) doesn't *or* does not

33. (13) lie

34. (11) well

35. (7) have

36. (9) I

37. (9) I

38. (11) poorly

39. (8) his (her)

40. (9) me

41. (13) too

42. (12) sweet

43. (13) let

44. (13) might

45. (9) we

46. (10) written

47. (10) begun

48. (13) too

49. (11) easily

50.   0

51. (7) prefer

52. (13) there

53. (13) too

54.   0

55. (2) was

56. (4) were

57. (10) seen

58. (8) he

59. (10) came

60. (11) softly

61. (8) his

62. (13) sat

63. (3) was

64.   0

65. (10) frozen

66.   0

67. (10) sang

68. (10) threw

69. (3) has

70. (10) asked

71. (7) has

72. (4) are

73. (9) me

74. (13) there

75. (6) doesn't *or* does not

76. (1) is

77. (4) are

78. (5) are

79. (7) doesn't *or* does not

80. (9) me

CAPITALIZATION
(pages 227–230)

	Rule	*Answer*
1.	(3)	S G
2.	(1)	W
3.	(3)	H N Y
4.	(3)	C C
5.	(3)	K C
6.	(2)	D H E
7.	(2)	J
8.	(5)	J
9.	(3)	G
10.	(5)	F J
11.	(3)	W S D K
12.	(2, 4)	S D
13.	(3)	T C
14.	(3)	E L
15.		——

16. (4)	K K K		45. (3, 5)	S B C		74. (3)	W O C
17. (3)	N		46. (2)	G J		75. (4)	M S
18. (3)	M B		47. (2)	P W		76. (3)	S L M R
19. (3)	F		48. (2)	C B		77.	—
20. (6)	I C N		49. (2)	S		78. (2)	G P
21. (2)	J L		50. (4)	G E C		79. (2, 5)	E M J
22.	—		51.	—		80. (2)	J
23. (2)	J M		52. (6)	H			
24. (3, 5)	D A		53. (6)	C M			
25. (5)	M D T		54. (4)	U L			
26. (4)	S P		55. (3)	C W			
27. (6)	D		56. (2)	P B			
28. (2, 6)	L D B A		57. (5)	L			
29.	—		58. (3)	L			
30. (3)	A		59. (4)	H C			
31.	—		60. (3)	A			
32. (3)	S		61.	—			
33. (6)	W		62. (2)	C J			
34. (2, 6)	T I M		63. (2)	J			
35. (2)	C E		64. (5)	J A			
36. (6)	G D		65.	—			
37. (3)	A E		66. (6)	C			
38. (4)	P B		67. (4)	S H			
39. (3)	R		68. (4)	M W C			
40. (4)	N R A		69. (4)	C B			
41. (4)	L S		70. (6)	L D			
42. (2)	G		71. (2)	M A			
43.	—		72. (2, 6)	C L J V			
44.	—		73. (2)	J			

(pages 227–230)

Note: Comma underlined thus <u>,</u> is optional; the sentence is correct either with or without the mark.

The total score in punctuation is the total number of lines in which correct punctuation marks *and no others* have been inserted (except as certain alternatives are allowed as indicated by the marks in parentheses). If the student has only three of four punctuation marks needed on a line or if he has all the punctuation and adds a mark, no credit is given. The total possible score is thus 80 points.

	Rule	Answer
1.	(1, 8)	strassburg, germany?
2.	(12, 1, 7)	exclaimed, "what lake!"
3.	(3)	The hudson, a york, is
4.	(1)	ceylon?
5.	(14)	we'll
6.	(12, 7)	"Tell did,"
7.	(14, 12, 7)	"If that's all," john said, "we go." (that's said,)
8.	(3)	Friday, the june,
9.	(1)	germans?
10.	(3)	july, a
11.	(8)	street, dolby, kentucky.
12.	(3)	Al smith, the candidate,
13.	(10)	college; then
14.	(11, 5)	following: history, english<u>,</u> and latin.
15.	(14, 6)	They're ready, but we'll

16. (4)   place, the

17. (9)   newburg; there (started; to)

18. (7)   (No punctuation needed)

19. (6)   (No punctuation needed)

20. (13)   called "in night."

21. (9)   heirloom; it

22. (3)   captain, our friend, met

23. (15, 5) Esther, jane, and girls'

24. (8)   8, 1933

25. (5)   Christmas, memorial day, and

26. (1)   succeed?

27. (9)   detoxal; it

28. (13, 11, 5) books: *dodsworth, babbitt,* and *arrowsmith.* (books; "dodsworth," "babbitt," and
              "arrowsmith.")

29. (12, 7) "We are," said the speaker, "at era."

30. (4)   tourists, let

31. (6)   (No punctuation needed)

32. (10)   spanish; then

33. (13)   "By a waterfall" is

34. (15, 3, 13) tennyson's poem, "in memoriam."

35. (6)   given, for

36. (4)   cleaning, since

37. (14, 10) didn't alps; still

38. (15, 9) presbyterian; he

39. (5)   rome, that politics, and

40. (9)   pay; it

41.   (No punctuation needed)

42. (14)   It's can't

43. (5)   Oranges, lemons, and

44. (7)   (No punctuation needed)

45.   (No punctuation needed)

46.   (No punctuation needed)

47. (7, 6)   wales, but

48. (12, 7)   "Please come," she wrote, "colonel here."

49. (6)   going, nor

50. (4)   words, the

51. (15, 14, 9)   soft; it's

52. (14, 13)   "I'm hurry"

53. (13, 11)   movies: *cimmaron* and *masquerade*. (movies, "cimmaron" and "masquerade.")

54. (14)   tomorrow, at o'clock.

55. (6)   washington, and

56. (12, 7)   "You brown," she

57.   (No punctuation needed)

58. (1, 9)   lisbon; which be?

59. (9)   mathematics; he

60. (14, 9)   You'll athens; you'll

61. (14, 10)   I'm tonight; besides it's

62. (12, 7)   "That youngster," said coach jones, "will year." (said, "coach year.")

63. (14, 6)   It's hard, but jim won't

64. (5)   June, july, and

65. (5)   quick, who ambitious, and

66. (14, 4)   If it's necessary, you

67. (14, 6)   didn't

68. (4)   prominent, she

69. (7, 12, 14)   "All right," he said, "we'll bank."

70. (14, 13, 4)   I'll *literary digest*, if ("literary digest,")

71. (2, 10)   mr. adams; then

72. (13, 9)   *lord jim;* he *victory*. ("   ")

73. (14, 4)   frank, she doesn't

74. (5)   washington, to oregon, and

75. (4)   society, thus

76. (6, 2)   st.

77. (14, 10)   I'll car; otherwise you'll

78. (15, 3)   Mary, you pershing's

79. (15, 5, 2)   one's conscience, to one's clothes, or mrs.

80.   (No punctuation needed)

SENTENCE STRUCTURE (pages 231–232)		SENTENCE STRUCTURE (*Cont.*)		SENTENCE STRUCTURE (*Cont.*)	
Rule	*Answer*				
1. (2)	2			27. (4)	1
2. (5)	2	16. (3)	3	28. (1)	3
3. (3)	1	17. (4)	2	29. (5)	3
4. (4)	2	18. (5)	2	30. (4)	3
5. (5)	2			31. (6)	3
6. (1)	3			32. (6)	1
7. (4)	3			33. (1)	1
8. (4)	1	19. (3)	1	34. (6)	2
		20. (5)	1		
9. (3)	3	21. (1)	1	35. (4)	2
10. (5)	2	22. (4)	2	36. (1)	2
11. (6)	3	23. (6)	1	37. (5)	3
12. (1)	1	24. (6)	3		
13. (2)	1			38. (2)	2
14. (6)	3	25. (1)	1	39. (1)	3
15. (6)	2	26. (1)	2	40. (5)	1

1. absence
2. ache
3. altogether
4. affect
5. accidentally
6. accept
7. across
8. advise
9. accommodate
10. already
11. angel
12. among
13. always
14. almost
15. angle
16. apparatus
17. auxiliary
18. athletic
19. argument

20. attacked
21. appearance
22. athlete
23. believe
24. balance
25. beginning
26. business
27. benefit
28. bicycle
29. commercial
30. chose
31. character
32. changeable
33. calendar
34. characteristic
35. college
36. choose
37. chief
38. certain
39. captain
40. coming
41. criticize
    (*or* criticise)
42. course
43. convenient
44. complimentary
45. compliment
46. comparatively
47. committee
48. conscience

49. conscientious
50. control
51. conscious
52. conspicuous
53. deceive
54. decide
55. definite
56. does
57. disappoint
58. disappear
    (*or* develope)
59. develop
    (*or* developement)
60. development
61. describe
62. descend
63. dining
64. discipline
65. doctor
66. dependent
67. don't
68. existence
69. experience
70. exercise
71. executive
72. except
73. enough
74. equipped
75. emigrant
76. embarrassment
77. embarrass

78. effect
79. eligible
80. fascinate
81. February
82. finally
83. formerly
84. forty
    (*or* fulfill)
85. fulfil
86. friend
87. grateful
88. grievous
89. grammar
90. governor
91. guess
    (*or* humourous)
92. humorous
93. hoping
94. here
95. hear
96. harass
97. irresistible
98. it's
99. immigrant
100. immediately
101. imagine
102. independent
103. interesting
    (*or* judgement)
104. judgment
105. judicial

106. knew
107. laboratory
108. laid
109. led
110. leisure
111. library
112. lose
113. loose
114. literature
    (*or* licence)
115. license
116. management
117. meant
118. misspell
119. mischievous
120. mortgage
121. minute
122. necessary
123. noticeable
124. nineteen
125. twenty
126. niece
127. occasion
128. occasionally
129. opportunity
130. omission
131. often
132. o'clock
133. omitted

134. occurred
135. parallel
136. probably
137. proceed
138. professor
139. prophecy
140. permanent
141. permissible
142. persevere
143. picnicking
144. precede
145. possession
146. planning
147. planned
148. piece
149. preference
150. preferred
151. privilege
152. preparation
153. principal
154. principle
155. prejudice
156. parliament
157. partner
158. perform
159. perhaps
160. quantity
161. quiet

162. quite
163. really
164. receipt
165. rhythm
166. rhyme
167. responsible
168. respectfully
169. repetition
170. religious
171. relieve
172. recommendation
173. recommend
174. recognize
175. receive
176. salary
177. separate
178. seize
179. secretary
180. schedule
181. scene
182. sincerely
183. shining
184. similar
185. shepherd
186. speech
187. sophomore
    (*or* skilful)
188. skillful
189. stationery

190. stationary
191. sure
192. stopping
193. studying
194. success
195. supersede
196. superintendent
197. stopped
198. surprise
199. syllable
200. tariff
201. there
202. their
203. they're
204. therefore
205. through
206. too
207. together
208. tragedy
209. two
210. twelfth
211. tries
212. truly
213. unnecessary
214. until
215. using
216. which
217. whole

218. women
219. weather
220. Wednesday
221. where
222. writing
223. usually
224. villain
225. village
226. won't
227. would
228. write

SUMMARY SHEET

Directions: When each of the following activities is completed, fill in the date below and, if it has a score, its score. This listing quickly indicates what has been completed and which tests need checking; after the course this will serve as a record of your test results.

Page	Title	Date	Result	Checked
4	Self-Insight Exercise	....	not scored	....
9	Student Data Sheet	....	not scored	....
11	Problem Check List	....	not scored	....
17	Practice with Cues	....	not scored	....
32	Practice with Survey Q3R	....	not scored	....
46	Final Examination Schedule	....	not scored	....
53	Examination Practice	....	not scored	....
58	Present Use of Time	....	not scored	....
59	Study Habits Questionnaire	....	.... score	....
61	Plan of Time Use	....	not scored	....
65	Study Conditions Questionnaire	....	.... score	....
69	Check List of Work Behavior	....	not scored	....
70	Evaluation of Study Conditions	....	not scored	....
76	Motivation Check	....	not scored	....
79	Motivation Write-up	....	not scored	....
83	Test of Library Information	....	.... score	....
87	Library Laboratory Exercise	....	.... score	....
88	Term Paper Library Project	....	.... grade	....
90	Evaluation of Past Term Papers	....	not scored	....
94	Evaluation of Classroom Behavior	....	.... score	....
101	Practice with Classroom Skills	....	not scored	....
107	Art Reading Rate	....	........%ile	....
107	Art Comprehension Accuracy	....	........%ile	....
107	Geology Reading Rate	....	........%ile	....
107	Geology Comprehension Accuracy	....	........%ile	....
107	Summary Evaluation of Reading	....	not scored	....
110	Rate Evaluation	....	not scored	....
111	Outside Reading Record	....	not scored	....
112	Rate Chart	....	not scored	....
114	Summary Evaluation of Comprehension	....	not scored	....
117	General Vocabulary	....	........%ile	....
121	Dictionary	....	.... score	....
124	Vocabulary Listing	....	not scored	....
126	Reading Tables	....	.... score	....
126	Reading Charts	....	.... score	....
126	Reading Maps	....	.... score	....